Mr. Jay of Bedford

JOHN JAY, THE RETIREMENT YEARS

1801–1829

Carol Brier

HERITAGE BOOKS
2016

HERITAGE BOOKS
AN IMPRINT OF HERITAGE BOOKS, INC.

Books, CDs, and more—Worldwide

For our listing of thousands of titles see our website
at
www.HeritageBooks.com

Published 2016 by
HERITAGE BOOKS, INC.
Publishing Division
5810 Ruatan Street
Berwyn Heights, Md. 20740

Copyright © 2016 Carol Brier

All rights reserved. No part of this book may be reproduced or transmitted in any form or by any means, electronic or mechanical, including photocopying, recording or by any information storage and retrieval system without written permission from the author, except for the inclusion of brief quotations in a review.

International Standard Book Numbers
Paperbound: 978-0-7884-5711-1
Clothbound: 978-0-7884-6425-6

"I shall retire accordingly; but I shall retain and cherish the warmest affection for my country, as well as the esteem which I entertain for many, and the good-will which I bear to all my fellow citizens."

John Jay to Richard Hatfield,
Albany 8th November, 1800

Table of Contents

Dedication	*iii*
List of Illustrations	*vii*
Acknowledgements and Preface	*xi*
1. Virtues, Talent, Patriotism and Into the Shades of Retirement	1
2. Let Us Be Resigned	47
3. A Pleasant Situation	97
4. Just and Necessary Wars	145
5. Our Mutual Esteem and Regard	173
6. We are Blessed with Many Enjoyments	213
7. The Last Inn	245
8. Legacy	285
9. Notes and Bibliography	301
10. Index	315

List of Illustrations

1. *John Jay*, by John Trumbull, John Jay Homestead State Historic Site, Katonah, N.Y. New York State Office of Parks, Recreation and Historic Preservation.

2. *Sarah Livingston Jay*, by Daniel Huntington after Alexandre Roslin, John Jay Homestead State Historic Site, Katonah, N.Y. New York State Office of Parks, Recreation and Historic Preservation.

3. *William Jay*, by Henry Antonio Wenzler, John Jay Homestead State Historic Site, Katonah, N.Y. New York State Office of Parks, Recreation and Historic Preservation.

4. *Peter Augustus Jay*, by Henry Bryan Hall, New York Public Library Digital Collections, New York, N.Y.

5. *Ann (Nancy) Jay*, by Gideon Fairman, John Jay Homestead State Historic Site, Katonah, N.Y. New York State Office of Parks, Recreation and Historic Preservation.

6. *Maria Jay Banyer*, by Charles Balthazar Julien Ferret de Saint Memin, John Jay Homestead State Historic Site, Katonah, N.Y. New York State Office of Parks, Recreation and Historic Preservation.

7. *John Jay II*, by Daniel Huntington, John Jay Homestead State Historic Site, Katonah, N.Y. New York State Office of Parks, Recreation and Historic Preservation.

8. *John Jay Residence, Bedford, N.Y.* by J. W. Barber and Henry Howe, Westchester County Historical Society.

9. John Jay -Twenty Pounds Reward, 17 September, 1802, Westchester County Historical Society.

10. *Village of Sing Sing and the Hudson River*, by W. H. Bartlett and R. Wallis, Westchester County Historical Society.

11. *The Clermont on the Hudson* by Charles Pensee, New York Public Library Digital Collections, New York, N.Y.

12. *Lindley Murray*, by E. Westoby, New York Public Library Digital Collections, New York, N.Y.

13. *Richard Peters*, unknown (Scan from 1904 book by Nellie Peters Black: *Richard Peters: His Ancestors and Descendents)*, New York Public Library Digital Collections, New York, N.Y.

14. *Napoleon Bonaparte, Premier Consul* by Francois Delpech, New York Public Library Digital Collections, New York, N.Y.

15. *The War of 1812, MacDonough's victory on Lake Champlain, and defeat of the British Army at Plattsburg by Genl. Macomb, Septr. 11th, 1814,* by Benjamin Tanner, New York Public Library Digital Collections, New York, N.Y.

16. *James Fenimore Cooper*, by Edward Scriven after Wesley Jarvis, New York Public Library Digital Collections, New York, N.Y.

17. *Gilbert du Motier, Marquis de Lafayette* by Ary Scheffer, - New York Public Library Digital Collections, New York, N.Y.

18. *Landing of Gen. Lafayette at Castle Garden, New York, 16th August 1824* by Sam Maverick Set, New York Public Library Digital Collections, New York, N.Y.

19. *DeWitt Clinton Mingling the Waters of Lake Erie with the Atlantic* by Philip Meeder, New York Public Library Digital Collections, New York, N.Y.

20. *View on the Erie Canal, 1829*, by J. W. Hill, New York Public Library Digital Collections, New York, N.Y.

21. *Benjamin Vaughan*, attributed to Thomas Badger, Vaughan Homestead Foundation.

Illustrations follow Chapter 4 Just and Necessary Wars after Page 171.

Acknowledgements and Preface

I wish to thank those who were instrumental in assisting me during the research and writing of this book particularly Jean Ashton and the staff and curators of the Butler Library Rare Book and Manuscript Division at Columbia University, where much of my research was conducted. Ronna Dixson of New York State Office of Parks, Recreation and Historic Preservation is due recognition for her assistance. The librarians of the Westchester Library System, in particular the Katonah Village Library, were exceedingly cooperative. Acknowledgement is also due the Westchester County Historical Society and its Executive Director, Katherine M. Hite and Librarian, Patrick Rafferty. The Bedford Historical Society and its Executive Director, Evelyne Ryan, as well as the staff of St. Matthews Church, Bedford, New York, should also be commended. Elise Haas, Publicity Director of the Keeler Tavern Museum in Ridgefield, Connecticut, also deserves my thanks. David G. Gallo, Esq. is commended for his contribution to the publication process.

In addition, this book would not have been possible without the cooperation, support and encouragement of the staff and volunteers of the John Jay Homestead State Historic Site, including Site Managers Linda McLean, Alix Schnee and Heather Iannucci, along with Interpretive Programs Assistants Julia Warger and Bethany White. Special recognition is given to the late William Pencak, Emeritus, Professor of American History at the Pennsylvania State University and Ohio State University, for all the support and encouragement he gave me to continue with my work on this book. James B. O'Hara and Kathleen Shurtleff of the United States Supreme Court Historical Society are also due recognition for their support and encouragement.

Lastly, this book would never have been possible without the patience, support and abiding confidence of my husband, Tom, who absolutely believed in what I was trying to accomplish in undertaking to write this book.

It is my sincere hope that this book will add to the documented history of John Jay, his legacy and his family. My research, primarily at Butler Library Rare Book and Manuscript Division at Columbia University, yielded information about John Jay during his retirement years that I believe is enlightening and relevant to the study of John Jay. This book contains new scholarship about John Jay which focuses on Jay's retirement to his farm in Bedford, New York. I believe that this final chapter in Jay's life is due the scrutiny and attention of present and future scholars. *Mr. Jay of Bedford* examines the challenges that John Jay faced during the last years of his life, and how his unique and admirable qualities that served him so well as a public official, became the mainstay of his final years. This book strives to examine and add to the reader's knowledge of John Jay, the man.

William Jay in his two-volume biography of his father, *The Life of John Jay,* published in 1833, gives us a greater glimpse into the last years of John Jay's life than most John Jay biographers and is a great source of personal information about the Jay family.

For those readers who are not familiar with the life of John Jay, I suggest you take the time to read the first chapter, *Virtues, Talent, Patriotism and Into the Shades of Retirement.* John Jay is best remembered for his notable accomplishments during his career as a public official. More importantly, his endeavors during his retirement to his beloved 'farm in Bedford,' his family, the Village of Bedford, his religious beliefs, his political views, and the republic he helped to create, are examined in this book. I have tried to detail the qualities in John Jay's character that enabled him to achieve success not only as a public official, but also in his retirement, and Jay's ability to continue to persevere, especially in times of adversity.

With the publication of *Mr. Jay of Bedford,* I also wish to dispel the notion held by some that John Jay was not the same person after his wife's death - that he was a "broken man." With this book, I contend that John Jay was the same person with the same character, beliefs, and commitment to the principles of justice for all, for which he labored his entire life, despite the loss of his wife, Sarah Livingston Jay. Theirs was an arranged match, as most marriages were at that time. It proved to be a union of two perfectly matched souls which enlightened and advanced the cause of American independence in so many ways.

There are a number of quotes from John Jay in this book which I believe are compelling and revealing of John Jay's character, along with observations made by family members and contemporaries. Jay was very specific in what he had to say and never left anyone in doubt as to his position on the issue at hand. The format of this book embraces the words of John Jay and his family, friends and compatriots with great joy. Their revelations are far more persuasive, in their own words, reacting to the moment at hand, than anything I could endeavor to write about John Jay. They speak for themselves and need no explanation. Such was the time in which John Jay lived and he dedicated himself, without reservation, to the cause of American independence. I have tried to present John Jay as he was and in his own words. This book focuses on John Jay, the man, and who better to testify to the facts of the man, than John Jay himself. I hope that my book will give recognition to the character that made John Jay the patriot and admirable person of sincere beliefs which served him so admirably throughout his life and have enhanced and nurtured his contribution to the United States of America.

It is to John Jay and his enduring legacy that I dedicate this book. May it enrich all who venture to explore the extraordinary life of John Jay, Founding Father.

Virtues, Talent, Patriotism - Into the Shades of Private Life

CHAPTER 1

In 1801 John Jay thought it "proper to retire from public life."[1] After a distinguished public career that encompassed more than a quarter of a century, John Jay was determined to put the life of a public official behind him and retire to his farm in Bedford, New York with his wife and family. Even Jay's wife, the former Sarah Livingston, desired a quiet life in the country to the duties that public life imposed on a spouse "…indeed my Love I more than ever wish for the time that will put a period to your public cares and permit the indulgence of retirement, rural quiet …."[2] Jay was forty-six years old when he expressed his intention to retire. He had served his country in so many positions, that Jay's attempt during retirement to document the numerous positions that he held as a public official covered almost ten pages. By his own account, it was indeed fitting and highly appropriate for Jay to retire to what he often referred to as 'my farm in Bedford'.

Any discussion of Jay's life should begin with his Huguenot heritage and his paternal grandfather, Augustus Jay, who came to the New World seeking religious freedom. Augustus was born in La Rochelle, France in 1665. When the rights of the Huguenots were abolished in 1685 with the revocation of the Edict of Nantes, Augustus left France, as did thousands of other Huguenots, and eventually settled in New York. He went into trade and quickly established a flourishing mercantile business which enabled him to marry in 1697 the 'exceedingly lovely' Anna Maria, daughter of wealthy New York merchant and brewer, Balthazar Bayard. John Jay's son, William, wrote of this union in his two-volume biography of his father "By his marriage Augustus became encircled with friends, who, from their situations were able …to promote his interest as a merchant, and his social happiness as a man."[3] Through his marriage, Augustus became connected to some of the most prominent and influential families in New York, particularly the Stuyvesants, the Philipses and the Van Cortlandts. Augustus and Anna Maria had one son, Peter, who was born in 1704.

As a boy, Peter was sent to Bristol, England to work in the

counting house of the Peloquin branch of the Jay family. He also learned the merchant trade by working alongside his father. Peter quickly established himself as a prosperous merchant and in 1728 he married Mary Van Cortlandt. By the time that John Jay was born in 1745, Peter and Mary had six children ranging in age from seventeen to eight. Some of the children were not in the best of health. Eve suffered from fits of hysterics and Augustus was considered to be slow. Peter and Anna lost their eyesight in a yellow fever epidemic which was rampant in colonial cities.

Out of family considerations, Peter left trade and moved his family to a farm, the Locusts. The farm was about 400 acres in Rye, which was located in Westchester County about 20 miles north of New York overlooking the Long Island Sound. The village of Rye was a typical, rural, colonial town complete with churches, farms and a small town center. Rye was located near the Boston Post Road which was a major route connecting New York with New England. Peter retired from trade and devoted a good deal of time to satisfying outstanding debts owed to British merchants for whom he was an agent. Perhaps the combination of rural life and his father's interest in finances may have had a strong influence on the young John Jay who himself would retire to a farm not far from his father's and become a farmer and financier, among other pursuits. John was also greatly influenced by the fact that his ancestors had emigrated from France for religious purposes and often with financial sacrifice. The persecution of his forbears in France by the Catholic church made a lasting impression on the young John Jay and he remained anti-Catholic for the rest of his life. Religion was also reinforced through the daily readings of the Scriptures and religious tracts by his father, a tradition that John Jay would carry on in his own household.

Jay received his initial education from his mother who taught him English and Latin. When Jay was eight, his father remarked "Johnny is of a very grave disposition, and takes to learning exceedingly well. He will soon be fit to go to a grammar school."[4] Jay was sent to New Rochelle, a Huguenot town in Westchester county not far from Rye, where he studied under the

Virtues, Talent, Patriotism - Into the Shades of Private Life

Rev. Mr. Stoupe (a/k/a Stouppe, Stoope) who was pastor of the local church which combined the French and Episcopalian churches. Stoupe also maintained a grammar school. For the next three years, John studied under the strict and often harsh conditions at the school with small rations, and frequent admonitions from Mr. Stoupe. During the winters, John often had to use pieces of wood to cover up the broken pains in the bedroom windows to prevent the snow from entering. Despite the Spartan conditions of the grammar school, John succeeded and his proud father remarked "I cannot forbear taking the freedom of hinting to you [the. Peloquins of Bristol] that my Johnny gives me a very pleasing prospect."[5] Young John left Mr. Stoupe and returned home to study under a tutor named George Murray to be prepared for Kings College, now Columbia University. Murray concentrated on classical studies with his pupil and in 1760 at the age of fourteen, John Jay entered Kings College. Jay's private schooling and young age were somewhat typical for the sons of the upper class at that time when there were no public schools and few well-established colleges. Kings College had received a royal charter from King George II in 1754 and Samuel Johnson, an Anglican minister and good friend of Peter Jay, became its first president. The college initially had strong Anglican ties and the original eight students attended classes in a building located in lower Manhattan at the intersection of Broadway and Murray Street, adjacent to Trinity Church where Jay was baptized and often worshiped. It was a logical choice for John Jay since his brother, Augustus, had been tutored by Samuel Johnson.

Jay's choice of a career in the legal profession may have been influenced by several factors. Some of his classmates included Robert R. Livingston, Jr. who would later become Jay's law partner; Egbert Benson, Peter Van Schaack, and Gouvenor Morris, all of whom achieved great success in either politics or the law. These men also became good friends of John Jay. Most of them would become participants in the American Revolution and members of the Federalist party.

Another strong influence on John Jay's choice of law as a career was his godfather and uncle, former Supreme Court Justice,

Virtues, Talent, Patriotism - Into the Shades of Private Life

John Chambers. Jay often dined with Judge Chambers and his wife, Anne, at their New York City home. When Judge Chambers died in 1764, he left half of his law books to John Jay. Years later, Jay would be the executor of the Will of Anne Chambers.

By 1763 Peter Jay acknowledged his son's career choice when he wrote to him "Your observation on ye Study of ye Law, I believe, is very just,...I hope you'll closely attend to it with a firm resolution...."[6]

Dr. Johnson stressed a curriculum in the classical tradition of Cambridge and Oxford with studies in Greek, Latin, philosophy, public law, and physical science. Johnson had also been influenced by the writings of John Locke and Isaac Newton. His departure from Kings College in 1763 led to the appointment of another Anglican minister, Miles Cooper, who stressed the importance of the classics but reduced the study of science.

On May 22, 1764, at the age of eighteen, John Jay received his bachelor of arts degree. The *New York Mercury* reported on the commencement exercise noting the excellent manner in which John Jay delivered his dissertation on the Happiness and Advantages arising from a State of Peace. Jay was also commended for a debate he argued on the subject of national poverty, opposed to that of national riches with Richard Harrison.[7]

There were no law schools in the colonies, so Jay became a clerk for an experienced lawyer which was the standard path for any aspiring attorney. The New York attorneys, in an attempt to restrict access to the profession and to increase fees, had agreed not to accept any clerks between 1756 through 1769. Realizing this, Peter Jay had inquired of his cousin, David Peloquin, who lived in Bristol, England, about the possibilities of John Jay finding a position there. Peloquin replied that clerks were required to pay a sum £200 and agree to clerk for a period of five years.

However, in 1764 the restrictions on hiring law clerks in New York were lifted. Before his graduation from Kings College, Jay had been negotiating for a position with Benjamin Kissam, a noted New York attorney with a thriving practice. Jay had agreed to apprentice himself to Kissam for the sum of £200 for a period of five years, with the last two years applied to the study of law.

Virtues, Talent, Patriotism - Into the Shades of Private Life

Jay began working in Kissam's office two weeks after graduation from Kings College.

The life of a law clerk was a true test of one's dedication to the law since it consisted of preparing pleadings and judgments, and the drafting of deeds and wills, all in long hand. After a day of writing, Jay was allowed to read law in Kissam's library from legal treatises and to read from his own law dictionary, *New Law Dictionary*, by Giles Jacob. Overseeing Jay's work during his apprenticeship was Lindley Murray, Kissam's senior clerk. In that position, Murray would have handled the court calendar, client billing and trial preparations. Murray, who was to become internationally renowned as a grammarian, recognized Jay's outstanding qualities when he said of Jay years later in his autobiography "His talents and virtues gave at that period pleasing indications of future eminence: He was remarkable for strong reasoning powers, comprehensive views, indefatigable application, and uncommon firmness of mind."[8] These qualities were soon recognized by Benjamin Kissam and a strong bond developed between the attorney and his junior clerk. Jay later said of Kissam that he was "...one of the best men I have ever known, as well as one of the best friends I have ever had."[9] In 1766 Kissam had to leave New York on business and left Jay in charge of the office. He wrote to Jay asking him about the affairs at the office and Jay replied in a very whimsical manner writing whatever came into his head first. The depth of their relationship was revealed in Kissam's reply "I just now received your long letter of the 12th Inst., and am not a little pleased with the humour and freedom of sentiment which characterize it. It would give me pain if I thought you could even suspect me capable of wishing to impose restraint upon you, in this high and inestimable privilege of friendship."[10]

Attorneys were bound by the agreement with the clerk to give legal instruction. Peter Van Schaack, who was to become one of John Jay's good friends and a clerk in the office of noted New York attorney, William Smith, Jr., commented on the education of law clerks at the time and his frustration with the attorney-clerk relationship. He noted the injustice by attorneys on their clerks for not explaining the law to the clerks. This often led the clerk to search for several hours until the applicable section of the law was found.[11]

However, a comradeship had developed among Jay, Kissam and Murray that apparently was unique to the profession when Kissam wrote confidently to Jay regarding his calendar at the Westchester County Courthouse in White Plains which he left for Jay with instructions on the work to be done.[12]

Jay progressed quickly under the tutelage of Kissam and Murray and in 1767 Jay received his Master of Arts degree from Kings College and was admitted to the New York Bar the following year. He went into practice with his good friend from Kings College, Robert R. Livingston, Jr.. Livingston was a member of the Clermont or 'Lower Manor of the Livingston family'. The two men practiced law for three years after which the partnership was dissolved probably because they discovered that their separate efforts could command an adequate share of business.[13]

During his tenure as a solo practitioner, Jay's practice was in civil litigation and was primarily in New York but also extended to Westchester and Dutchess counties. By 1774 he had become one of the most prosperous attorneys in New York.

Jay was also a charter member of "The Moot", a legal debating society formed in 1770 by the leading attorneys in New York. The club was formed for conversation and the furthering of the careers of its members.[14] Jay acquired much expertise from the club's prominent members which included William Livingston, Richard Morris, William Smith, James Duane, Egbert Benson, Robert R. Livingston, Benjamin Kissam and Peter Van Schaack. On one occasion, Jay found himself debating with his mentor, Benjamin Kissam. These debates no doubt helped Jay to hone his public speaking and debating skills for the future.

During this time, Jay also served as a Clerk to the Boundary Commission for the settlement of the disputed boundary between New York and New Jersey. His appointment was due to the efforts of Benjamin Kissam. Serving on a commission of diverse individuals and working with agencies from the colonies and the British colonial service gave him invaluable experience for

Virtues, Talent, Patriotism - Into the Shades of Private Life

future positions in international relations.

Jay's life was not all the practice of law and debating societies. He found time to establish an active social life with membership in New York's "Social Club" which met at Fraunces Tavern during the winter months and at Kips Bay in the summer. Jay was also a member and manager of the New York Dancing Assembly which met at the City Arms. This nearly led him into a duel with a rejected applicant to the club. Though duels were not uncommon at this time, Jay suggested that arbitration by other members of the club would be preferable to a confrontation.[15] Already Jay's preference for a peaceful solution to a problem and his discretion were coming into evidence.

At this time, Jay's thoughts turned to marriage. He sought the hand of one of Peter De Lancey's two daughters. The De Lancey's were rich and powerful leaders of conservative politics in New York and were friends of the Jays with a shared Huguenot heritage. It is understood that Jay's first marriage proposal was rejected on the grounds that the young lady preferred another suitor whom she later married and the other sister also rejected Jay for preference to another. However, sometime between 1772 or 1773, Jay met Sarah van Brugh Livingston. Sarah's father, William Livingston, was fond of Jay and invited him to the Livingston home in Elizabeth, New Jersey where he was charmed by Sarah. Sarah was one of five daughters of William Livingston, a retired attorney and former member of the Moot. The Livingston home was "Liberty Hall" newly built by William Livingston. As the name would suggest, William Livingston was anything but a conservative or Tory. It was at Liberty Hall that Jay met a young, ambitious man from the West Indies named Alexander Hamilton. The two men would have a major impact on the cause of American independence and the formation of the federal republic.

Jay seemed captivated by the sixteen-year old Sarah who was considered by many to be beautiful and vivacious. Her personality was the perfect complement to Jay's serious and reserved character. Sarah accepted Jay's proposal of marriage which delighted Peter Jay when he wrote to William Livingston

Virtues, Talent, Patriotism - Into the Shades of Private Life

"Tho' we have not the pleasure of knowing the young Lady, yet the confidence that we have in our son's Prudence, satisfies us of the Propriety of his choice."[16] They were married at Liberty Hall on April 28, 1774. Jay was twenty-nine and Sarah eighteen, and despite the difference in age, they were devoted to each other. He called her 'Sally' and his letters to her began with, 'My dear Sally' and she responded prophetically by ending one of her letters to him with "Farewell my best beloved. Your wife till death, and after that a ministering spirit."[17] Sarah was to prove to be a perfect mate for Jay, not only as a wife and mother, but as an avid supporter for American independence. With his marriage, Jay had forged another link with the Livingston family.

While Jay and his family strongly supported American rights, they did not advocate a break with England, at least at this time. This was an evolutionary period of political change for Jay which eventually led to his commitment to the revolutionary cause. The year 1774 was to be a turning point in Jay's life both private and public. While he and his wife were honeymooning in rural New York visiting relatives, events in the colonies were taking a very serious and decided turn towards a break with England. Several days before their wedding, New York held its own 'Tea Party' with the dumping of the cargo of the East India Company ship, *London*, into New York harbor to protest the Tea Act which imposed a tax on all tea imported by the Company to the colonies. New York's 'Tea Party' was very similar to the one held in Boston on December 16, 1773. Many in the colonies considered the new tax to be a violation of their right to be taxed only by their own elected officials.

Several weeks after the New York event, the first of the "Intolerable Acts" was passed by Parliament in retaliation for colonial opposition to the Tea Act. The British responded by closing Boston harbor. The Boston Committee of Correspondence appealed to the other colonies for aid for the citizens of Boston who were suffering due to the closing of the port. The New York conservative faction formed a Committee of Twenty-Five which favored the closing of the port of New York to force the British to open the port of Boston. However, New York's conservative merchants feared the political and economic consequences of such a move and organized the Committee of Fifty to which John Jay was elected. The Committee, which soon became the Committee of Fifty-One, strove to prevent New York from becoming involved in any non-importation plan and to maintain a correspondence with the other colonies. Jay himself was active in the Committee's efforts to relieve the suffering of the people of Boston. Still hoping and working for reconciliation with England, Jay even confided to his friend, John Vardill, of his availability for an appointment to a royal but modest and honorary, judicial post but only if it offered a more lucrative position than the one he already had. Jay said he would be glad to resign the tedium of his present position for *Otium cum Dignitate*. [18] The royal appointment never came to pass and John Jay and his wife, Sarah, would soon find their lives for the next quarter of a century shaped by the events of the coming revolution, American independence, and the new republic.

The desire in the colonies for some form of pan-colonial congress resulted in the First Continental Congress to which John Jay was elected as a representative from the province of New York. His father-in-law, William Livingston, was a delegate from New Jersey. On September 4, 1774, the First Continental Congress convened at Carpenter's Hall in Philadelphia to take up the issues of the closing of the port of Boston and the suspension of the government of Massachusetts Bay Colony. Most delegates were not known beyond their colony but Samuel Adams of Massachusetts Bay, George Washington of Virginia and John Dickinson of Pennsylvania had established reputations throughout the colonies. The oratory of Virginia's Patrick Henry for a political break with England did not sway John Jay as he hoped to work for a moderate approach to distinguish himself from the loyalists but he opposed the radicals who favored independence. Jay was appointed to a committee which resulted in his drafting *The Address to the People of Great Britain*, in which he appealed for recognition by the British voters of the unconstitutional nature of the Intolerable Acts stating no one or any power has the right to take anyone's property from them without their consent[19] and that the British government had established slavery in the colonies.[20] Jay wrote the *Address* as one Englishman to another and in a warning to England stated that the colonists would never allow themselves to be debased or subjugated by England.[21] These were strong words for the circumspect Jay, who a few months before was interested in a judicial appointment from the Crown. Jay's plea for moderation and conciliation with England was not a call to arms in a revolution against the mother country but a plea for a restoration of harmonious relations between England and the colonies which was the hope of every American.[22] He had established himself as a leading moderate and differentiated himself from the loyalists and radicals. Jay pursued a course of a restoration of peace, at least for the present. Yet his *Address* expressed republican ideas that were to become part of the new nation about to be born.

On April 20, 1775, Jay was elected by the New York Provincial Congress to the Second Continental Congress. News of the battles of Lexington and Concord reached New York one day after these momentous events. With the convening of the Second Continental Congress in May, Jay was recognized as a leader of the moderate faction. His legal training and literary skills, along with his discretion and pragmatic approach to the problems before the Congress, made him a popular choice for a number of committees. Of particular importance was Jay's work in drafting a petition to the King known as the *Olive Branch Petition*. Congress was still pursuing a course of moderation and conciliation with Great Britain and it was the final draft of John Dickinson of Pennsylvania that was adopted by the Congress. The *Petition* was replete with phrases of the longing for independence by Americans [23] and the restoration of unity and accord[24] and ends with a hope for a secure and permanent reestablishment of relations between Great Britain and its American subjects. The *Petition* was signed by all delegates individually and not as the Congress. No reply to the *Address* was ever received by Congress.

Recognition of Jay's importance in the Congress led to his becoming a member of a Secret Committee of Correspondence with the goal of obtaining foreign support for the colonies. The Committee's success resulted in covert aid from the French and Dutch which enabled the Americans to pursue the Revolution.[25] Jay's position on this committee aided him in developing and refining his diplomatic skills which would be utilized for important future assignments in Spain and France.

In January of 1776, Jay left Congress to be with his pregnant wife, Sarah, who was in Elizabeth Town, New Jersey. On January 24, 1776, the Jay's first child was born. He was named, Peter Augustus, after his grandfather and great grandfather. Mrs. Jay's health was delicate as described by Jay in his letter to Robert Livingston on January 26th and in the same letter, Jay also expressed some concern for his wife.[26] Childbirth was a dangerous procedure for mother and child at that time with a high death rate for both. Jay was also concerned about the poor health of his father, but by March his concerns for his growing family had been allayed and he returned to Philadelphia. He resumed his work for the Secret Committee of Correspondence arranging a correspondence with the committee's agent in Paris, Silas Deane. Jay and Deane corresponded by using a formula for invisible ink developed by Jay's older brother, Sir James Jay, who had been knighted by King George III in 1763 in recognition of his fund raising efforts on behalf of Kings College.

Jay remained in Congress until April, 1776 when he was elected to the New York Provincial Congress. He vacated his seat in Congress fully expecting to return shortly but the pace of events leading to independence would overtake Jay and many other moderates. The primary goal of the New York Provincial Congress was to see to the governing of the Province while continuing to work for peace with Great Britain. Events in Philadelphia to adopt a resolution for independence concerned Jay's moderate colleagues and he was urged to return to Philadelphia to help forestall the adoption of the Declaration of Independence. Jay remained in New York and on July 9th the New York Provisional Congress received a letter from the New York delegates in Philadelphia along with a copy of the Declaration of Independence. Jay drafted the reply to the Congress that same day

Virtues, Talent, Patriotism - Into the Shades of Private Life

"While we lament the cruel necessity which has rendered that measure unavoidable…we approve the same, and will, at the risk of our lives and fortunes, join with the other colonies in supporting it."[27] Jay, being pragmatic, had resigned himself fully to the cause of American independence.

As a member of the New York Provisional Congress, Jay was also involved in work to detect conspiracies in New York, exposing a plot to assassinate Gen. George Washington. Jay also worked to neutralize Loyalist sympathies in New York which resulted in his interrogation of people suspected of being loyal to the crown.

By the fall of 1776 General Sir William Howe had defeated the Americans in the Battle of Long Island which ultimately resulted in Washington withdrawing his troops from New York leaving the city, Long Island, Staten Island, the port of New York and parts of the Hudson Valley as far north as Yonkers under British control. Jay's parents fled north to the Hudson River Valley to the safety of Fishkill and the New York State Provincial Congress retreated to Kingston where John Jay joined them. The safety of Jay's wife and son was of grave concern to him when he wrote his wife "My dear Sally, are you yet provided with a secure retreat in case Elizabethtown should cease to be place of safety. I shall not be at ease till this be done."[28] Yet, Jay's wife and son were also removed to Fishkill for their safety and resided in other areas of the Hudson Valley during the early days of the revolution.

During this period, Jay was appointed to a committee of the Provincial Congress to draft a new constitution for New York State. The committee met intermittently and Jay's draft was for the most part adopted on April 20, 1777. This first constitution was to serve New York for the next fifty years and was one of the models for the Federal Constitution for the nation ratified in 1787. New York's constitution provided for a bicameral legislature. The executive was given veto power in conjunction with a Revision Council composed of judges and legislators. Executive appointments to State positions were to be approved by the Senate. Jay was responsible for the adoption of secret ballots, rather than a voice vote, to reduce the influence of the wealthy on their tenants.

Virtues, Talent, Patriotism - Into the Shades of Private Life

Jay endorsed the new constitution vigorously despite some reservations he had about the document, including his unsuccessful attempt to disenfranchise Roman Catholics by requiring them to publicly renounce the authority of the Pope. The state constitution reflected Jay's views for checks on the power of the executive with council approval for various appointments. Jay believed in popular participation in the government with tax payers having the franchise. The new constitution expanded slightly the number of persons qualified to vote.[29] The gradual elimination of slavery was an issue that would have to wait and was not addressed in the new constitution to Jay's regret.

On May 3, 1777 the Provincial Congress elected Jay the first Chief Justice of the New York State Supreme Court of Judicature. His charges to the jury were endorsements of the revolution and the New York constitution. In the first session of the Court Jay wrote insightfully by urging every resident of the New York State to read the constitution. He reasoned that when people are aware of their rights, they will know when they have been violated and will be prepared to defend those rights.[30] The Supreme Court faced the immense task of administering criminal law during a revolution when the state was divided into two warring camps.

Jay was a successful attorney in the field of civil law but he found criminal law distasteful when he wrote to Gouveneur Morris how disagreeable it was for him to try criminals and that this was the most repugnant part of his duty on the Supreme Court of New York State.[31]

Relief came to Jay through the New York State Constitution and a thirty year boundary dispute with Vermont over the lands north of Massachusetts and west of the Connecticut River. At one point Massachusetts joined in the dispute. All three states petitioned the Continental Congress for relief. Jay had not resigned his seat in the Continental Congress but he was still Chief Justice of the New York State Supreme Court and the state's constitution prohibited state office holders from holding more than one office at a time. Article XXV of the Constitution provided an exception whereby the Chief Justice might, in a State emergency, continue in that post and represent the state as a delegate to the Continental Congress 'upon special occasions'. The Assembly and Senate agreed that the dispute with Vermont was a special case and Jay went on to represent New York in the Congress. There were considerable political and property rights at stake and the Jays had extensive land holdings in the disputed areas along with many other prominent New York families as well as his alma mater, Kings College. For two years, Jay opted to remain in New York and work for the establishment of a new government in which he played a major role after which he was to assume a more prominent role in the national government of the new nation.

When Jay arrived in Philadelphia in December of 1778, the Congress was in a heated debate over the controversial activities of Silas Deane, the American agent in Paris attempting to obtain financial aid from the French. When the president of the Congress, Henry Laurens, resigned over the dispute, Jay was elected president of the Continental Congress which made him the highest official in the land.

The office of president afforded Jay limited authority with extensive administrative duties. Jay's correspondence increased to such a degree that he retained two clerks to assist him in addressing the many fiscal, military, constitutional and diplomatic issues before Congress. As president of the Congress, Jay presided over congressional proceedings while retaining his vote as a delegate. The considerable debating skills that he acquired from his years as a member of the Moot, were not put to use. However, Jay was refining his diplomatic skills holding discussions with Conrad Gerard, the French minister, and working behind the scenes for peace with France. The result was a Franco-American alliance with French recognition of American independence and its commercial rights.

Jay's separation from his wife began to weigh on her and writing from Persipiney, New Jersey, Mrs. Jay commented almost sardonically to her husband "I had the pleasure of finding by the newspaper that you are honored by the first office of the Continent, and I am still more pleased to hear this appointment affords general satisfaction."[32] Obviously tired by the prolonged

Virtues, Talent, Patriotism - Into the Shades of Private Life

separation from her husband she inquired "...I am solicitous to know how long I am still to remain in a state of widowhood;...."[33] and continued with "...I should not have been Roman matron enough to have given you so entirely to the public,..."[34] Jay did find a house for his wife in Philadelphia where she joined him and acted as hostess to many diplomats thereby supporting her husband in his diplomatic endeavors as she would continue to do for a number of years with great success.

By 1779 events in Europe were to have a direct bearing on the course of Jay's career as a public official and set him firmly on the path of diplomacy. In April, 1779, Spain issued an ultimatum to Great Britain offering to mediate the war between France and Great Britain. Without waiting for a reply, Spain secretly ratified the Convention of Aranjuez with France thus committing Spain to war with Great Britain. The Americans became alarmed over the secret treaty and the effect it had on its alliance with France. The Americans felt that the French had not made provision for sharing fishing rights off the coast of Newfoundland in the secret treaty with Spain. After sessions in Congress, presided over by Pres. John Jay, Congress appointed Jay Minister Plenipotentiary to Spain. Jay's emergence as a promising diplomat through his efforts as a member of the Secret Committee of Correspondence and his work on the Franco-American alliance were no doubt recognized by Congress in its selection of Jay for this mission to Spain. His primary goals were to secure a loan of five million dollars from Madrid, obtain free navigation of the Mississippi River for America to its southern boundary, secure fishing rights on the banks and coast of Newfoundland and have the British evacuate their troops from United States territory.[35]

Sarah Jay, in her decision to accompany her husband to Spain, set a new standard in the pattern of behavior for women to join their husbands in their overseas missions. In doing so, she would support her husband in the coming years of crucial diplomatic efforts that would lead to American independence. Not even the wives of Silas Deane or John Adams chose to accompany their husbands overseas. The letters of John and Sarah during the first years of his life in public service reflect a dissatisfaction with

Virtues, Talent, Patriotism - Into the Shades of Private Life

the long separations the two had to endure. In the end, she was supported by her family in her decision to accompany her husband. Her brother, William, Jr. wrote to his sister encouraging her in her mission and he believed that she would honor her country and family by her actions.[36] Sarah's mother, Susannah French Livingston, echoed her son's words when she wrote to Sarah "Viewing you in the way of your duty and happiness to accompany your best friend...."[37]

The Jays set off for Spain aboard the American frigate *Confederacy* and were accompanied by Jay's Secretary of Legation, William Carmichael; his personal secretary and Jay's brother-in-law, Henry Brockholst Livingston; Jay's teenage nephew, Peter Jay Munro; and Conrad Gerard, the retiring French minister to the United States and his wife. Crossing the Atlantic during the winter storm months was dangerous enough but the passengers aboard the *Confederacy* were prime targets for the British if they had been captured. The ship put into Martinique due to storm damage. Here the Jays saw the harsh brutality of life for slaves who toiled on the island's sugar plantations bound with chains and neck collars. Jay bought a 'Negro' boy of fifteen, named Benoit, whom Jay later manumitted when Benoit reached adulthood and could manage for himself. This was a practice Jay used with some of his slaves until 1820, when only free men and women worked at Jay's farm.

The Jays arrived in Spain at Cadiz on January 22, 1780. John Jay embarked on a difficult mission with the Spaniards and was to summon all of his diplomatic skills which Mrs. Jay noted in a letter to her mother during the final days of the crossing her abiding love and admiration for her husband and his fine qualities.[38] This was an insightful observation of her husband's considerable talents which would be used so skillfully by him in the coming years in defense of his country.

Spain was not supportive of the American cause, fearful that the rebellion would spread to its own colonies in Central and South America. The Spanish were also deeply concerned with the American settlers in the Spanish territory between the Appalachian Mountains and the Mississippi River. Spain was very protective

Virtues, Talent, Patriotism - Into the Shades of Private Life

of Florida, one of its prized possessions, which now bordered the new state of Georgia. American expansion into Spanish territories was a prime concern for Spain and they would not have been at all disappointed if the Americans were defeated in their cause. Count Floridablanca, the king's Minister, gave Jay little hope for success in his mission. Added to this was Spain's denial of a formal recognition to Jay's mission because Spain did not recognize America's independence from Great Britain. On a personal level there was the tragic death of the Jay's second child, Susan, only one month after her birth in July of 1780. Jay's staff was also the cause of much irritation and great disappointment to him. William Carmichael, the Secretary of the Legation, did not like Jay and Carmichael's inability to settle his financial accounts increased the difficulty of the relations between the two men. Brockholst Livingston did little to aid Jay's mission with his public ridicule of Congress which may have been prompted by his military service and the sometimes seeming neglect in which Congress treated the military. Such behavior was improper for a diplomat and it was Sarah Jay who took her brother to task at dinner one evening, with several diplomats in attendance. Lastly, Lewis Littlepage was sent to Spain to join the Jay family but instead of studying French and the arts, Littlepage took an interest in the ladies and the art of war, ultimately becoming a mercenary. The seemingly doomed mission to Spain ended mercifully for Jay when in May of 1782 he was called to Paris to join his fellow Americans as one of the American Commissioners to negotiate a peace treaty with Great Britain after the American victory over Gen. Cornwallis and the British forces at Yorktown.

    Samuel Flagg Bemis, the noted diplomatic historian, in observing Jay's mission to Spain wrote said that Jay's arrival in Spain and his departure from Spain were the most important moments of his mission.[39] Despite not achieving one of his stated goals, Jay gained valuable diplomatic experience during his mission to Spain. He was the first American representative to that country and did acquire some insight into Spanish policies and finances. Not recognized by the Spanish government as the representative from the United States, Jay displayed great patience and dedication in carrying out a thankless mission. The diplomatic education Jay received in Spain would prove to be invaluable experience in Paris.

When Benjamin Franklin, the American Ambassador to France, deemed his preliminary discussions with the British agent, Richard Oswald, to have reached a critical and serious stage, he thought it necessary to have the American commissioners present. He wrote to Jay "here your are greatly wanted, for messengers begin to come and go, and there is much talk of a treaty proposed, but I can neither make, nor agree to propositions of peace, without the assistance of my colleagues."[40] Franklin assured Jay that he would be of 'infinite service'. The other American commissioners were John Adams, the first American commissioner, who was in Holland taking up his post as the newly appointed ambassador to the Dutch court and did not join the other commissioners until October of 1782. Another American commissioner was Henry Laurens who had been captured by the British at sea and was imprisoned in the Tower of London and not released until the preliminary peace treaty was signed. Thomas Jefferson, the fourth commissioner, remained in America.

Realizing that he could not attain his goals for his mission to Spain, Jay left for Paris with his wife and daughter, Maria, who was born on February 20, 1782 in Spain. They arrived in France in April of that year. Jay and his family settled in a house near Franklin in the Paris suburb of Passy where another daughter, Ann, was born in August of 1783. Although Jay had been appointed one of the commissioners to negotiate a treaty with Great Britain in 1781, he had remained in Spain in the hope of obtaining a loan from the Spanish government until he realized the futility of his mission.

The Jay's social life in France was quite different from the diplomatic and social ostracism they had encountered in Spain. Mrs. Jay's fluency in French and her outgoing personality and sense of fashion contributed to her social success. The Jay's quickly became part of the diplomatic scene and they received many invitations to social events including invitations from the Marquis de Lafayette. As the wife of a recognized diplomat,

Virtues, Talent, Patriotism - Into the Shades of Private Life

Sarah embraced the role of hostess at the many social events the Jays held, a role which she would play many times in the future with great success. She was a dutiful wife, mother and hostess as would be expected of someone in her position. Her decision to be with her husband inspired the wives of other Americans attached to the peace commission to accompany their husbands to France, including Alice De Lancey Izard of the Westchester County De Lancey family.

    Before Jay entered into the formal negotiations, he insisted that the British treat the commissioners as representatives of the United States of America, thereby guaranteeing British recognition of American independence before the formal negotiations commenced and that Great Britain's unconditional recognition of American independence be part of the treaty. Jay remained implacable on this point and issues throughout the negotiations and he conducted himself in a very organized and lawyer-like manner. Shortly after the Jays arrived in Paris, Franklin became ill and Jay was fully in charge of the negotiations until Franklin recovered and the two constituted the *de facto* American negotiators. However, Jay was to assume a critical role in the negotiations. Benjamin Vaughan, who was a British peace commissioner and who held extensive talks with Jay and Franklin in the hope of reaching a settlement, thought that Jay possessed many fine qualities that would stand him in good stead during the negotiations.[41] Using all his diplomatic skills and judgment, Jay disregarded instructions from Congress concerning soliciting advice from the French during the negotiations. Jay realized from his mission in Spain that the French were concerned more with their own interests in Europe than in any commitment to the United States.[42] By taking this position, Jay entered into secret negotiations with the British, excluding the Comte de Vergennes of France, a move which surprised and angered some in Congress. Undeterred, Jay himself drafted the Preliminary Articles of Peace and after several revisions, the Articles were signed on November 30, 1782. During the interim, John Adams pressed issues primarily concerning fishing rights and compensation for Loyalists. The final peace treaty signed on September 3, 1783 by

Virtues, Talent, Patriotism - Into the Shades of Private Life

all belligerents confirmed the preliminary treaty of 1782.[43] The United States had won a great victory including its independence from Great Britain, fishing rights off the Great Banks, the extension of its western boundary from the Appalachian Mountains to the Mississippi River and the recovery of claims by creditors against the new nation.[44] John Adams later wrote to Jay with the highest praise for his efforts "A man and his office were never better united than Mr. Jay and his commission for peace."[45] John Adams further expounded on the 'neophyte' American commissioners when he commented "Undisciplined marines as we were..." and that "...we were better tacticians than we imagined."[46] The Treaty of Paris was an historic victory for the Americans, but John Jay and his countrymen would work hard to insure the terms of the treaty for several decades. Richard B. Morris, the noted Jay scholar, thought that Jay's diplomatic skill in negotiating the Treaty of Paris ranks as one of the greatest achievements in American diplomatic history.[47]

After the signing of the treaty, the Jays remained in Paris while Jay and the other American commissioners attempted to negotiate new trade agreements with the European powers, but Prussia was the only interested nation. In March, 1784 the formal ratification of the peace treaty by Congress had arrived and the Jays made plans to return to America. Jay made a brief visit to England to settle some family affairs and on May 16, 1784, and after nearly five years in Europe, the Jays set sail on the American ship the *Edward*, and arrived in New York to a tumultuous welcome. The city of New York presented Jay and others, including Gen. Washington and Gov. Clinton, with the "Freedom of the City in gold boxes." In the Official Congratulations from New York City to John Jay, the city echoed the sentiments of the nation "Among these worthy patriots you, Sir, are highly distinguished. ... you have executed the important trusts committed to you with wisdom, firmness and integrity, and have acquired universal applause."[48] Jay then thanked the City expressing his happiness on his return and his hopes for America "If our views be national, our union preserved, our faith kept, war however improbable provided for, knowledge diffused, and our federal government rendered efficient, we cannot fail to become a great and happy people."[49] Another honor was bestowed on Jay by Congress while on the ocean voyage home - he had been elected Secretary for Foreign Affairs. Jay had expressed his wishes to retire from public life and resume his legal career, but at the urgings of Charles Thomson, Secretary of Congress, to fill the need for strong leadership in the new nation and the high regard in which Jay was held by Americans, Jay accepted the position. He took the oath of office on December 21, 1784. He was confronted immediately with violations of the Treaty of Paris with the British refusal to withdraw troops from the Northwest Territory (the area north of the Ohio River bounded by the Mississippi and the Great Lakes) and the difficulty of British creditors to sue American debtors in State courts. British creditors were being denied relief granted to them by Article IV of the Peace Treaty, and as a result, the British felt justified in not withdrawing troops from the Northwest Territory. These two issues would finally be resolved a decade later by the Supreme Court when Jay was Chief Justice and his efforts in negotiating the Jay Treaty with England.

Jay also initiated discussions that led to the establishment of consular posts with China so that American merchants could participate in the lucrative China trade. Jay attempted to resolve the issue of free navigation for Americans of the Mississippi River, something he had sought from the Spanish as minister to Spain and as a peace commissioner. As Secretary of Foreign Affairs, Jay had discussions with the Spanish charge d'affaires, Don Diego de Gardoqui. Jay concluded that it might be prudent for the United States to temporarily forego its claims to navigate the Mississippi River, if Spain would enter into a commercial agreement with the United States. Jay's plan met with opposition from Congress for sacrificing free navigation of the Mississippi River, which was essential to American expansion in the West, in favor of Atlantic coast interests. The proposed plan was tabled by Congress.

Then there was the issue of the Barbary pirates that confronted Jay. Pirates from the north African states of Morocco, Algiers, Tunis and Tripoli seized vessels in their sphere of influence, enslaved the crews and demanded ransom from their governments. The United States, with no standing army or navy, had no other choice but to pay 'tribute' for the release of Americans held captive. Jay sought to raise the ransom through private channels and from state governments but without success.

During this period, Jay had many social duties to perform and he was ably assisted by his wife, Sarah. The Jays built a house at No.8 Broadway in New York City and it was here that Mrs. Jay firmly established herself as a leading hostess in the city. "Mrs. Jay's Dinner and Supper List for 1787 and 1788" reflected the guests invited to the numerous events she planned, usually a dinner every week, and included the diplomatic corps, leading colonial families and noted statesmen of the time. The experience of living in Europe and being introduced to European customs benefited the Jays in their entertaining as a guest duly noted at a dinner reception at the Jay residence:

> Yesterday we dined at Mrs. Jay's in company with the whole corps diplomatique. Mr. Jay is a most pleasing man plain in his manners. But kind, affectionate, and attentive; benevolence is stamped in every feature. Mrs. Jay dresses showily, but is very pleasing on a first acquaintance. The dinner was a la Francaise, and exhibited more of European taste than I had expected to find.[50]

Clearly, European living had made an impression on the Jays, especially Mrs. Jay. These dinners were a success on another level for they no doubt afforded Jay and his important guests an opportunity for discussions on a range of topics.

During his tenure as Secretary of Foreign Affairs, Jay proved himself to be a highly capable administrator. He instituted a filing system for correspondence and state papers that remained in practice well into the nineteenth century. However, it had become increasingly obvious to many, including Jay, that the ineffectual Articles of Confederation needed to be replaced by a new government and constitution. Jay was often frustrated with Congress and its inability to act on his recommendations. He considered the national government weak and ineffectual complicating his duties in foreign matters. In a letter to Thomas Jefferson, Jay spoke about the weakness of the present government and the need for a stronger one "A form of government so constructed has inconveniences which I think will operate against the public or national interest until some cause not easy to be predicted shall produce such a modification of it as that the legislative, judicial and executive business of government may be consigned to three proper and distinct departments."[51] Jay's enunciation of a federalist form of government and support for the Philadelphia Convention of 1787 to draft a new constitution was confined to correspondence with trusted individuals rather than open criticism. Jay wrote definitively to Washington about the need for a new government "Let Congress legislate. Let others execute. Let others judge."[52]

In all respects, Jay continued in his post with unswerving duty to his position, to his country and to God when he said "All that the best men can do is, to preserve in doing their duty to their country, and leave the consequence to Him who made it their duty; being neither elated by success, however great, not discouraged by disappointments however frequent and mortifying."[53]

Jay was not a member of the New York delegation to the Philadelphia Convention. He was defeated in the state Senate due to his strong federalist leanings in support of the adoption of the Federal Constitution drafted by the Philadelphia Convention and now put before the states for ratification. In 1787 and 1788 Jay joined forces with Alexander Hamilton and James Madison in a series of essays, *The Federalist*, written anonymously under the name of Publius, and in support of the ratification of the Constitution in New York State. Jay authored essays numbers two, three, four, five and sixty-four that dealt with the difficult position the United States had been placed in with regard to foreign affairs. In the second *Federalist* paper, Jay wrote that the Americans and North American continent were ideally suited to each other.[54] He further deplored the divisiveness that [55] which

Virtues, Talent, Patriotism - Into the Shades of Private Life

Jay believed was the result of the Articles of Confederation. Jay and his fellow Federalists favored a strong national government, a separate federal judiciary with a supreme court as a court of final appeal, and a system of checks and balances on the three proposed branches of the federal government: the legislative, the executive and the judicial. Illness prevented Jay from writing more essays but the effect of the essays contributed to a public dialogue over the ratification issue. Jay also authored a pamphlet, *An Address* to *the People of the State of New York,* which was a powerful defense for the new Constitution. Writing under the name, A Citizen of New York, Jay stated in conclusion:

> If the people of our nation, instead of consenting to be governed by laws of their own making and rulers of their own choosing, should let licentiousness, disorder, and confusion reign over them, the minds of men everywhere will insensibly become alienated from republican forms and prepared to prefer and acquiesce in governments which, though less friendly to liberty, afford more peace and security.[56]

Jay's Address, which focused more on the current political situation, was written for the average reader. It was published in the spring of 1788 and had a great effect in gaining support for the ratification of the Constitution. Jay sent a copy of the Address to George Washington who was impressed with the 'good sense, forcible observations' of the document and the effect it would have on the Antifederalists. Jay then turned his attention and talents to the ratification of the Constitution in New York State at the Poughkeepsie Convention. Jay was joined by Alexander Hamilton and Robert R. Livingston, Jr. in leading the fight for ratification against the Antifederalists led by Gov. George Clinton. On July 26, 1788, the delegates voted thirty to twenty-three to ratify the Constitution. George Washington, who was following the ratification very closely, wrote to Jay "With peculiar pleasure I now congratulate you on the success of your labours to obtain an unconditional ratification of the proposed constitution in the Convention of your State...."[57] Jay replied to Washington about his steadfast conviction to federalism "The division of powers of government into three departments, is a great and valuable point gained, and will give the people the best opportunity of bringing the question whether they can govern themselves to a decision in their favor."[58]

Jay remained in his position as Secretary for Foreign Affairs until his resignation in 1789. He continued to act as Secretary at the request of Pres. Washington until Thomas Jefferson returned from France to assume the position of Secretary of State.

When Jay returned to New York from the successful negotiations leading to the Treaty of Paris, it was his intention to retire to his farm in Bedford with his wife and family. He wrote to his friend Robert R. Livingston, Jr. that his believed his public career was at an end since America had obtained its objectives.[59] Yet, Jay realized that the new nation would need the services of experienced men such as himself. He left open the door to continuing in public service, placing his sense of public duty above personal desires, when he wrote to General Schuyler "If on my return, I find it my duty to devote more of my time to the public, they shall have it, though retirement is what I ardently desire."[60] In that same spirit, Jay urged Gen. Washington to abandon his retirement to Mount Vernon and accept his appointment as a delegate from Virginia to the Federal Convention and not remain on the sidelines as an observer at this all too important juncture in America's history "...I am persuaded that you cannot view them with the eye of an unconcerned spectator."[61]

As president, Washington realized that the legitimacy of the new Constitution was of primary concern and he gave a great deal of thought to his appointments, especially to the Supreme Court. Article III and other Articles of the Constitution mandated the creation of a Supreme Court with judges nominated by the president, confirmed by the Senate to serve for life during good behavior with an unspecified salary that could not be diminished.[62] In the Federal Judiciary Act of 1789, the Supreme Court would

Virtues, Talent, Patriotism - Into the Shades of Private Life

consist of a Chief Justice and five Associate Justices. Each state was to have a Federal district court with its own judge who lived in the district. The next level was the Circuit Court, one for each state, and the courts were grouped into three circuits; eastern, middle and southern circuits. Each Circuit Court would be presided over by two Supreme Court Justices and the district judge for the state in which the Circuit Court was sitting. It was the hope of Congress that the Supreme Court Justices would help to promote the new government for the good of all, by extending the law to every citizen's home and the Courts to their doorsteps.[63]

The Circuit Courts met twice a year in the spring and the fall, thereby requiring the Justices to ride circuit to the courts. The Justices were away from their homes for extended periods of time and traveling during the worst months of the year in February and August over crude, bumpy and often muddy roads. The Justices often had to stay in local taverns where the food was poor and the sleeping accommodations assigned up to twelve others in a single bed. The Chief's salary was $4,000 and the Associate Justices were paid $3,500 out of which they were to pay for their traveling expenses, which left very little money at the end of the year.

Washington realized that the new federal judiciary was independent and the last court of appeal, answerable to no other authority, unlike the British judiciary and the judiciaries of several states. His criterion for the six nominees were based on character, reputation, legal background and experience, geographical interests, Revolutionary War experience and lastly, only men who supported the Constitution.[64] It appeared that James Wilson of Pennsylvania, John Rutledge of South Carolina and Chancellor Robert R. Livingston of New York were prime candidates for the position of Chief Justice, but Washington offered the post to Jay who was known throughout the country for his impeccable character. In offering the position to Jay, Washington said he relied on his own judgment and expressed a high level of confidence in Jay's loyalty, especially his close association with Washington during the Revolution, Jay's tenure as president of the Continental Congress and his credibility. Washington's nominations for the Supreme Court, John Jay, John Rutledge,

Virtues, Talent, Patriotism - Into the Shades of Private Life

James Wilson, William Cushing of Massachusetts, Robert H. Harrison of Maryland, and John Blair of Virginia, were sent to the Senate for confirmation the day Washington signed the Judiciary Act of 1789. Without any hearings, the Senate confirmed all of Washington's nominations to the Supreme Court two days later.

As Chief Justice, Jay established the rules of practice before the Supreme court, much as he had done as Chief Justice of New York years earlier. His rule for admission of attorneys to practice before the court was three years of practice before the highest courts of the state of their residence and a "fair" professional character. Jay thought it best to continue some of the practices that had been adopted after the Revolution, including the wearing of black robes and elaborate judicial wigs for the judges. Jay was deeply religious and he supported the New England tradition of having a clergyman offer a prayer at the opening of each court session. Realizing that the Antifederalists were skeptical of the new federal judiciary, fearing that it would deprive state courts of their jurisdiction in some areas of law, Jay, eschewed the suggestions of parades or opening ceremonies for the courts. He wanted the focus to be on the workings of each court to render impartial and fair judgments to all.

On February 1, 1790 the first session of the Supreme Court was held in New York City in the Old Royal Exchange building on Broad Street near the intersection of Water Street. There was an assemblage of state judges and other members of the bar as well as local dignitaries at the Court's first session. Chief Justice Jay and Associate Justices William Cushing and James Wilson were present. It is interesting to note that Justice Cushing wore a judicial wig but quickly dispensed with it after observing that his colleagues were wearing traditional wigs which Justice Cushing opted for as well. There is no record of exactly what type of robe was worn by the judges but one newspaper account reported that Jay wore a black silk judicial robe trimmed with salmon fabric.[65] A robe of such a description is now preserved at the Smithsonian Institute in Washington, D.C. as being, 'Chief Justice John Jay's Judicial Robe.'[66] Several newspapers reported how elegant the justices looked in their robes which met with the

Virtues, Talent, Patriotism - Into the Shades of Private Life

approval of the crowd.[67] Lacking a quorum, but having made a favorable first impression, the court adjourned. The new court had attracted great attention with the public and there were numerous accounts of the first session in many newspapers, in New York and Pennsylvania.[68] The following day, Justice James Blair and Attorney General Edmond Randolph arrived. Over the next several days the court held sessions, and completed some administrative work with the appointment of a Clerk of the Court, the Court Crier, adoption of the Court's seals, formulation of the rules of the Court and the admission of attorneys to practice before the Court.[69]

The Court adjourned on February 10th and the members of the Supreme Court were entertained by the Grand Jury of the District Court at Fraunces Tavern. Toasts were drunk to federal judiciary and the Constitution.[70] The proceedings of the Court's first session were printed in many newspapers from Massachusetts to Georgia, and treated as a major event.[71] The new court had obviously attracted much attention and its proceedings were of great interest to the public.

Jay and other members of the Supreme Court questioned the wisdom of Congress in the Judiciary Act of having the justices of the Supreme Court ride circuit. Judge Iredell, who was assigned to the Southern Circuit comprising Georgia, and North and South Carolina, had to ride circuit twice a year and appear at the sessions of the Supreme Court twice a year as well. He wrote to Jay of his doubts about riding circuit and being able to perform his duty as a Justice of the Supreme Court.[72] Jay commented that, "the circuits press hard on us all" and Judge Johnson resigned from the Supreme Court after two years due to the rigors of riding circuit. The Justices also objected to a conflict of interest in hearing cases in the Circuit Courts and reasoned that should a decision from a Circuit Court be appealed to the Supreme Court, two of the six Justices would be reviewing their decision from the lower court. The Justices made annual appeals and submitted drafts to Congress to revise the federal court system and abolish circuit riding. The Judiciary Act of 1792 granted some relief to the court providing that no judge should be assigned to ride any circuit he had not already ridden.[73] This resulted in the Justices taking turns riding circuit. Jay and Iredell rode the Southern Circuit in 1793. Although Iredell was not favorably disposed to Jay on a personal basis, he later said of Jay to his wife that Jay was a more likable person once you got to know him.[74] Jay, missing his wife and family, took his wife and his son, Peter Augustus, with him when he rode circuit in 1791.

While riding circuit, Jay kept a diary noting various taverns, weather conditions, agricultural pursuits and the rise of new factories. On occasion, he was met by a welcoming committee of local officials and sometimes stayed with acquaintances rather than at a tavern. At one home he noted in his circumspect manner "heard many anecdotes, not to be written."[75] He corresponded with his wife and spoke of the rigors of riding circuit and how much he missed his family but he also found time to meet with local people and bought a telescope from a Revolutionary War veteran.

Throughout his tenure as Chief Justice, Jay impressed people but not with his personal appearance as one eye-witness in Boston noted:

> His height was a little less than six feet; his person rather thin, but well formed. His complexion was without color, his eyes black [they were really blue] and penetrating, his nose aquiline, and his chin pointed. His hair came over his forehead, was tied behind, and lightly powdered. His dress black. The expression of his face was exceedingly amiable. When standing, he was a little inclined forward, as is not uncommon with students long accustomed to bend over a table. His manner was very gentle and unassuming.[76]

However, unassuming and ordinary John Jay may have been in his appearance, it was his character and enduring credibility that impressed people. Joseph Loring, a Boston merchant, was also unimpressed with Jay's understated appearance but observed that appearances can be deceiving since Jay was said to be a man of talent and compassion.[77]

During Jay's tenure, the Supreme Court asserted that the Court would not provide any extra-judicial or advisory opinions. Jay played a major role in this evolution of the Supreme Court emerging as a separate but equal branch of the federal government and in stressing the sanctity of checks and balances among the three branches of the government under the Constitution. On August 3, 1793 Jay and four other members of the Court who were present, signed a letter addressed to Pres. Washington in which the Court stressed the concept of checks and balances in the federal government:

> These being certain respects checks upon each other, and our being judges of a court in the last resort, are considerations which afford strong arguments against the propriety of our extra-judicially deciding the questions alluded to, especially as the power given by the Constitution to the President, of calling on the heads of departments for opinions, seems to have been purposely as well as expressly united to the executive departments.[78]

The new federal government was in its infancy and many aspects of the separation of powers had to be resolved. Jay's answer to the president on the issue of extra-judicial opinions was compelling and defined the issue of a separate and independent judiciary by establishing the precedent that the Supreme Court would not give opinions on issues not before the Court.

Jay used his charges to the grand jury not only to instruct the jury about the case before the court, but he used every opportunity to give resounding endorsements to the federal system of government. He discussed various aspects of federalism and the new constitution and urged the jurors to be patient with the

Virtues, Talent, Patriotism - Into the Shades of Private Life

new government stressing its many positive aspects over the old Confederation. Many of the charges to the Grand Jury were published and well received by the public. One of the court's spectators observed how respected Jay is and the importance of his addresses to the Grand Jury.[79]

Although the Supreme Court rendered few decisions, Jay himself worked on 400 cases while riding circuit. One of the major questions confronting the courts at this time was the issue of the payment of war debts owed by Americans to British merchants and whether state laws were invalid or constitutional. This was an issue Jay dealt with as a Peace Commissioner and Secretary of Foreign Affairs and now had to grapple with the issue as Chief Justice. In the case of *Ware v. Hilton*, the issue before the court was whether British creditors could sue American creditors in a Circuit Court. Mindful of America's treaty obligations, Jay ruled in favor of the British petitioners, strongly supporting the new Circuit Courts. His was the minority opinion. The Court ruled that a Virginia statute contravened the Treaty of Paris with Great Britain. When the case was appealed to the Supreme Court three years later, the Court upheld Jay's opinion, even though he was no longer on the Court and during the interim he had negotiated a treaty with Great Britain that settled the issue.

Perhaps the most notable case decided while Jay was on the Court was *Chisholm v. Georgia*. This case involved a state's sovereign immunity, and original jurisdiction of the Supreme Court. The state of Georgia was sued in the Supreme Court for debts incurred by the State of Georgia during the Revolutionary War and the creditor was from the state of South Carolina. The judges followed the Constitution which gave the Court jurisdiction in cases between a state and citizens of another state and upheld the Court's jurisdiction in the case. The Court recognized the right of a citizen of one state to bring a suit in the Supreme Court against another state. In his opinion regarding state sovereignty Jay stated that sovereignty derived from the people and so too the sovereignty of the country was also derived from the people, a notion that was expressed some twenty-six years later by Chief Justice John Marshall in the landmark case of *McCullough v.*

Maryland. Jay's reasoning in this case was a strong endorsement for the Constitution and the federal system of government. The case caused such an uproar in the country, viewed by many as an assault on state's rights, that the Eleventh Amendment to the Constitution was ratified stating that no State could be sued by the citizens of any other state in the Supreme Court.

Jay was steadfast in his belief of a strong federal government during his time on the Supreme Court. He had made significant strides in establishing the supremacy and independency of the Supreme Court and in defining its role in the new federal government during his brief time on the court, as well as establishing precedents and administrative procedures. However, in 1794, Pres. Washington once again had need of Jay's negotiating skills.

The British were not honoring their treaty commitments under the Treaty of Paris regarding vacating their military posts in America. In the Northwest Territory, many Americans thought that the British were arming the Native American tribes in the area who were rebelling against the new settlers. To complicate matters, the British would have to surrender their access to the profitable fur-trading routes in giving up their military posts. Then there was the problem of British impressment of American sailors.

Pres. Washington wanted to exhaust all peaceful means to settle the dispute with Great Britain and he did not hesitate to turn to Jay for assistance by asking him to accept an appointment as Envoy Extraordinary to Great Britain. Jay had not sought this position and he realized the dangers of negotiating with Great Britain, having to gain concessions on both sides and the effect any unpopular treaty would have on his popularity and his political future. Before rendering his decision, Jay wrote to his wife that there was a movement to send him to England to negotiate a treaty with the British to avoid another war and that he was torn between his duty to this county and his personal wishes to avert a war. In considering the importance of the occasion, he knew that his wife would agree with him. He went on to state the difficulty in accepting the position and that he did not seek this mission but

Virtues, Talent, Patriotism - Into the Shades of Private Life

would do his duty.[80]

    Jay sailed from New York to a large cheering crowd and gun salutes with his son, Peter Augustus, who had recently graduated from Columbia College. Jay landed in England on June 8, 1794 and after a brief tour of England, took up residence in London at the Hotel Royal on the Mall. While in London, he and his son were welcomed and entertained by British society. Favorable reports of Jay had been sent to London by British agents in America and Jay had many British and American friends in England. He was presented to the King and Queen and received endless invitations to dinner parties, theatre outings and weekends at numerous estates. He was often in the company of Sir John Sinclair and the two exchanged views on numerous agricultural and horticultural subjects culminating with Jay's unanimous election to the British Board of Agriculture.

    In the midst of this social whirl, Jay began negotiations with Lord Grenville, the British Foreign Secretary and leader of the House of Lords. In November of 1794, a treaty, the Treaty of Amity, Commerce and Navigation, more commonly known as the Jay Treaty, was signed and secured the much hoped-for peace for the United States, but at a price. The British agreed to evacuate the frontier posts and the treaty also guaranteed the payment of British war debts as had been previously agreed to in the Treaty of Paris in 1783. Jay had obtained the right of American merchants to trade in the British West Indies but only in vessels of less than seventy tons, thus rendering them incapable of making a trans-Atlantic crossing in such a small vessel which severely restricted American foreign trade. While the treaty was ratified, it was widely condemned throughout the country for its restrictive trading clause and Jay was burned in effigy across the country. At a rally in New York City, the following was exhibited in a window "Damn John Jay! Damn every one that won't damn John Jay!! Damn every one that won't put lights in his windows and sit up all night damning John Jay!!!"[81]

    Although the treaty secured a much needed peace for the United States, it did widen the gulf between the Federalist and Republican parties in the country with the treaty regarded as a

Virtues, Talent, Patriotism - Into the Shades of Private Life

Federalist treaty. Jay had performed the thankless task of negotiating an unpopular treaty under difficult circumstances but he had secured peace for his country at a time when it was ill prepared to go to war with Great Britain and risk the independence of the new nation. Jay was well aware of the assignment he had accepted and the reception the treaty he signed would meet with in America. He wrote to Pres. Washington from London in 1795 that any treaty he negotiated would not meet with universal approval.[82] He went on to further state philosophically his profound belief "The time will come when all books and histories and errors will be consumed, and when from their ashes truth only will rise and prevail and be immortal."[83]

When Jay returned to New York City, he learned that he had been nominated for the governorship of the State of New York and early returns gave all indications that he had been elected governor. In 1792, Jay had challenged George Clinton for the governorship of New York, but lost in a hotly disputed election with returns from upstate counties favorable to Clinton having decided the election. The Federalist party in New York was eager to end George Clinton's hold on the governorship. He was New York's first and only governor for eighteen years and in John Jay, the Federalist party believed they had the right candidate for the office. Jay did not actively seek the governorship in 1792 and again in 1795 but made it understood to his supporters that he was available for the office. He was elected governor by a clear majority of 1,589 out of a total 25,373 votes cast.

Jay resigned his position as Chief Justice on June 29, 1795, and on July 2, 1795, he was sworn in as governor. No longer would Jay have to endure the rigors of circuit riding and he could now be closer to his family.

Almost immediately after taking office, Jay was confronted with a major issue. While the newspapers were denouncing Jay and his treaty with Great Britain, a yellow fever epidemic had broken out in New York City. While many people fled the city, Jay and his family remained in New York at the governor's new residence, Government House, with a commanding view of New York harbor. Jay insisted on remaining

Virtues, Talent, Patriotism - Into the Shades of Private Life

in the city with his family during the epidemic so as not to cause further alarm by evacuating to a safer place. The cold weather checked the spread of the epidemic after almost 700 people died. Jay recommended, because he was not sure that he had the authority to issue a proclamation, that Thursday, the 26th of November be set aside 'as a day of prayer and Thanksgiving.' This was the first Thanksgiving Day in New York State. To try and stem future outbreaks of the disease and relieve the conditions of those in quarantine, Jay wrote to Richard Varick, the mayor of New York City, and urged that Bedloe's Island be used as a 'lazaretto', or sick house, to quarantine sick persons. Jay then sponsored legislation which was enacted by the state legislature.

In Jay's first address to the State Legislature, he promised a fair and non-partisan administration which he carried out to the surprise of both the Federalists and the Clintonians (or Democratic-Republicans) parties. During his two terms as governor, not one state official had been dismissed from office due to political affiliation. His administration has been praised as one of able men and honest service.[84] During a discussion with the Council of Appointment that oversaw all state appointments, Jay interrupted a member speaking zealously of a candidate's political experience saying that the question is whether the candidate for the office is fit for the office.[85] Jay also issued pardons rarely and not to those with political connections, even denying a pardon to the son of a Revolutionary War hero who had been convicted of forgery and sentenced to life in prison. Jay refused the pardon stating that the guilt in the case had been clearly established.

Jay also turned his attention to the reform of the state's penal code, utilizing his legal experience by urging the repeal of flogging as a means of punishment and by limiting the death penalty to cases of treason, murder and robbing churches. While the legislature was considering such legislation, Jay exercised his executive power to issue stays of execution until the legislation was passed and the convicted individuals could benefit from the new law.

Yet, Jay was not successful in some of his recommendations to the legislature, as when he called attention to the inadequate salaries of the chancellor and justices of the state's Supreme Court. The notion of pensions in this instance was not adopted but the salaries were later increased. Jay was successful in the construction of the state's first prison, additional assistants for the State Attorney General and the redistricting of the state in recognition of the state's additional voters.

The gradual abolition of slavery in New York was a goal Jay had advocated for many years and hoped, now as governor, to see such a law passed. While not being directly involved in the debate and never speaking publicly about the law each time it was introduced to the state legislature, Jay did sign a bill into law in 1799. The law provided that the children born of slaves in New York after July 4, 1799, would gain their freedom when reaching the age of twenty-five for women and age twenty-eight for men. The law also prohibited the exportation of slaves from New York. Although Jay could not take credit for actively working for the passage of such a law, it was passed by a majority of Federalists who revered Jay and his record as a public servant and an advocate for the abolition of slavery. Jay may have served as the inspiration for the passage of the bill. Personally, Jay continued to own slaves until, in 1820, the federal census indicated there were no slaves in the Jay household in Bedford.

In the waning days of his second term as governor, Jay made a strict interpretation of the state's constitution as its chief magistrate and refused to convene a special session of the legislature to select the electors for the contested presidential election of 1800. The newly elected state legislature was to be convened in November of 1800 with the Jeffersonian Republicans holding a majority. Jay rejected a plan suggested to him by Alexander Hamilton for a special session which would be controlled by Federalists, who favored John Adams for president, to select the federal electors to the Electoral College. Jay was not pleased at the prospect of the election of Thomas Jefferson as president over Federalist and friend John Adams but nevertheless, he rejected Hamilton's obvious 'political' plan and took no further action.

In the last days of his presidency, John Adams appointed

Virtues, Talent, Patriotism - Into the Shades of Private Life

many Federalists, often called the 'midnight judges', to the federal judiciary. When Chief Justice Oliver Ellsworth resigned from his post, Adams wrote to John Jay in December of 1800 that he had nominated Jay for the post of Chief Justice "In the future administration of our country, the firmest security we can have against the effects of visionary schemes or fluctuating theories, will be in a solid judiciary; and nothing will cheer the hopes of the best men so much as your acceptance of this appointment. You have now a great opportunity to render a most signal service to your country."[86] In responding to Adams, Jay wrote of his doubts about the present judiciary system "I left the bench perfectly convinced that under a system so defective it would not obtain the energy, weight, and dignity which are essential to its affording due support to the national government, nor acquire the public confidence and respect which, as the last resort of the justice of the nation, it should possess."[87] Jay then stated that his health and his plans for retirement prevented him from accepting the nomination. What happened next is worthy of discussion, for John Jay's letter was delivered to Secretary of State John Marshall who then gave it to Pres. Adams. After a brief discussion of another candidate for Chief Justice, Adams turned to Marshall and said that he would have to nominate Marshall for the office of Chief Justice.[88] For the next several decades, John Marshall, as Chief Justice, would play a major role in the history of the United States and further establish the Supreme Court as a separate and equal branch of the federal government.

    In 1797 the state legislature decided to convene in Albany and Jay rented a house there at 60 State Street where Jay and his family lived and entertained as befitting his office. Among the new acquaintances the family made was Goldsborough Banyer, Jr., the son of a prominent colonial official. Jay's daughter, Maria, formed an attachment with the young Banyer, and they were married in Albany in May of 1801. At the time of the wedding, Sarah Jay's health began to decline and she left for Lebanon Springs to take the waters and recuperate in the fine air. Jay was in the midst of the closing days of his governorship and preparing for retirement from public life after twenty-eight years of public

Virtues, Talent, Patriotism - Into the Shades of Private Life

service. He attended many dinners and receptions and received a citation from the Federal Freeholders of the City of New York in which they paid a "....grateful tribute to your virtues, talents and patriotism...that in the great events which accomplished the American Revolution, you were among the most conspicuous, and that your abilities, patriotism and energy, then and since, have been repeatedly displayed with luster, as well as in the councils of this state and of the United States, as in the diplomatic trusts confided in your trust."[89] The Mayor and Alderman of Albany presented Jay with a Freedom of the City and their proclamation praised Jay for his long years of service to the nation and the state and, reflected on his impending retirement, stating that they "...cannot forbear at the moment of your departure from this city to retire voluntarily from an elevated official situation into the shades of private life, ..."[90] Yet, John Jay, with all his 'virtues, talent and patriotism' was resolved to fulfill a long standing wish to retire to his farm in Bedford. While his lifestyle changed dramatically with retirement, Jay himself retained many of the admirable qualities that he acquired during his career as a public official. Jay always had the highest regard for the law. As a law clerk, his dedication and patience were evident in the often tedious work he was assigned to do. Lindley Murray noted Jay's other fine qualities such as his reasoning, hard work and firmness of mind. His debating and public speaking skills were developed and refined when he was a member of the Moot. His participation in the Boundary Commission to settle a dispute between New York and New Jersey helped Jay to develop a sense of diplomacy that would become evident later in his life. As a member and later president of the Continental Congress, Jay's legal training, literary and leadership skills were recognized by the Congress and served him well. These qualities later emerged in Jay's work with the New York Provincial Congress in drafting New York's first constitution and becoming its first Chief Justice. In the field of diplomacy, Jay's patience, dedication, and resolution were first in evidence during his mission to Spain and later during the Treaty of Paris negotiations and his tenure as Secretary for Foreign Affairs. *The Federalist Papers* and the *Address to the People of New York*

Virtues, Talent, Patriotism - Into the Shades of Private Life

displayed Jay's literary skills and strong reasoning powers. Jay's sense of duty to his country enabled him to persevere during the arduous years of circuit riding and to undertake the thankless task of negotiating the Jay Treaty. In all his endeavors, Jay's keen sense of circumspection guided his actions and thinking. Lastly, Jay was utterly devoted to his wife and children and though he was away from home many times, their importance in his life is evident in his correspondence. His strong religious beliefs would continue to sustain him through many difficult times. Now that Jay was finally going to embark on a life of retirement at his farm in Bedford, the qualities that served him so well during his years as a public servant would sustain him for the rest of his life.

Virtues, Talent, Patriotism - Into the Shades of Private Life

---

[1] John Jay. Memoranda of John Jay n.d. No. 402136C, JJCU.

[2] Sarah Jay to John Jay, 7 July 1799, JJH.

[3] William Jay. JJWJ I:7.

[4] Peter Jay to James Jay, July, 1752. JJWJ I:9.

[5] Peter Jay to David and John Peloquin, 24 October, 1753., JJCU.

[6] Peter Jay to John Jay, 23 August 1763, HPJ I:1.

[7] *The New York Mercury*, 5 May 1764, JJFM 31.

[8] JJGP 14.

[9] John Jay to John Adams, 16 February 1788, JJCU.

[10] Benjamin Kissam to John Jay, 25 August 1766, HPJ I:7.

[11] Peter Van Schaack to William Smith, Jr., n.d., Paul M. Hamlin, *Legal Education in Colonial New York*, (New York 1939), 43.

[12] Benjamin Kissam to John Jay, n.d., Ibid, 44.

[13] JJWJ I:16.

[14] Hamlin, *Legal Education in Colonial New York*, 202.

[15] JJWS 30.

[16] Peter Jay to William Livingston, 31 January 1774, JJCU.

[17] Sarah Jay to John Jay, 22 April 1794, JJCU.

[18] John Jay to John Vardill, 23 May, 1774, 1JJRM 129-30; *Otium cum Dignitate* - Leisure with dignity. www.merriam-webster.com/dictionary/

[19] John Jay, Draft, *Address to the People of Great Britain*, 1JJRM 136-37.

[20] Ibid, 136.

[21] Ibid, 137.

[22] Ibid.

[23] *The Olive Branch Petition*, 3-19 June 1775, 1JJRM 153.

[24] Ibid.

[25] Herbet Alan Johnson, *John Jay 1745-1829*, (Albany, 1970) 12; 1JJRM 195; JJFM 79-80.

[26] John Jay to Robert Livingston, 26 January 1776, New York Historical Society, Gilder Lehrman Institute of American History, John Jay Papers, New York, NY.

[27] Resolution of New York Convention Approving Declaration of Independence, 9 July, 1776, HPJ I:72-3.

[28] John Jay to Sarah Jay, 29 July 1776, Private Collection.; also available at JJCU.

[29] Richard B. Morris, *John Jay The Nation and the Court*, (Boston 1967), 10-12; Johnson, *John Jay*, 14-15.

[30] John Jay, Charge to the Jury of Ulster County, New York, 9 September 1777, JJFM 101.

[31] John Jay to Gouveneur Morris, 29 April 1778, JJCU; 1JJRM 475.

[32] Sarah Jay to John Jay, 28 December 1778, JJCU.

[33] Ibid.

[34] Ibid.

[35] 1JJRM 650.

[36] William Livingston, Jr. to Sarah Livingston Jay, 16 October 1779, 1JJRM 677; Jennifer Janson. *Sarah Livingston Jay 1756-1802: Dynamics of Domesticity, Patriotism and the American Revolution.* West Virginia University, Spring, 2007.: 7.

[37] Susannah French Livingston to Sarah Livingston Jay, 9 October 1779, ; Janson. *Sarah Livingston Jay 1756-1802.*: 8.

[38] Sarah Livingston Jay to Susannah French Livingston, 12-26 December 1779, 1JJRM 680-81.

[39] Samuel Flagg Bemis. *American Secretaries of State and Their Diplomacy I-X* (New York 1928) I:197; JJFM 142.

[40] Benjamin Franklin to John Jay, 23 April 1782, JJCU.

[41] Benjamin Vaughan to Earl Shelburne 3 October and 1 November 1782, 2JJRM 336.

[42] 2JJRM 241-44; Johnson, 25-6.

[43] *The Definitive Treaty of Peace Signed at Paris, September 3, 1783*, 2JJRM 461-65.

Virtues, Talent, Patriotism - Into the Shades of Private Life

---

[44] Ibid.

[45] John Adams to John Jay, 24 November 1800, JJCU.

[46] 2JJRM 459; John Adams to Elbridge Gerry, 14 December, 1782, Adams Family Papers, Massachusetts Historical Society, Boston, MA.

[47] Morris. *John Jay The Nation and the Court,* Preface ix-x.

[48] *Official Congratulations from New York City to John Jay*, September 11, 1784, HPJ III:127.

[49] John Jay to New York Council, 4 October 1784, JJCU.

[50] Mrs. William Smith to Mrs. John Adams, 20 May 1788, Mrs. Ellet. *The Queens of American Society* (Philadelphia 1867), 75.

[51] John Jay to Thomas Jefferson, 21 February 1787, HPJ III:231-32.

[52] John Jay to George Washington, 7 January, 1787, Library of Congress, The George Washington Papers 1741-1799, Washington D.C.; HPJ III:227.

[53] John Jay to Dr. Richard Price, 27 September 1785, JJCU.

[54] John Jay, *Federalist Paper #2.* (New York 1961) 38.

[55] Ibid.

[56] John Jay, *An Address to the People of the State of New York*, 1788, HPJ III: 294.

[57] George Washington to John Jay, 3 August 1788, JJWJ II:106; HPJ III:352.

[58] John Jay to George Washington, 21 September 1788, JJWJ II: 108; HPJ III:360.

Virtues, Talent, Patriotism - Into the Shades of Private Life

---

[59] John Jay to Robert R. Livingston, 22 April 1783, National Archives, Washington, D.C.; HPJ III:44; John P.Kaminski and C. Jennifer Lawton. *Duty and Justice at 'Every Man's Door: The Grand Jury Charges of Chief Justice John Jay*, 1790-1794. Journal of Supreme Court History 31: 3, 235 (2006).

[60] John Jay to General Schuyler, 16 September 1783, HPJ III:82.

[61] John Jay to George Washington, 16 March 1786, HPJ III:186.

[62] U.S. Constitution, Article III, Section 1.

[63] William Patterson's Notes for Remarks on Judiciary Bill [June 23, 1789], DHSC IV:416; Maeva Marcus. *George Washington's Appointments to the Supreme Court*. Journal of Supreme Court History 4: 3, 244 (1999).

[64] DHSC IV: 416; Marcus. *George Washington's Appointments to the Supreme Court*. :245.

[65] Charles Warren. *The Supreme Court in United States History I-II* (Boston 1922) I:48n.

[66] JJFM 305.

[67] Warren. *The Supreme Court in United States History*, I:48n.

[68] Warren. *The Supreme Court in United States History*, I:46n.

[69] Ibid, I:46-48.

[70] JJFM 306.

[71] Ibid.

[72] Warren. *The Supreme Court in United States History*, I:86.

[73] Joshua Glick. *Comment on the Road: The Supreme Court and the History of Circuit Riding.* Cardozo Law Review, April (2003): 1753

[74] JJFM 321.

[75] John Jay, 25 May 1790, *Circuit Court Diary,* 16 April, 1790-August 1792. JJCU.

[76] JJGP 238.

[77] Kaminski and Lawton, *Duty and Justice at 'Every Man's Door'*: 239.

[78] Chief Justice Jay and Associate Justices to President Washington, 8 August 1793. JJCU; HPJ III:488-89.

[79] Henry Jackson to Henry Know, Boston, 7 November 1790. DHSCI, 113-14; Kaminski and Lawton. *Duty and Justice at 'Every Man's Door'*: 243.

[80] HPJ IV:3; also available at JJCU.

[81] .Ibid, 4: JJGP 282.

[82] John Jay to President George Washington, 25 February 1795; HPJ IV:161..

[83] Ibid, 161.

[84] JJFM 408.

[85] Ibid.

[86] John Adams to John Jay, 19 December 1800. HPJ IV:284.

[87] John Jay to John Adams, 2 January 1801, HPJ IV:285.

[88] Leonard Baker. *John Marshall A Life in Law.* (New York and London 1974), 353.

[89] Committee of the Federal Freeholders of the City of New York to Governor Jay, New York 13 January 1801. HPJ IV:286-7.

[90] The Mayor and Alderman of the City of Albany to Jay, May 11, 1801.JJCU.

Let Us Be Resigned

CHAPTER 2

For many years during his career as a public official, John Jay had longed to retire to what he often called 'my farm in Bedford.' He had served his country in many positions from 1774 through 1801 without interruption, frequently separated from his family and on difficult assignments. In 1795 Jay wrote to his wife, Sarah "...much of our lives is spent. A few years of leisure and tranquility are very desirable. Whether they will fall to our lot, cannot be known....If they come, let us enjoy them: if not, let us be resigned."[1] He was joined in his desire for retirement as Sarah Jay had expressed her desire for "retirement, rural quiet...."[2]

Jay's retirement to Bedford, was preceded by years of attention to the development of the property of some 750 acres which he acquired through inheritance and acquisition. The property in Bedford first came into the Jay family through Jay's mother, Mary Van Cortlandt Jay, which she inherited from her father's estate when Jacobus Van Cortlandt purchased land from the Native American Sachem, Katonah, in 1703. When John Jay's father, Peter Jay, died in 1778, he left a devise to his son John of "the choice of any one of my farms at Bedford."[3] Jay chose a property of some 500 acres appraised at £1219.15 which was added to by purchases of land from his brothers. Jay's farm in Bedford was about twenty miles northeast of his father's farm in Rye, where John Jay grew up and was now the home of his brother, Peter and his wife, the former Polly Duyckinck. Jay leased his farm to tenants.

Jay's Circuit Court Diaries, from his tenure as Chief Justice, indicate that Jay stopped at the farm on occasion while riding circuit "Fri 16 April 1790 Set out on northern Circuit - Lodged with my brother at Rye - Cloudy and chilly - went to Bedford - wind at northeast & raw - dined at Holly's [a local family at Mt. Holly, now Mt. Holly Road, in Bedford] - then went to my farm."[4] Jay's visits to his farm prior to his retirement in 1801 usually had a specific purpose, such as improvements to the farm, in addition to breaking his riding circuit. Jay was intent on retiring to the country some day and expressed his desire when he

Let Us Be Resigned

wrote to his friend and Federalist, Timothy Pickering "From early Youth it was my Desire and Intention to live in the Country, as soon as Prudence and Prosperity would permit me."[5]

During this pre-retirement period, the farm was cared for by Maj. Samuel Lyons, Jay's farm manager, and the land was worked by tenant farmers. In 1787, Jay signed a contract with John Cooley, a builder from Bedford, for the construction of "...a house with a piazza and a kitchen adjourning thereto...."[6]. The Agreement, written in Jay's hand, evidenced Jay's legal background. It included diagrams of the house along with instructions for shutters, sashes, chimney finishings and no wainscoting, with work to be completed in a "...neat sufficient and workmanlike manner...."[7] with construction to be completed by November of that year. Another contract was signed with a local mason which again laid out the construction plans to Jay's detailed specifications, including the foundation, height of the ceilings, thickness of the walls, painting and plastering, and the construction of the "chimnies."[8] Construction of the new house was fully completed by 1790 allowing Jay to stay there more frequently. Jay's new house was evidently admired by his brother Peter for in his Will dated September 21, 1797 Peter made provision for a house to be built for his widow "which house shall be in all respects as my brother John Jay has built on his farm at Bedford."[9]

Jay saw to every phase of construction of his house and was very precise in the building materials. When a shipment of 20,000 shingles from Moses Vail of Albany was not to Jay's liking, he wrote to his son-in-law, Goldsborough Banyer, Jr., to handle the matter. The shingles were delivered via a sloop to Elijah Hunter at Sing Sing Landing [now Ossining, NY], were of inferior quality and were pine and not spruce as Jay had ordered.

Jay took a decided interest in all aspects of the farm from an early date as he noted in his Circuit Court Diary, "11-14 Octr 1791 Set out on <u>Eastern</u> circuit - went to Rye - Went with my Son to Bedford, & sent in my Brothers (sic) Waggon the Ram sent to me by Mr. Renselaer & the Lamb from Tunecliff - also abt a Bushell of black Walnuts & a number of young Locust Trees."[10]

Let Us Be Resigned

He also gave directions for the construction of a hay house, the sewing of a potato patch and the construction of a bridge over a brook.

While Secretary of Foreign Affairs, Jay turned his attention to experiments with salt as a manure, or fertilizer as it was called, on onions, carrots, turnips and flax, noting the results with each crop:

> In June 1786 I salted one Bed of Onions, one Bed of my Carrots, & one bed of my early Turnips, laying the salt under the Surface, in the centers of the Intervals between the Rows at some distance from the Roots, that the Salt might have Time to be dissolved, & attend before the fibrous Roots should reach it. The Carrots of the Salted bed, evidently grew much larger & better than the rest, but I could not perceive that the Salt was at all beneficial to the Onions or Turnips.[11]

Jay also made entries in his Circuit Court Diaries about livestock and crops he noticed while riding circuit. This was the scientific age with experimentation and development of new equipment, new crops and new methods of farming to increase production in all areas of farming. Jay was to maintain his avid interest in scientific advancements that would help to increase production on his farm where he often conducted experiments. While he was not in the forefront of scientific experimentation, he corresponded for many years with his good friend and leading authority and experimenter in all aspects of farming, Judge Richard Peters, on subjects relating to manures, livestock and new crops.

Jay availed himself of every opportunity to broaden and share his knowledge on all aspects of farming. While in London in 1794 to negotiate a treaty with Great Britain, Jay met and

Let Us Be Resigned

corresponded with Sir John Sinclair of the British Board of Agriculture on a number of subjects and visited Sinclair at his country estate to inspect some of his sheep. Jay also submitted a paper on the effects of salt as a manure on flax to the British Board of Agriculture. In 1795 Jay sent fifty apple trees to Edmund Burke. Jay and Burke met while in London the previous year, where they discussed the pleasures of apple trees and planting trees in general.

The rigors of public office did not deter Jay from his commitment to a quiet life in the country nor his meticulous plans for developing his farm. Perhaps his joy of planting trees, a legacy from his father, was best expressed by Jay in a letter to his son, Peter Augustus, in 1792:

> It always gives me pleasure to see trees which I have reared and planted and therefore I recommend it to you to do the same - planting is an innocent and rational amusement - my father planted many trees, and I never walk in their Shade without deriving additional pleasure from that circumstance - The time will come when you will probably experience similar Emotions.[12]

Jay was keenly aware of the importance of local manufacturing from raw products. John Ralls owned several mills on the Cross River, just north of Jay's farm and in 1792 Ralls sold four mills to Jay. Jay had purchased a griss mill, a saw mill, an 'oyl' mill and a fulling [mill for the cleansing of cloth for weaving]. After repairs to the mills, the griss mill became operational in 1794.

Once construction had begun to enlarge the main house on his farm for his family, Jay embarked on the construction of a new home for his farm manager, Maj. Samuel Lyons, who had been living in the main house. In 1798 construction began on a brick cottage for Maj. Lyons not far from the main house. Jay was concerned with the water supply and drainage on his farm and so the new house for Maj. Lyons included a pump. Construction of a

Let Us Be Resigned

stable was begun in 1801 and the additions to the main house were nearing completion with an office, a kitchen wing, gambrel roof and the central hall stairway moved to the rear of the house. Maj. Lyons was directly involved in the construction of both houses, but Jay's son, Peter Augustus, was the overseer during the construction. Peter Augustus made several visits to Bedford to make sure that Maj. Lyons and the other workers were doing the work expected of them. His father had no tolerance for delays of any kind. When John Jay left Albany to supervise the work on the farm, he did so with a determination and commitment that was characteristic of him. He wrote to his wife "Except going to meeting on Sundays, I have not been ever once from home since I came here."[13] While Jay expressed satisfaction with Maj. Lyons' work on the management of the farm, Jay confided to his wife "…yet I find myself engaged by it, and in it from Morning to night."[14] Jay was precise in his wishes for the remodeling of the house and he displayed as much dedication to this project as he did in every task he undertook as an attorney and later as a public official.

    When completed, the house was three stories high, with a piazza. It was situated on a slight rise which afforded views of the surrounding countryside and mountains. It was a simple and comfortable farmhouse, well built with the best materials but was not at all in the grand manner of a 'seat' such as Mount Vernon or Monticello. Jay desired a simple and quiet life at his farm in Bedford, surrounded by his family and the many friends who came to visit during his retirement.

    The town of Bedford is about fifty miles north of New York City being first settled in 1681. It was a two or three day journey by stage from New York or a day's sail by boat up the Hudson River in good weather. The town was rural with a population of over 2,000 people which varied little between 1790 (2,470) to 1810 (2,374) based on the federal census for that year. [15] Bedford was primarily a farming community. Along with White Plains, it was one of the two county seats. In 1787, a courthouse was built on the village green and is one of three Westchester county courthouses built before 1800 still standing. There was a

Let Us Be Resigned

small post office in Bedford which was one of four post offices in Westchester County at the time. Many of the buildings in the town of Bedford were fairly new since much of the town, including the Meeting House, had been burned by the British during the Revolutionary War in a raid led by troops of Col. Banastre Tarleton's infamous British Legion. John Jay was informed of the burning of Bedford by George Washington who wrote to Jay on July 31, 1779.[16]

Bedford was on the New York and Danbury, Connecticut post road where the mail was delivered by stage. The stage brought the mail once a week as Jay noted to his wife "The post goes from here every Thursday, and comes in every Saturday - so that we can send Letters only once a week...."[17] 'Way Mail', or outgoing mail, was picked up at the post office by a post rider and deposited at the next post office for a price of two cents a letter. Post offices were often in stores and mail was left on a counter where people would go through the recently delivered mail looking for their own mail.[18] This practice so disturbed John Jay, that he often asked a trusted friend or family member to personally deliver his letter to the recipient and advised the recipient in the letter who would be the bearer of the letter. He disliked the idea of his mail being examined, possibly opened and read by strangers which happened on occasion. Perhaps Jay's discretion stemmed from his public experience which often demanded a need for secrecy.

By 1807 newspapers such as the *Westchester Gazette, Peekskill Advertiser, Somers Museum* and *Westchester and Putnam Gazette* were in print and provided Jay and his fellow townspeople with additional news including national and international events.[19]

Bedford enjoyed a number of toll roads connecting the town to other regions of the country. The Albany, Danbury and Boston Post Roads were the major roads in the area. They were used not only for mail but for shipping goods to market and for stagecoach travel. Taverns and inns were built along these roads as accommodation for the travelers. By 1825, stage service from Bedford to New York had increased to three days a week for a

Let Us Be Resigned

cost of $1.50 for each trip and there was also stage service from Danbury to Bedford which was extended to White Plains.[20] The isolation that Jay had described to his wife in 1801 had been somewhat alleviated by the change in stage travel.

In 1784 Bedford turned its attention to its local roads by establishing thirty-one "path masters" to oversee the construction and maintenance of local roads. This was an honorary position and the path masters were assigned to manage certain roads which included seeing that residents maintained the road along their property during the year for which they were assessed. Residents were expected to clear the dirt roads adjacent to their property with their own equipment when the roads became impassable. When the roads were blocked with snow, teams of oxen were hitched to a cement slab which the teams dragged to clear the roads.[21]

Other turnpikes or 'toll roads' were built by private turnpike companies to enable the goods produced by local farmers and mills to reach the ports along the Hudson River. The Croton Turnpike and the Somerstown Turnpike linked Bedford and other parts of Northern Westchester to Sing Sing (now Ossining), the major Hudson River port for the area.[22] Local farmers drove their cattle to New York City on the hoof but produce was shipped down river often from Capt. Elijah Hunter's cove at Sing Sing Landing and to other ports north such as Albany by a sloop. Most of the farm produce from the towns of North and South Salem, Bedford, and portions of Putnam County and to the Connecticut state line were shipped from Sing Sing Landing and Sparta, another landing in the area.[23] John Jay often chose Capt. Elijah Hunter to have his goods shipped down river, a preference that may have begun in the Revolutionary War. Capt. Hunter fought in the Revolutionary War and served as Assistant Commissary of Forage in Bedford for the 2nd New York Militia. This was the same militia in which John Jay served as a colonel, a position he retired from in December of 1776 to engage in espionage. During the winter of 1778-1779 Hunter was thought to have been part of the network of spies established by John Jay in Westchester county. Hunter became a secret agent reporting to Jay. He gained

Let Us Be Resigned

the confidence of Sir Henry Clinton and Governor William Tryon for two years while he passed on military information to John Jay and ultimately to Gen Washington. Hunter boldly asked Sir Henry for an escort of British redcoats for a trip he intended to make to Westchester County. At the end of the war, Washington gave Hunter a Certificate of Service, which was rarely granted to anyone engaged in espionage.[24] Hunter bought property in Sing Sing after his property in Bedford was burned during Tarleton's raid during the Revolutionary War. He then set up a trading business operating a sloop from a cove at Sing Sing Landing.[25]

Goods from mills in Bedford owned by local men such as Henry Haight, Squire Wood, John Burr Whitlock and John Rundle were also shipped via sloop. Marble quarries in Tuckahoe, Sing Sing, Hastings and Thornwood supplied New York with marble for many of its buildings with the marble being shipped down the Hudson on a sloop.[26] The word sloop is derived from the Dutch word "sloep"[27] and the sloops sailing the Hudson River from New York to Albany and ports along the Hudson were the mainstay of transporting goods and for travel. The Hudson River sloop had a single mast with a mainsail and was steered with a long rudder. The sloops were usually 65-75 feet in length and could carry up to 100 tons. They offered swift passage, traveling about five miles per hour and a sloop leaving the Battery in New York City at 6am could reach Newburgh by noon, a distance of sixty miles. The captain was usually the owner of the sloop he sailed and the goods being shipped, along with children and infirm adults, were often entrusted to his care. On the return trip from New York, the sloops were laden with manufactured goods, hardware, shoes, textiles and kitchenware which were not available in the rural areas. John Jay and his family relied heavily on the Hudson River sloops for travel and for obtaining many goods that were not available to them from their farm production or local purchase.

The Jay family was no exception in using the sloop for travel as Jay noted in one letter to his son in New York City, Peter Augustus Jay, about the departure of his daughter, Maria, from Albany "Maria left us yesterday in Capt. Trotter's Sloop."[28] Jay's meticulous attention to detail even extended to his

Let Us Be Resigned

preference for which sloop should be used for travel and the shipment of goods up the Hudson for delivery to him when he wrote to his son, Peter Augustus "Desire Mr. DePeyster to send for me two Barrels of Ale to Sing Sing, either by the Sloop *Volunteer*, or the Sloop *General Delavan*, to the care of Squire Wood."[29] Squire Wood was a mill owner and local merchant with a store on Cherry Street doing business under the name of Wood and Whitlock in Bedford. Squire Wood often saw to the delivery of goods to the Jay farm via ox cart.[30] Peter Augustus Jay lived in New York City where he practiced law and served as his father's agent in procuring goods and tending to business matters.

John Jay saw to numerous details of the move from Albany to Bedford, selling his family's new coach and having a saddle made for his son, William, who was to stay behind in Albany to prepare for admission to Yale. Jay also had to tend to William's tuition, school supplies and clothes. With his attention to every detail, Jay asked his son, Peter Augustus, to see that a personal need of his is attended to"…I desired you to have a wig immediately made for me by Winslow - remember this - I wish to avoid the inconvenience of traveling with a Wig Box."[31] Jay would eschew the changes in men's fashions in the coming years preferring his traditional attire of breeches when he wrote he desired only 'neatness + utility'.[32]

By May of 1801 the house was nearly completed and John Jay and his daughter, Nancy, arrived at Bedford. He wrote to his wife, "…we arrived at Sing Sing & having sent on some of the most necessary articles of furniture etc. we came here last evening we found the house had been white washed and well leaned…Five wagon loads with our Effects have been brought with but little injury…tomorrow a number of teams will set out for more."[33] In addition to seeing to the furniture, Jay was pleased to inform his wife "…a place for a Kitchen Garden has been fenced and ploughed, so that we shall not be so destitute of Vegetables as we apprehended."[34] As mistress of the house, Sarah Jay would have to plan the meals with the cook and the kitchen garden would furnish the Jays with fresh vegetables and herbs. This was one detail that Sarah would not have to worry about when she arrived

Let Us Be Resigned

at Bedford.

Later that year, Jay saw the end of an irksome problem with a local blacksmith, Daniel Gregory, who had erected his house and shop on the highway about two miles north of the village of Bedford. According to Jay "…that this man living near my farm, & this encroachmt being under my Eye whenever I go there, I could not reconcile it to my official Duty to let it continue to pass unnoticed - I have frequently apprized him of the consequences - he had no place to move -…"[35] Jay did not want to give the impression "…that I press too hard on a poor man…"[36], since he was still governor of New York and he thought of himself as a reasonable person. In the spirit of desiring to end the stalemate, he offered to pay for one acre of land of Daniel Gregory's choosing, not to exceed $50.00. In October of 1801 Jay received a receipt from Daniel Gregory for "…50 Dollars as a Gratuity to assist me in refitting the House I removed from the Hiway.[37] Clearly, John Jay went to great lengths to see that no detail was overlooked in getting his house in order for his retirement and doing so in a manner that he had employed with great success many times as an attorney and public official.

While the house was being readied by John Jay and his daughter, Nancy, they were paid a visit by Jay's brother, Peter and his wife, Polly, who lived at the Jay farm in Rye. They were greatly impressed with the house and how settled John and Nancy seemed to be at that early stage of the move.

Peter was John Jay's elder brother and he and his sister, Anna Marika, lost their eyesight as children during a small pox epidemic in New York City where the Jay family was living at the time. John's father, Peter, moved the family to Rye when John was a few months old. Jay's brother, Peter, inherited the Rye farm on the death of their father. He lived there for the rest of his life, along with Anna Marika. Although blind, both brother and sister persevered and despite their disability, led remarkably accomplished lives. They were highly respected by all who knew them. Marika became an expert seamstress and tended to the housekeeping herself.[38] Her brother, known as Blind Peter, was taught cabinet making and made all types of furniture for the

Let Us Be Resigned

house. He was an accomplished horseman and rode over his farm daily, stopping to open the gates by himself. His sense of hearing and touch became acute and it was said that he knew his friends and family by their step and by feeling their hands. Peter's heightened sense of touch never failed to amaze people especially when some visiting guests, including his brother John, were debating whether a large stand was made from a massive tree or several boards. When Peter entered the room, he quickly settled the matter by placing his finger in the middle of the table on the joint which was barely visible.[39] Timothy Dwight, the theologian, future president of Yale and a family friend, wrote of Peter's "...possessing a fine mind, and an excellent character,...being highly respected and beloved by his acquaintance. He directs all his own concerns with skill and success, and often with an ingenuity and discernment which have astonished those by whom they were known."[40] Dwight also recounted how Peter detected a flaw in a new fence being made for his garden and pointed out the bulge in the fence to the gardener.

    When Marika died in 1791, Peter became lonely. Although he was fifty-seven, he prevailed upon his family and friends to find him a wife. Polly Duyckinck was a spinster from a prominent New York Dutch family and was approached about a marriage to Peter. She became indignant when Peter asked to feel her face to determine her appearance when they first met. Polly reluctantly agreed to Peter's request. She found him to be "kind, and gentlemanly, and agreeable...."[41] After the marriage, she was sometimes called "Auntie Jay" by some.[42]

    There was a tall case clock owned by Peter engraved with his initials. It was said that Peter would open the glass case and feel the hands of the clock to judge the time. Today, his clock is at his brother John's house in Bedford, now the John Jay Homestead State Historic Site.[43] During his retirement, John Jay and members of the family often made the twenty-mile ride Rye to spend time with Peter and Polly.

    While John and Sarah Jay looked forward to retirement in the country, some family members did not take up residence at the farm in Bedford until some time later. Nancy was nineteen at the

Let Us Be Resigned

time she moved to Bedford with her father who was fifty-five. Peter Augustus was a twenty-four year old bachelor practicing law in New York City. Maria Jay Banyer, age twenty, was married and living with her husband, Goldsborough Banyer, Jr., in Albany.

William Jay was twelve and had remained in Albany to attend a school run by the Rev. Thomas Ellis of St. Paul's Episcopal Church to prepare for his entry into Yale. His fellow class mates were from wealthy Federalist families which included the Van Rensselaers and Livingstons as well as the future author, James Fenimore Cooper. William and Cooper became life-long friends[44] Sarah Louisa was only eight and had accompanied her mother, who was not well, to convalesce at a spa.

Sarah Jay was stricken with an illness in 1796 and went to the spa at Lebanon Springs, northeast of Albany, to recuperate. By 1800, Sarah was so ill that she returned to Lebanon Springs to take the waters and refreshment from the mountain air. While recuperating, she did not neglect her duties as mistress of the house when she visited the Quaker settlements in the area "I have purchased of them some very clever sheets towels and ticken & likewise very pretty shirting for servants at a very reasonable rate."[45] She spoke of climbing the tallest mountain in the area and that bathing "gives me a charming glow & occasions a quick circulation."[46] Sarah longed to be in Bedford with her husband when she wrote to him "...I am more than ever desirous of being there - then we may roam together & together inhale the salubrious breeze--"[47] However, John Jay thought that the house was not yet ready for an invalid when he wrote to Sarah "The noise and hurry of Carpenters, Masons and Laborers in and about the house...were inconveniences to be submitted but not to be chosen by convalescents or invalids."[48]

After returning to Albany, Sarah Jay suffered another set back in August of that year with bouts of delirium. Her speech was affected as well as her right hand and arm. Spiced wine was prescribed by the doctor and as she improved, Jay's prognosis was "at present her Prospects of Recovery are fair---."[49] By 1801 Sarah had journeyed to Oak Hill, a Hudson River mansion built by one of Sarah's Livingston relatives, John Livingston, and one of

Let Us Be Resigned

twelve houses built by the Livingston family members in the Hudson River Valley. Her sister, Catherine, was at Oak Hill as well. Sarah wrote to her husband about her illness "...-the fever sister hinted to you she thought I had, harassed me every night with an excessive heat in my back & and extreme restlessness notwithstanding increased doses of opium."[50] She also wrote of using laudanum for sleeping and had an erratic pulse and a general weakness that prevented her from dressing herself. Sarah did show signs of improvement with a good appetite and exercise and she expressed her pleasure at the letters she had received from her husband and daughter, Nancy "- No cordial could have had so salutary an effect upon my spirits as the dear letters I recd from you both."[51] Sarah also spoke of her rheumatism "...were it not for the swelling in my right heel which continues very obstinate, I should not be in the least lame."[52] As her health continued to improve, she still thought of the farm in Bedford when she wrote to her husband about a visit from her brother, Brockholst, and discussed at length the iron oven he had installed in the jam of his kitchen fireplace and the many benefits derived from it. Sarah suggested that John give it consideration for their house in Bedford. In July, being impatient at the separation from her family, Sarah boarded a southbound sloop and traveled down the Hudson River and overland by stage to stay with Peter and Polly at Rye. By December of 1801, Sarah was at last at Bedford "I can truly say I have never enjoyed so much comfort as I do here."[53] She wrote delightfully to her daughter Maria about the mild weather that permitted Nancy to plant 'peach stones' in the garden and "I must not omit mentioning that my health continues to improve-."[54]

    In February of 1802, John Jay traveled to New York City to sit for a portrait requested by the city council. Before returning to Bedford, he stopped at Peter's house in Rye to break his journey due to a severe storm. Sarah's letter to Jay on March 2nd was full of news about the house, the staff and the snow. It seemed that Sarah's health had been restored and she was settling in very nicely at the farm. On May 5th Sarah wrote to Maria about a visit in August and September and stating "And I can with the greatest

Let Us Be Resigned

sincerity assure you that my health & appetite increases daily--& that I really & truly feel very well indeed."[55] Then suddenly, her health began to fail and on May 18th, Sarah Livingston Jay died with her husband and children at her side. She was forty-five years old. Jay led his children into an adjoining room, and from the family Bible he read from the fifteenth chapter of Paul's first letter to the Corinthians with the victory of immortality over death:

> We shall not all sleep, but we shall all be changed. In a moment, in the twinkling of an eye, at the last trump; for the trumpet shall sound, and the dead shall be raised incorruptible, and we shall be changed. For this corruptible must put on incorruption, and this mortal must put on Immortality. So when this corruptible shall have put on incorruption, and this mortal shall have put on immortality, then shall be brought to pass the saying that is written, Death is swallowed up in victory.[56]

Jay was a devout, literal Christian. He believed in the Bible taking every word as the absolute truth. His faith had sustained him throughout his life and he believed that our earthly existence was a preparation for eternal life. For the remainder of his life, his correspondence gives little indication that Jay outwardly expressed sorrow for his wife's death, but in 1802, Jay revealed his feelings in a letter to William Wilberforce in writing "...I feel her absence."[57] Most other references to her death were in terms of his wife having departed this world for a better place which he utterly believed. He wrote to a friend "Conversation, Books and Recollections, still enable me , with the Blessings of Providence...to glide on placidly towards that ocean, to which the Stream of Time is bearing us all--"[58] He sometimes had conversations with 'the Mighty Dead' as he referred to his departed family members and friends. Jay may have had apprehensions about her health when he described the prospects of her recovery in 1801 as 'fair' and wrote to her about being 'resigned' to whatever time is left to them for their retirement.

Sarah had been the perfect complement to Jay for in many

Let Us Be Resigned

respects her personality was the exact opposite of his. She was beautiful, outgoing, and a vivacious hostess. John on the other hand was serious and more introverted. As a young attorney, Jay, in a rare moment, discussed his personality with Robert Livingston when he wrote of the effect his shyness and proud character had made him more serious.[59] Jay considered himself 'pertinacious' rather than flexible. As for his role in life Jay thought of himself as fit for 'a College or a Village' and as for acquaintants, he thought himself 'careless of all but a few' and deriving pleasure from 'few' objects. Yet Sarah acted as a foil for her husband, drawing him out by complementing his many talents. Her family background and education along with her patriotism gave her the impetus to break with tradition and accompany her husband on his diplomatic missions to Europe which kept them away from America for five years.. As the wife of a diplomat, she represented the best virtues of American women with dignity and patriotism to her country. The many separations they endured allowed her to take charge of managing the household. She had a keen political mind that developed during the Revolution and often gave her husband advice in many areas including personal matters and politics. As a leading hostess in New York City, she invited many important people of the time to the Jay house on Broadway. Sarah Jay had redefined the role of women in American society.

   She was interred in the family vault at or near the church of St. Marks in-the-Bouwerie in New York City. On June 2, 1802 the *New York Herald* printed the following tribute to Sarah Livingston Jay:

> At Bedford, after a short and severe illness, in the 45th year of her age, Mrs. Sarah Jay, wife of His Excellency, John Jay, died and entered into the gates of Eternal Life. All who had the happiness of an intimate acquaintance of Mrs. Jay, will bear tribute to the uncommon merits of the woman,-her placid, cheerful temper and the

Let Us Be Resigned

> tenderness of a mother.
> From an admiring world she chose to fly;
> With Nature then retired, and Nature's God,
> The silent paths of wisdom trod;
> And banished every passion from her breast,
> But those the gentlest and the Best.
> Whose holy flames with energy divine;
> The virtuous heart, enliven and improve,
> The conjugal and the maternal Love.[60]

As a final remembrance, Maria noted on the back of her mother's letter of May 5, 1802 "From my dearest Mother--The last letter she ever wrote to me. She departed this life the 18th of the same month."[61]

After Sarah's death, Jay mourned the passing of his beloved wife, but he was not a broken man in spirit. His wife's sudden death may not have been an unexpected event given Jay's assessment of their retirement with resignation at what might happen. Then there was the issue of Sarah's health which had been delicate for some time and Jay was cautiously optimistic about her prospects of recovery.

He devoted himself to his family, farm and correspondence for there was much to occupy his time. The farm had been leased to tenant farmers for many years and was in desperate need of attention. Over the next few years, Jay had to oversee the construction of a carriage barn and cider mill along with the installation of lightning rods. He saw to developing livestock and crops and planting trees as well as maintaining meticulous accounts of all expenses. He extended bonds to individuals and was scrupulous about the payment of interest and principal. He approached managing his farm in the same lawyer-like manner with his characteristic style of precision that had served him so well throughout his public career and would assist him in the transition to a retirement bereft of his wife. Jay was also motivated by a sense of duty and commitment infused with

Let Us Be Resigned

his deep and abiding faith. Attention to every detail was the hallmark of his character and very little escaped his attention. When peaches and apples were taken from his orchard, or rails were taken from his fences, he offered rewards, but only on the conviction of the offender(s).[62] On another occasion, he was obliged to write to Maj. Samuel Lyons about Lyons's daughter, who, with the assistance of another, shook Jay's walnut trees and made off with the nuts.[63]

When his health and the weather permitted, Jay spent most of his time outdoors on horseback overseeing the operation of his farm. Jay wanted his life on the farm to be simple and frugal as befits a republican. While his farm manager saw to the cultivation of the farm, it was Jay who oversaw the improvements and instructed the workmen and always insisted on the best materials available without ostentation. He wanted his family to have the best and saw to their comforts but his frugality was tempered with generosity.

Each day he would assemble his family, guests and staff and lead them in morning and evening prayers. A visitor to the Jay farm described the moment as being heaven itself.[64] As to his life on his farm in Bedford, Jay once said with religious fervor and an inner sense of determination to continue on his life's journey "I have a long life to look back upon and an eternity to look forward to."[65]

Jay took comfort from his five children even when they were not at Bedford which was often the case. Sarah Louisa Jay left Bedford after her mother's death and lived in Albany with her sister Maria, where she attended an academy for continuing her education. Jay would later write to 'Sally' about her education saying "I am not anxious that you should be called a 'learned Lady' but it would mortify me to have any of my children classed with the ignorant and illiterate. I am particularly solicitous that they should be well versed in the Science of living agreeably and comfortably <u>here</u> and happily <u>hereafter</u>."[66] Yet Jay was also keen that his daughter be well versed in history, geography and arithmetic and not neglect her attention to drawing, dancing and music, skills and accomplishments that a well brought up woman

Let Us Be Resigned

would be required to have if she was to marry, have children and manage a large household. Such were the expectations for women of Sarah Louisa's social status.

William was at Bedford when his mother died and in 1803 he went to Yale College which was undergoing a transformation under the leadership of Rev. Timothy Dwight. Dwight preached the virtues of the New Testament and orthodox faith. He was against Deists and the 'infidel philosophy' of the French Revolution, the latter being in concert with Jay's opinions on the 'tragedy of the French Revolution'. Under Dwight's religious and political [Federalist] leadership and his teachings, Yale became one of the largest institutions of higher learning. Jay made arrangements for William to stay at the home of Professor Henry Davis. Jay revealed some of his thoughts about child rearing and education, giving indications of the effects the Rev. Stouppe and Kings College had on him. Jay wrote to Davis about William "He has hitherto been so good a boy as to render any degree of severity unnecessary."[67] Jay further stated "Habits of punctuality and industry are so important through life that they cannot be too early and carefully formed."[68] He enclosed fifty dollars for clothing and other expenses with a weekly allowance for William of twenty-five cents and tuition of six dollars.[69] Since William would be fourteen in June of that year, Jay expressed a wish for William's studies to be completed by the time William reached his eighteenth birthday and asked for periodic accounts of William's progress. During matriculation, William was reunited with his friend, James Fenimore Cooper until Cooper was expelled after two years for fist fighting. Another classmate was John C. Calhoun of South Carolina and ultimately the two men would find themselves on opposing sides of the abolition movement.

Upon graduation from Yale, William went to Albany to study law under attorney John B. Henry, a staunch Federalist. William's eyes soon proved too weak for the prodigious amount of reading required in the law. With doctors offering conflicting opinions ranging from wearing green tinted glasses, to no glasses at all to seeking medical advice in England, William returned to Bedford in 1809, despairing of a career in law. His father feared

Let Us Be Resigned

that William's career path would be that of a farmer, but William became active in many causes beginning with assisting in the establishment of the American Bible Society, serving as first judge in Westchester County and being actively involved in the temperance, antislavery and antiwar movements. For many years William Jay distinguished himself by his participation in the American Antislavery Society and the Peace Society. Clearly, William Jay had been greatly influenced by his father's Federalism and anti-slavery beliefs.

William remained at the farm in Bedford for the rest of his life and assisted his father in the management of the farm. In 1812 he married Augusta McVickar, daughter of a New York City merchant. They were married by a relative, the Rev. John McVickar, at the village of Bloomingdale which was located on Manhattan Island in the Hudson River in the area of what is now 96th to 114th streets. The couple visited Maria Jay Banyer at Albany during their wedding trip. William was anxious to return home to Bedford as Augusta had not met John Jay and she was concerned about meeting her new father-in-law. Maria had written to her sister Nancy about Augusta "…she seems however perfectly happy at the idea of living in Bedford & every way exposed to accommodate the wishes of the family. I really believe that you will find her a very agreeable & estimable companion."[70] William and Augusta lived at the Bedford farm where they raised their family of six children.

Peter Augustus was forced to leave his New York law practice due to a pulmonary condition he contracted in the fall of 1802. Fearing tuberculosis, he followed the advice of doctors and spent the next two winters in Bermuda and Europe and two years with his father at Bedford. After recovering his health, Peter resumed his legal practice and became one of New York City's leading attorneys with an elite, international clientele. In 1807, at the age of thirty-one, Peter became engaged to his second cousin, Mary Rutherford Clarkson. Mary was the daughter of General Matthew Clarkson, who served with distinction during the Revolutionary War and participated in Washington's retreat from Long Island, the Battle of Saratoga and the siege at Yorktown. He

Let Us Be Resigned

was a good friend of John Jay who admired Clarkson for his 'virtue and purity'. Both were vestrymen for Trinity Church and were members of the New York Manumission Society, the American Bible Society and many other charitable organizations. When Jay learned of the engagement, he wrote to Gen. Clarkson of his approval of the match, expressing his respect and esteem for the Clarkson family.[71] A wedding guest, John Cox Morris, gave a rare and vivid account of the wedding performed at the Clarkson home on Pearl and Whitehall Streets in lower Manhattan on July 30, 1807. According to Morris, the wedding was attended by the elite of New York including John Jay, who rarely left Bedford, the LeRoy's, Bayards and Rutherfords. Doctor Moore [a relation of Augusta McVickar Jay], Bishop of the Protestant Episcopal Diocese, performed the ceremony. Nancy Jay was one of the bridesmaids. Here is the full account of the wedding and reception:

> The Bride had on a white silk dress covered with white crepe or gauze with pearls in her head and on her neck and arms. The Brides Maids in elegant white dresses; the groomsmen in white waistcoats, drab small clothes, flesh colored silk stockings and different colored coats....The Groom in the same underdress with a light colored Coat. The Bride was frightened out of her senses. She saw nobody, but with her eyes fixed on the floor...; it was not until near the close of the evening that she raised her eyes to look at anyone. After the ceremony tea and coffee and a great variety of refreshments were handed about. A cold collation was placed upon a side table down stairs of which the elderly Ladies and Gentlemen partook....[72]

Peter and his wife settled in a house on Broadway where

Let Us Be Resigned

they raised their family. Peter carried on the Jay family tradition of public service as President of the New York Manumission Society. He served in the New York State Assembly helping to arrange for the financing for the construction of the Erie Canal. He was also Recorder for the City of New York, a Westchester County judge, Westchester delegate to the New York State Constitutional Convention in 1821 and President of the New York Historical Society, to name a few of Peter Jay's attainments. His speech at the 1821 Constitutional Convention was notable for his support of suffrage for free African Americans and is discussed in another chapter of this book.

John Jay kept detailed journals of all produce from the farm and the expenses and on one occasion, he asked Peter to obtain supplies for him, displaying his characteristic desire for specific and detailed instructions "I wish to have two Blank Books, with two Quires [24-25 sheets of paper or one-twentieth of a ream] of the best Fools Cap Paper in one and 3 quires in the other - let them both be ruled for accts and bound in Calf - "[73] Another set of instructions from Jay focused more on the expense, even if it was for a former president of the United States "President Adams was so obliging as to send me a Volume containing the Proceedings of the late Massachusetts Convention for amending their constitution - purchase for me a Volume of our Convention - Let it be decently but not splendidly bound; and send it by Reynolds or Calhoun - "[74]

Sarah Jay, if she had lived, would have taken up the position as 'mistress' of the house. It was her daughter, Nancy, who filled that position and with great dedication and love for her parents when she earlier wrote to her mother that she found great satisfaction in tending to the needs of her parents.[75]

Nancy and her sister, Maria, received an education that befitted young ladies of their social status. Although John Jay had strict thoughts about the education of women, Nancy and her sister, Maria, attended the Moravian School in Bethlehem, Pennsylvania. The school was the first academy for girls in the colonies and was founded by Countess Benigna van Zinzdorf in 1742. It was during the Revolutionary War that the school came

Let Us Be Resigned

into prominence and attracted the attention of many American army officers who chose to send their daughters to the school. The school stressed that education was a sacred responsibility and encouraged a rational approach to women's education. The curriculum included religion, English and German, history, geography, arithmetic, sewing, knitting and other feminine pursuits to prepare upper class young ladies for a proper role in life. Accounts from the school that were sent to John Jay for Maria's education detail the materials that were needed for her education. Nancy's schooling called for accounting sheets, grammar books, hymnal and music books; embroidery silk, ribbons and needles; paints, quills, blank books and paper.[76] Nancy and Maria were also expected to play an instrument, draw, paint, and press flowers as part of their education. These refinements were expected of women from their social status.

    Religion played a central role at the school, where Nancy kept a prayer journal, which was a major influence on her throughout her life. In expressing her faith, Nancy later wrote of the 'Rev. Mr. F., having visited the farm at Bedford. She spoke glowingly of his morning and evening devotions and Sunday sermon having a profound effect upon all, speaking of God's love and wisdom.[77] Nancy was clearly inspired by her father's piety when she wrote to her brother Peter Augustus in 1816 about their father being the embodiment of the Scriptures and the profound effect it has had on his family.[78]

    Devotion to one's family was one of Nancy's strong traits and it guided her in the role she assumed at her father's farm, forsaking marriage and a family, to be by her father's side as his helpmate. Her faith led her to be concerned for the welfare of all, excepting none. Nancy was expected to run the household and train and supervise the servants as well as see to their personal needs. She had to manage the provisioning of the house and she kept her own account book of expenses from the monthly sum allotted to her by her father. Nancy would often have her father write to Peter Augustus when it was time to order household items. Many of John Jay's letters to Peter spoke of Nancy advising her father of the supplies needed on the farm from

Let Us Be Resigned

Franklin stoves, to a marble mantelpiece, tobacco, wine, brandy, ale and Madeira, silver, flatware for the table, an electric shock machine for Nancy and a flower book for her sister Maria, to name but a few items. Relatives, friends and notables visited the farm and Nancy had to act as hostess, seeing to their needs and comfort. Ladies in Nancy's position were also expected to cook some delicacies on occasion and gifts of food such as cheese, oysters, rusks and a recipe for honey cake were exchanged by Nancy and other ladies in her family, with John Jay obligingly tending to the transmittal letters. Nancy also saw to the interior decorating of the house. While she and her father were preparing the house for Sarah's arrival, John Jay wrote to his wife how much enjoyment he and Nancy received from their efforts to decorate their new home.[79] When it came to painting and hanging wallpaper, Nancy and her friends and relatives took a hands on approach, as was the custom, with the ladies in hanging the wallpaper "I know Nan is anxious to have her dining room painted and smarted up."[80] and "I wish I were here with you to paint the cornices."[81]

Augusta's entry into the household did not displace Nancy's position as the mistress of the house. Most of Augusta's time would be spent in bearing and rearing six children. In 1818, the house was enlarged to accommodate William and Augusta's children and a schoolhouse was built in 1826. A tutor, Mr. Van Kleek, was hired to teach the children. Augusta would instruct the younger children at home while the older ones would study with Mr. Van Kleek at the schoolhouse which was set on top of a hill in back of the house. However, Maria's hope that Augusta would be a 'companion' to Nancy did not come to fruition. Over the years, a feeling of disharmony had developed between Nancy and Maria about their feelings toward Augusta. While Nancy and Maria expressed remorse over the developments and wished for warmer relations among the three, Maria wrote in her diary of Augusta's attitude when an injury to John Jay's hand developed into a life-threatening infection "…my feelings were much depressed by the real or imagined…coldness of one who should have felt for us & perhaps did, tho' she did not express it…."[82] Later that same day after taking Communion at the house, Maria noted further in her

Let Us Be Resigned

diary that she "...felt disposed to embrace each of the family...one in particular whom I sincerely love tho' I fear there is little reciprocity of affection..."[83] On the other hand, Augusta's letters reflect a deep affection for her father-in-law when she wrote to John Jay "Believe me dear Papa, I shall ever retain a grateful recollection of all your kindness to me & the children, & it will increase the happiness of my life it I can, even in an inferior degree promote the comfort of yours - I am ever your affectionate child, Augusta Jay."[84] It might have been that Augusta's major concerns were primarily for her husband and children. She also came from a very religious family with relatives in the clergy and she had a pious and reserved nature which may have explained the strained relations with Nancy and Maria. It might also have been the case that since Maria and Nancy revered and admired their father greatly, they may have felt that Augusta did not outwardly express her feelings for John Jay in her relations with him. This conflict of imbalance in feelings would not be resolved until some time in the future, despite hopes to the contrary by Nancy and Maria.

As Nancy assumed the position of running the household, she shared her love of gardening with her father. Botany and gardening were areas of great interest at the time and Nancy and her father were no exception. The east coast of the North American continent was still being explored with new species of flora being discovered and cultivated. Botanists were also cataloging the new discoveries of native flora sent back from the Lewis and Clark expedition. Nurseries were offering new flowers, fruits and vegetables led by John Bartram of Philadelphia and William Prince of Flushing, New York, both of whom counted George Washington, Thomas Jefferson and James Madison as customers as well as the Jays. Seeds and roots were constantly being exchanged by members of the Jay family. Nancy took particular joy in her rose garden and its twenty-one varieties of roses 'all quite distinct'. Susan Ridley, a cousin of Nancy, spoke of Nancy's love of gardening and how Nancy devoted so much time and pleasure to her garden, carefully nursing every bed.[85] On one occasion, John Jay could not resist commenting about Nancy's

Let Us Be Resigned

garden and one flower in particular "Your flowers look well - among them there is a white Poppy which exceeds any Poppy that I remember to have seen."[86]

Yet John Jay had the responsibility of running a farm and his letters are replete with news of varieties of fruit and vegetables that were planted on his farm such as peach, apple, cherry and pear orchards, grape vines, quinces, strawberries, raspberries, watermelons, potatoes, acorn squash, rye, corn, buckwheat, speltz, sweet potatoes, and pumpkins. Jay often relied on his son William to arrange for the ordering of new trees, shrubs and seeds. Most of the orders were placed through the Prince Nursery in New York City. In October of 1789, John Jay had accompanied then Pres. George Washington and Vice Pres. John Adams to the Prince Nursery by barge when New York City was the capital of the nation.[87] William Prince gained a wide reputation for his nursery during the Revolutionary War when the British occupied New York and enjoyed the protection of Gen. Lord Howe and his troops. Many British and Hessian officers had nursery stock from Prince's Nursery shipped to Europe.[88]

After Jay's retirement, William would often write to his brother Peter for the nursery stock desired for the Bedford farm "Papa wishes you to desire Prince to send him as soon as possible in order that they may be planted before the ground freezes, the following tress viz. 1 Larch or deciduous fir; 2 Siberian Crab; 2 Balsom fir or Balm of Gilead, I Double flowering Chinese apple; and 1 Black and 1 White Tartarian Cherry,...."[89] When the stock arrived, it usually fell to William to oversee the planting "I have been very busy the last week in setting out young Locust Trees, and have planted about <u>Seventeen hundred</u>."[90]

Although the farm had been occupied by tenant farmers for many years, Jay worked hard to transform his property into a working farm. He wrote glowingly of his efforts ten years later to Maria "You would be surprised to see the orchards---they are literally bending and breaking under a prodigious Burthen of Fruit. I do not recollect any former Year in which there was so much."[91]

As a farmer, Jay devoted much time to raising crops and livestock experiencing both success and failure. He once referred

Let Us Be Resigned

to his efforts at growing wheat by saying "To sew Wheat here, is like taking a ticket in a Lottery - more blanks than prizes - the Fly destroys more than we reap."[92] With his farm, Jay displayed the patience and determination he acquired during his public career. Jay was undaunted and not the least bit resigned to the wheat situation, and he corresponded frequently with his friend of fifty years, Judge Richard Peters, who was renowned for his agricultural experiments and innovations. The two men met in Philadelphia during the Revolutionary War when Peters was a delegate to the Continental Congress and a member of the Board of War which oversaw the administration of the Continental Army. After the war, Peters served as a delegate to Congress under the Articles of Confederation and later became the Speaker of the Pennsylvania State Senate. In 1792, Pres. Washington appointed Peters a Judge for the U.S. District Court of Pennsylvania. Peters served in that position until his death in 1828 and was highly regarded in the field of admiralty law.

Peters was in many ways the opposite of Jay. While Jay wanted to live quietly and simply on a farm, Peters had an elegant estate, Belmont, overlooking the Schuykill River with views of Philadelphia. The Palladian style mansion, with its formal gardens, became a favorite retreat of Pres. Washington along with John Adam, Thomas Jefferson, James Madison and Lafayette. Peters sang and composed music and was a gourmand and famous host. He was known for his witticisms and puns. Peters had a sharp nose and chin, and as he aged, they became more prominent. When a friend suggested that the two might quarrel, Peters replied "Very likely, for hard words often pass between them."[93] Yet Peters admired Jay's 'Settled Plan of Life' but he admitted to Jay that he needed some 'Hobby Horse to ride'. Peters was very much a part of the scientific revolution and through his experiments in agriculture and animal husbandry, he gained an international reputation. Washington praised Peters when he wrote to Sir Arthur Sinclair that Richard Peters is one of the leading 'theoretical' farmers in America.[94]

Peters, like many other farmers including Jay, experimented with different types of manures or fertilizers. In his

Let Us Be Resigned

book, *Agricultural Enquiries on Plaister of Paris,* first published in 1797, and remains in print to this day, Peters discussed his highly successful experiments with the new fertilizer which he began in 1783. Peters was extremely thorough and wrote about the amounts of Plaister, a form of gypsum, to be used per acre; the increase in crop production which led to increased livestock; the texture of the Plaister to be 'moderately pulverized'; how light, dry and loamy soils benefited most from applications of the fertilizer; the time of year for applying the Plaister to the soil; the crops, wheat, rye, barley, Indian corn, buckwheat, peas, potatoes, cabbage and clover; and the type of Plaister he preferred which was from the Montmartre section of Paris where the French became the first to work the gypsum quarries and hence the name 'Plaister of Paris'.

Washington was among the many notables and average farmers of the time who wrote to Peters for advice. He recounted his lack of success with Plaister at Mount Vernon and Peters explained that the clay soil at Washington's plantation was not suitable to Plaister. Nevertheless, Washington requested several copies of Peters' books to send to Sir John Sinclair in England.

Jay also experimented with Plaister and ground shells and found the shells had increased productivity in a poor lot near his house planted with clover and Spear Grass. Jay wrote to Peters of his experiment. He had the shells ground into a powder which Jay spread along with Plaister near his house and noted the results of his little experiment "…-as the Dry Weather came on, the little Square became less and less verdant, and is now brown and parched, while the plastered ground Which begins with a Yard of it, remains, green."[95] Jay repeated the experiment the next year but only on grass and asked Peters for his advice on the effects of Plaister on vegetables; which vegetables benefit from the application of Plaister; the quantities of Plaister to be used and what season is best. Peters replied to Jay that Plaister was, 'calcerous Earth & Oil of Vitriol' and it had sulphuric acid as a base which attracts and holds water longer than ground shells. Peters explained that he had discontinued using ground shells which required a greater application than Plaister and that he used

Let Us Be Resigned

Plaister to great effect "...on Garden Esculents continually. I know of none not benefited by it. But Vines & leguminous Plants, it seems more efficacious. Even young Trees receive Advantage from it."[96] Jay responded to his good friend, recognizing Peters' contributions to the field of agriculture by complementing him "I think it has greatly improved in our Country since the Revolution."[97]

Jay had an avid interest in experimenting with new crops and fertilizers to increase production and held the position of nominal president of the Westchester Agricultural Society. However, it was Peters who conducted in depth scientific experiments and published his findings in many journals. In 1785 he was one of the founding members and a future president of the Philadelphia Society for the Promotion of Agriculture. The Society maintained relations with other agricultural societies in America and in Europe and was one of the most respected of its kind on both sides of the Atlantic. The Society sent seeds for new crops to farmers, established a library, and published its findings through its journal, *Memoirs*. Peters was a prolific writer and the Society published 87 of his papers in its journal. Such was the fame and stature of Richard Peters that in 1811 Jay wrote to Peters asking for several copies of the second volume of the Society's *Memoirs* "I mean to place a set in our Town Library and to distribute others among certain Persons in the neighbourhood who in my opinion would make proper use of them."[98] Jay later wrote to Peters about the *Memoirs* "I am told that it is read with <u>great</u> avidity, and I suspect with proffit."[99]

Peters' experiments with Plaister of Paris had helped to revolutionize agriculture in America. Many farmers had been unable to raise enough fodder to feed their livestock during the winter months. The use of Plaister had enabled farmers to increase the production of crops and to employ crop rotation allowing for adequate supplies of feed for their livestock year round.

Farmers, including John Jay, would benefit from the introduction of new breeds of livestock, particularly sheep. Sheep were largely imported from England but did not flourish in

Let Us Be Resigned

America due to the harsh winters and the fleece from the English sheep did not produce much wool. Wolves were a real and present danger in many areas of the country, including Jay's farm. However, with the introduction of the Tunis sheep in America and Peters' efforts raising sheep, horticulture had been transformed.

In 1799 the Bey of Tunis made a gift of ten Tunis sheep to George Washington. Only a ram and a ewe survived the ocean voyage and Secretary of State, Timothy Pickering, gave the sheep to Richard Peters for breeding. The Tunis sheep, one of the oldest breeds, were characterized by their cream colored coat, accented by cinnamon/red head and legs. They were also known as broadtail sheep since their tails had fatty deposits and the breed was prized for the quality of mutton and fine wool. Washington replenished his flock at Mount Vernon with Tunis sheep and Jefferson had Tunis sheep grazing on the front lawn of the White House. The Tunis sheep were cross-bred with other breeds which produced the American Tunis, which is still bred by farmers to this day. After experimenting with the Tunis sheep, Peters wrote his *Memoir on the Tunis, broad-tailed Sheep* which was published in this country and in international journals. Peters noted the many favorable characteristics of the breed including the high quality cloth made from the fleece, the outstanding quality and quantity of mutton, the requirement of less food than other breeds, the rams readily mate with ewes of other breeds, and they bear the cold and hot climates very well. As a gourmand, Peters also turned his attention to the tail of the Tunis "Its tail (which I have known, when prepared for cooking, to weigh from six to eight pounds) if properly dressed, is a feast for an epicure. The tail of a young beaver, which I have enjoyed when I dared to indulge in such food…is the only rival I know."[100]

There was one other quality of the Tunis sheep that attracted John Jay's attention, as well as many other farmers. According to Peters' *Memoir* "…I never saw a breachy Tunis sheep."[101] By 'breachy', Peters meant that the sheep stayed in their pasture and did not jump the stone walls or fences. This prompted Jay to write to Peters about his desire to have some for his farm:

Let Us Be Resigned

> I had often heard of broad tailed sheep, and seen some of them, but supposed them to be a rather singular than a useful Breed. You have corrected that Error, and I should, like to have some of them, if they would remain quietly in fields fenced only by Stone Walls - My farm was, from its first Settlement occupied by Tenants - they left me no Trees fit for Rails, nor can I obtain a supply in this Neighbourhood. The stones they could not destroy - and they are the only Materials I have for Fence…You say the Tunisians are quiet - Tell me whether you think they may be trusted within Stone Walls - if they may - I shall, in case I live till Spring, be inclined to purchase two or three of them to begin with.[102]

Jay wanted only two sheep since he was concerned about the 'dogs', a problem that cost Peters a beloved sheep named 'Selma'. Jay and Peters settled on a price of $25 a piece for a ram and a ewe and Peters assured Jay that the Tunisians would get along with Jay's 'crooked leg'd' sheep. Jay and Peters made this bargain in 1810 when Jay suffered from rheumatism, a 'bilious' stomach and a 'blockage' of the liver along with other ailments such as the common cold and the flu. Jay regularly expressed concern for his mortality despite his perseverance and yet he accomplished much during his retirement.

At this time Jay maintained a flock of Merino sheep, prized for the exceptional quality of its wool, and which the Spanish had prevented from being exported until Napoleon's invasion of Spain in 1808. The other sheep that Jay had were the otter or Ancon sheep with crooked legs. Jay wrote to Peters about the two breeds "…and to but what are here called <u>otter</u> sheep, they have short crooked legs and are not Beauties…but they are orderly and stay at home , and that is more than can <u>always</u> be said of the

Let Us Be Resigned

Beauties [Merino]."[103] The otter or ancon sheep were first bred by a Massachusetts farmer, Seth Wright, who noticed an abnormality of unusually short legs in one of his new-born rams. This was attributed to a lack of cartilage between the joints resulting in a dwarf-like appearance in the sheep. Because the new breed could not jump fences, they attracted the attention of many farmers, including John Jay. This quality allowed the breed to gain in popularity, but other mutations including poor health caused the breed to decrease in acceptance.

Jay seemed very satisfied with the Tunis sheep until eight years after receiving the pair from Peters he wrote "I wish I could give you a good account of my Tunisian Sheep - but the dogs have put it out of my power."[104] Years later, the Tunisian sheep were almost wiped out during the Civil War to be replaced in popularity by the Merino sheep.

This episode with sheep serves to highlight Jay's commitment to his farm and to be open-minded to advances in agriculture. While he conducted experiments on his farm, his correspondence indicates his willingness to try new crops and to share new information with others. Yet, for the first years of his retirement, the burden of running the farm was virtually his responsibility alone. His son William later became a great support to John Jay in this area when William abandoned his hopes for a career in law and said with resignation upon his return to Bedford "I have for a long time since looked upon the pursuits of agriculture as those in which I am destined to be engaged; and a life of retirement as that which it pleased Providence to allot to me."[105] Admitting that he was ignorant on the subjects of agriculture and animal husbandry, William made notes on the work to be done on the farm and the appropriate season for the work and became the Secretary of the Westchester Agricultural Society.

Although the farm occupied much of Jay's attention, his love and devotion to his family never wavered but helped to sustain him. His letters to his family were usually signed in the same manner "Your very affectionate father, John Jay." Yet, the early years of his retirement were soon and all too often

Let Us Be Resigned

punctuated with the loss of loved ones. His brother Peter died in 1813 and John Jay described to Maria his last visit with his brother at Rye:

> When I arrived at Rye I found that the Doctr had little or no Expectation of your uncle's Recovery -- after executing the Day before, certain codicils to his Will, he said 'now I am ready.' on asking him the day after my arrival, how he did, he answered 'I am going fast - thro' the mercies of my Saviour I shall receive everlasting Life and Happiness in less than two Days' - with this Declaration the whole of his conduct and conversation corresponded exactly.[106]

It is interesting to note that John Jay referred to his brother's composure while dying. The Jays believed in salvation and eternal life but the manner in which one died was an integral part of their faith and a testament to one's piety. One's struggles through life were a passage to eternity and so your final moments should be ones characterized by the strength of your faith and your acceptance of eternity which is how Peter Jay died. Peter Augustus Jay echoed his father's beliefs when he wrote to his sister Maria about their uncle's death "May we die with as much Composure as he has done."[107]

The farm in Rye, after some legal reviews of Peter Jay's Will and Codicils, was left to John Jay who then conveyed the farm to his son, Peter Augustus in 1822. Peter's widow, Polly, lived on the farm until her death in 1821. Accounts show that Peter Augustus and his wife Mary, paid many bills for Polly and made improvements to the farm while Polly was alive.

Jay's youngest daughter, Sarah Louisa, who was called Sally, was sickly and suffered from a nervous disorder. Remedies from tar water, electric shock treatment, blisters applied to the breast, emetics, snake root tea, vinegar and brandy baths, and laudanum were of no avail to exact relief from her disorder. In

Let Us Be Resigned

April of 1818 Sally was with her sister Maria at Maria's house in Manhattan when Sally became gravely ill with a fever and swelling of her limbs. Once again, John Jay expressed his deep religious beliefs and resignation to whatever should happen when he wrote to Maria and Nancy who were nursing Sally "We have reason to believe that she is prepared for a better world; and that is a happy circumstance as it respects us, as well as it respects her."[108] At times she seemed to be recovering but finally succumbed. After Sally's death, Peter Augustus wrote to his father that "She retained her Senses to the last, knew her Situation and was perfectly composed and tranquil."[109] Writing to the Rev. Samuel F. Jarvis, Jay expounded on his faith but expressed his feelings about the loss of his daughter "The removal of my excellent Daughter from the House of her earthly, to the house of her heavenly Father leaves me nothing to regret or lament on her account - Her absence is nevertheless a Privation which I feel very sensibly…and that this temporary Separation will terminate in a perpetual Reunion."[110] Here again, is an example of Jay's deep religious beliefs. He believed in salvation and eternal life. In his correspondence concerning his wife's death, he usually referred to her having 'departed this life' and always believed that she had gone to a 'better place'. These beliefs he openly expressed when Sarah Louisa died. There would be other moments when Jay and his family would be faced with the loss of a loved one but persevered with a deep religious conviction of salvation.

However, it was Maria who suffered so many losses which were felt very deeply and with great empathy by John Jay. In November of 1804 Maria gave birth to a son. This was her first child and John Jay's first grandchild. It was quite common for letters at that time to be written over a period of days, given the intermittent mail service. Jay began his letter about Maria's 'dear little boy' and how he had derived much pleasure from writing the long letter to her. The next paragraph, however, refers to his receipt of a letter from Maria's husband that evening breaking the news of the death of the infant boy. Since his grandson's death was just two years after his wife's passing and so poignant, Jay was moved to openly expressed his grief at Maria's loss:

Let Us Be Resigned

> You can judge my Feelings on the occasion - It has cast a Gloom on both Families - I have to lament the Departure of my only Grandson, as well as the affliction of my dear and affectionate Daughter. It is natural that such Events should excite Grief in a high Degree - I know this by Experience, and I know by Experience also that no consolation is to be derived from any other Source, than acquiescence in, and Resignation to the Will of God....[111]

Jay's grief is palpable in this letter as well as his belief in God but his grief is more open and not as subtle, muted and reserved than in later years when his brother Peter and daughter Sarah Louisa died. When writing to Maria about grief over the loss of her son, Jay referred to 'Experience' indirectly recalling his wife's death. Jay also spoke of the loss "...for the Comforts we lose by his absence" but takes comfort in his belief of their reunion some day "...eternal and Happy shall we all be to arrive finally at the same blest abode,...." Jay closed the letter by saying to Maria "It is among my greatest Blessings that all my Children love me, and love one another."[112] Jay's love for his children and his strong faith no doubt helped Jay to live with the 'resignation' of the loss of his wife but not his will to persevere in this life.

On December 19, 1805, Jay happily wrote to Maria "I congratulate you most cordially on the Birth of your Daughter -- May she be a Blessing to her Parents & all of her Connections - ..."[113] Maria named her little girl, Sarah, after her sister, Sarah Louisa, which pleased John Jay greatly and met with his 'approbation'. Yet in the same letter, Jay spoke of how much more joyous the birth of Maria's child would have been had Maria's 'Mama' been alive "...and I think with you, that had your Mama been still with us, she would have largely participated in, and increased our Joy on the Occasion."[114] It would seem that as happy as Jay and Maria were about the birth of Sarah Louisa, their

Let Us Be Resigned

joy was tinged with melancholy. Melancholy is an emotion that is often experienced at very happy times in people's lives. This happy news aroused such feelings with Jay at a time when Christmas and his birthday were being celebrated. However, the faith and convictions of Maria and John Jay would be tested again and only too soon in the new year.

In January of 1806 Maria informed John Jay that her husband, Goldsborough Banyer, Jr., had been diagnosed with 'the diabetes' and that he had departed for New York City to seek the advice of Dr. Samuel Bard, a noted physician. By March, Jay was gladdened that Mr. Banyer's physicians had hope of his recovery and that he was in no danger with his thirst and nausea having abated somewhat. Jay encouraged Maria "...to be resigned composed and cheerful, both for your own Sake , and that of your dear little Daughter - distressed Mothers make bad nurses, in more Respects than one."[115] By June, Mr. Banyer's condition worsened and John Jay went to New York City to be with his son-in-law. Writing to his son Peter Augustus, Jay described the condition of Mr. Banyer:

> I have seen Mr. Banyer - one of his Biles is large and <u>hard</u> and painful - from the point there is a little Discharge, as from a broken pimple...Those Biles I fear indicate more Evil than Good, by depriving him of Sleep and Exercise and appetite - Hence it is probable that his Debility will increase, and afford Reason for serious apprehensions -[116]

Jay also expressed concern for Maria, who accompanied her husband to New York. Jay mentioned that he planned to visit Mr. Banyer after breakfast that day. The next day, June 6th, at five o'clock in the afternoon, Jay wrote to 'My dear Father Papa Banyer' [Goldsborough Banyer, Sr.] of his son's condition and that several other doctors had been called in for consultation. Jay was with his son-in-law at this time after learning from the doctors that morning that it was unlikely that there would be a recovery. He wrote to his daughter Nancy who was also in New York , on

Let Us Be Resigned

the morning of June 6th "...the opinion of his Physicians, terminated our Prospects of his Recovery - I have not since left him, and I am now working in his Chamber - shall leave this Letter open - but from every appearance fear that I shall so add the painful information that he is no more."[117] On the evening of June 6th, Goldsborough Banyer, Jr. died. Jay wrote to Goldsborough, Sr. in Albany and informed him "The painful Event alluded to in my Letter to you of the 5 Inst: took place last night."[118] After expressing his condolences, Jay spoke of his concern for Maria "Her long and affectionate attentions have not been favorable to her Health. I hope for the best - The Child thank God! is well."[119] Jay then went to say that he 'shall consent' to Maria and the child returning to Banyer, Sr., as soon as she was well enough.

    Jay remained in New York and was there to receive Banyer, Sr. when he arrived on Jun 13th. Jay commented about the manner in which the old gentleman learned of his son's death upon arriving in New York, since "...it was here that he received the first Tidings of his Sons's death, instead of hearing of it from Sloops going up the River, as was supposed wd be the Case - ..."[120] It was a common practice for news to be exchanged between sloops sailing up and down the Hudson River and Jay had thought that Mr. Banyer would have learned of his son's death from one of the north-bound sloops. Mr. Banyer was eighty years old at the time, which was an advanced age, as well as being blind. Jay though commented on his mind being 'quite sound and strong'.

    Maria returned to Albany with her daughter and father-in-law and later expressed her feelings about her husband's passing which exhibited her deep religious feelings "...but earthly happiness took its departure with my Banyer never again to become an intimate of my heart yet I firmly believe that all is for the best, and look forward to another & better world."[121] Her strong faith remained a guiding principle for her throughout the remainder of her life and help to sustain her especially in the coming months.

    When Maria returned to Albany with her daughter, Sarah Louisa was plagued with 'extreme salivation' which the doctors diagnosed as 'some glandular infection'. Maria took solace in her

Let Us Be Resigned

daughter who was a comfort and joy to her. Her cousin noted the effect that little Sally had on her grandfather Banyer as a "...pleasure diffuses itself over his countenance...."[122] Yet, in October little Sally became hoarse which was initially diagnosed as the common cold. Over the next few days, she became more hoarse and began to cough violently and her breathing became difficult. Maria's doctor, Dr. Stringer, was sent for " and his Countenance as soon as he saw the Child indicated so much alarm that Maria terrified asked him if he had ever seen a person recover who was so ill. - -He candidly owned that he had not - ...."[123] Several other doctors were called in and thought that her condition was not 'desperate' and had the child bathed, administered emetics and snakeroot tea which did little to relieve the child's symptoms and caused her to vomit continually which brought up large amounts of phlegm. An unsuccessful attempt was made to bleed her and another doctor was consulted whose opinion was that bleeding was the only hope for little Sally. She was bled twice with great quantities of blood taken from the child "But all was too late and after gradually growing worse and worse the poor child expired at five o'clock on Saturday afternoon retaining her senses perfectly to the last."[124]

    Peter Augustus Jay arrived in Albany shortly after Sally's death to be at his sister's side and wrote to John Jay "...Her disorder was the Hives which is very prevalent here. Three other Children were buried on Monday and three more Yesterday who all fell victims to this disease."[125] Peter also commented on the "...immense current of Visitors who according to an abominable Custom of this place flocked to console Maria."[126] Peter's use of the words 'abominable Custom' is interesting. It is not known exactly how the Jay family mourned the loss of a loved one but one might guess that it was a private event given Peter's comment. Various customs of the period were to have commemorative pieces of jewelry, such as a ring, broach or pin made for members of the family and scarves for other mourners. A broach surrounded by pearls containing a braid of hair from Peter Augustus and his wife Mary was made for the occasion of Peter's death. A special edition of the New Testament was also printed to

Let Us Be Resigned

be distributed to the family. It should also be remembered that Albany was first settled by the Dutch and it was a Dutch custom to have the house of the deceased open to all mourners with refreshments. This may have accounted for Peter's reaction to the 'custom' in Albany.

As John Jay prepared to travel to Albany with Nancy, he wrote with deep empathy to Maria "I feel more for you than I can express - to you such feelings are too familiar and need not be described - we both want Consolation - and there is but one source from whence it can be derived, and to that we are permitted to have access."[127] Within seven years Maria had lost her husband and both of her children to premature deaths. Yet she confided to her father a month after the death of her daughter "…as of my severe deprivations severe they indeed are and at times almost overwhelming me, but the God in whom I confide has most graciously supported me and I trust will not forsake me."[128]

Religion would continue to sustain Maria throughout the rest of her life yet her grief was so deep that when she died fifty years later, little Sally's playthings were among Maria's personal effects.[129] Maria would continue to live with her father-in-law in Albany until his death in 1815 at the age of 91. She was financially secure with an income of $2,000 a year by the terms of her husband's Will. She also traveled, making a memorable trip to Niagara Falls with her sister, Sarah Louisa, and brother, William, traveling by steamship and coach. By 1818, she had taken up residence at Bedford where she lived for almost eleven years. Yet Maria suffered from nervous disorders and severe headaches as she fell into what appears to be depression which took its toll on her mentally and physically for the remainder of her life.[130]

In 1805 Maria sought some consolation for her losses with the burial of her infant son in the meadow at the Jay farm at Rye.[131] The following year, Maria's husband was buried alongside his son. Then in 1807, John Jay had the remains of the those who had been buried in the family vault at St. Marks-in-the-Bouwerie interred at Rye with one headstone to mark the grave bearing the inscription "Remains from Family Vault in New York 1807."[132] This was the beginning of the Jay Family Cemetery,

Let Us Be Resigned

which John Jay established legally by drawing a deed in 1815 when he inherited the Rye farm on the death of his brother Peter.

John Jay's life during his retirement years was punctuated with many incidents of sadness and loss. With a resignation to these sorrowful events, Jay continued to persevere and fill his life with accomplishments. His love and devotion to his family and friends were great sources of strength and interest for him. He continued to pursue his commitment to worthy causes, not with a sense of resignation, but with a resolve and dedication to do what he thought was right and proper as he had done all of his life. In 1805 Jay wrote to his friend, Lindley Murray, reflecting upon his circumstances and retirement from public life. He expressed 'real satisfaction' with the 'freedom and leisure' he now enjoyed. He spoke of the 'tranquil retirement' of his life and his lack of 'disappointment' from it. He was sanguine in acknowledging that he experienced 'cares and anxieties' common to all and rejoiced that he was given such an 'agreeable situation in life'. Jay then concluded with much pragmatism "The truth is that although in numerous respects I have abundant reason to be thankful, yet in others I experience the necessity and the value of patience and resignation."[133]

Let Us Be Resigned

[1] John Jay to Sarah Jay 13March, 1795, Carol E. Brier. *Joseph Cusno: the Sicilian Immigrant and the Jays of Bedford.* The Westchester Historian 87: 2, 8 (2011).

[2] Sarah Jay to John Jay, 21 July 1799, JJCU.

[3] Abstracts of Wills on File in the Surrogate's Court, City of New York, Vol. IX.

[4] John Jay. *Circuit Court Diary,* JJCU.

[5] John Jay to Timothy Pickering 24 December 1808, JJCU.

[6] Agreement between John Jay and John Cooley, 17 February 1787, JJCU.

[7] Ibid.

[8] Contract with Mr. Winian (?) for masonry work at Bedford, March 15, 1787, JJH.

[9] Last Will and Testament of Peter Jay, September 21, 1797, JJH.

[10] John Jay. *Circuit Court Diary,* JJCU.

[11] John Jay. Bedford 1786, *Extract Respecting Salt as a Manure,* JJCU.

[12] John Jay to Peter Augustus Jay, 25 April 1792, JJCU.

[13] John Jay to Sarah Livingston Jay, 16 June 1801, JJCU.

[14] Ibid.

Let Us Be Resigned

[15] Frederick Shonnard and W.W. Spooner. *History of Westchester County,* (New York, 1900), 533.

[16] George Washington to John Jay, 31 July 1779, The New York Public Library; Dorothy Humphreys Hinit and Frances Riker Duncombe. *The Burning of Bedford July 1779*, (Bedford, NY, 1974), Introduction Page.

[17] John Jay to Sarah Livingston Jay, 16 June 1801, JJCU.

[18] Francis R. Duncombe and other Members of the Historical Committee Katonah Village Improvement Society. *Katonah The History of a New York Village and Its People,* (Katonah, NY, 1997), 79.

[19] Ibid, 80.

[20] James Wood. *The History of the Town of Bedford to 1917,* Reprinted from *The History of Westchester County New York,* (Bedford, NY, 1925), 646.

[21] Ibid, 59-60.

[22] Ibid, 80.

[23] Philip Field Horne. *A Land of Peace - The Early History of Sparta a Landing Town on the Hudson,* (Ossining, NY, 1976), 27.

[24] John Bakeless. *Turncoats, Traitors & Heroes Espionage in the American Revolution,* (New York 1998), 241-43.

[25] Greta A. Cornell. *The Ossining Story 175 Years on the Hudson, The History of the Village of Ossining.* (Ossining, NY 1988), 9.

[26] Susan Cochran Swanson and Elizabeth Green Fuller. *Westchester County,* (Elmsford, NY 1989), 52.

[27] Allan Keller, *Life Along the Hudson,* (Tarrytown NY, 1985) 96.

[28] John Jay to Peter Augustus Jay, 15 April 1799, JJH; also available at JJCU.

[29] John Jay to Peter Augustus Jay, 28 October 1823, JJH; also available at JJCU.

[30] Duncombe et al. *Katonah The History of a New York Village and its People,* 87-8.

[31] John Jay to Peter Augustus Jay, 15 April 1799, JJH; also available at JJCU.

[32] Hugh Howard and Roger Strauss III. *Houses of the Founding Fathers the Men Who Made America and the Way They Lived,* (New York 2007), 247.

[33] John Jay to Sarah Livingston Jay, 17 May 1801, JJH; also available at JJCU.

[34] Ibid.

[35] John Jay to Cadwallader Colden, 2 April 1800, JJH.

[36] Ibid.

[37] Gregory's Rect for a Gratuity of 50 Dolr, 5 October 1801, JJCU.

[38] James Fenimore Cooper, ed. *Correspondence of James Fenimore Cooper I-II,* (New Haven 1922), I:30.

[39] Charles W. Baird. *History of Rye, NY Chronicle of a Border Town, Westchester County, New York Including Harrison and White Plains till 1788,* (New York, 1871), 481.

[40] Ibid.

[41] Cooper. *Correspondence of James Fenimore Cooper,* I:31.

[42] Ibid, 29.

[43] Elizabeth Betts Leckie. *A Furnishing Plan for John Jay Homestead State Historic Site,* (Friends of John Jay Homestead, Katonah, NY 1992), 74.

[44] Robert Emmet Long. *James Fenimore Cooper,* (New York 1990) 15.

[45] Sarah Livingston Jay to John Jay, 28 July 1800, JJCU.

[46] Ibid.

[47] Ibid.

[48] John Jay to Sarah Livingston Jay, 16 June 1801, JJCU.

[49] John Jay to Peter Augustus Jay, 12 August 1800, JJH.

[50] Sarah Livingston Jay to John Jay, 27 May 1801, JJCU.

[51] Ibid.

[52] Sarah Livingston Jay to John Jay, 17 June 1801, JJCU.

[53] Mrs. Ellet. *Queens of American Society,* 84.

[54] Sarah Livingston Jay to Maria Jay Banyer, 2 December 1801, JJCU.

[55] Sarah Livingston Jay to Maria May Banyer, 5 May 1802, JJCU.

[56] JJWJ I:241.

[57] JJWJ I:242.

[58] John Jay to Richard Peters, 9 January 1815, JJCU.

[59] JJFM 37.

[60] Laura Jay Wells. *The Jay Family of La Rochelle and New York Province and State*, (New York, 1938), 33.

[61] Sarah Livingston Jay to Maria Jay Banyer, 5 May 1802, JJCU.

[62] John Jay. 17 September 1802, JJCU: Westchester County Historical Society, Elmsford, NY.

[63] John Jay to Maj. Samuel Lyons, 30 August 1802, JJH.

[64] JJFM 430; JJWS 371.

[65] JJWJ I:248.

[66] John Jay to Sarah Louisa Jay, 18 January 1808, JJCU.

[67] John Jay to Professor Henry Davis, 10 February 1803, HPJ IV:297.

[68] Ibid.

[69] *The Laws of Yale College in New Haven, in Connecticut: Enacted by the President and Fellows,* (New Haven 1808) Chapter XII:II, 34.

[70] Maria Jay Banyer to Ann Jay, 12 October, 1812, JJH; also available at JJCU.

[71] John Jay, ed. *Memorials of Peter A. Jay Compiled for his Descendants,* (Printed for Private Circulation 1929), 61.

[72] John Cox Morris to Sarah Sabina Morris, 30 July 1807, Wells. *The Jay Family,* 39.

[73] John Jay to Peter Augustus Jay, 22 July 1811, JJCU.

[74] John Jay to Peter Augustus Jay, 4 February 1822, JJCU.

[75] Mary Beth Norton. *Liberty's Daughters The Revolutionary Experience of American Women, 1750-1800, (*Boston and Toronto 1980), 97.

[76] Accounts for Maria Jay and Ann Jay from the Moravian School, Bethlehem, Pennsylvania 12 May, 1795-23 December, 1796, JJCU.

[77] Ann (Nancy) Jay to Miss F., Sabbath, November, 1819, John McVikcar. *A Christian Memorial to Two Sisters, (*Memphis, TN 2012), 7.

[78] JJFM 430.

[79] Jan Horton. *Three Sisters, Nancy Jay,* JJH, 10.

[80] Sarah Louisa Jay to John Jay, 12 April 1814, JJH.

[81] Mary Rutherford Jay to Ann (Nancy) Jay, 28 January 1807, JJH.

[82] Diary of Maria Jay Banyer, March 1827, JJH.

[83] Ibid.

Let Us Be Resigned

[84] Augusta McVickar Jay to John Jay, 8 July 1816, JJCU, Class of 1925.

[85] Leckie. *A Furnishing Plan for John Jay Homestead State Historic Site,* 26.

[86] John Jay to Ann (Nancy) Jay, 15 July 1810, JJCU.

[87] *Encounters with America's Premier Nursery and Botanic Garden. Thomas Jefferson's Monticello,* Twinleaf Journal, January 2004, 5; *Prince Family Nurseries ca. 1737-post-185`. Bulletin of the Hunt Institute for Botanical Documentation, Carnegie Melon Institute,* 21(1) Spring 2009, 4.

[88] Ibid 3 and 5.

[89] William Jay to Peter Augustus Jay, 13 October 1813, JJH; also available at JJCU.

[90] William Jay to Peter Augustus Jay, 21 April 1817, JJH; also available at JJCU.

[91] John Jay to Maria Jay Banyer, 14 August 1810, JJH; also available at JJCU.

[92] John Jay to Richard Peters, 9 January 1811, JJCU.

[93] Richard Peters and Samuel Breck. *A Collection of Puns and Witticisms of Judge Richard Peters, The Pennsylvania Magazine of History and Biography* I :3, 367 (The Historical Society of Pennsylvania, 1901).

[94] George Washington to Sir John Sinclair, 12 June 1796, The George Washington Papers 1741-1799, the Library of Congress, Washington, D.C..

[95] John Jay to Richard Peters, 30 August 1808, JJCU.

Let Us Be Resigned

[96] John Jay to Richard Peters, 18 September, 1808, JJCU.

[97] John Jay to Richard Peters, 24 July 1809, JJCU.

[98] John Jay to Richard Peters, 9 January 1811, JJCU.

[99] John Jay to Richard Peters, 16 October 1811, JJCU.

[100] Richard Peters. *Memoir on the Tunis broad-tailed Sheep,* Philadelphia Society for Promoting Agriculture, II (Philadelphia, 1811) and The Annual Register, or a View of the History, Politics and Literature, For the Year 1810, (London, 1812): 644.

[101] Ibid.

[102] John Jay to Richard Peters, 21 November 1810, JJCU.

[103] Ibid.

[104] John Jay to Richard Peters, 25 January 1819, JJCU.

[105] William Jay to John Jay, 19 August 1809, JJH; also available at JJCU.

[106] John Jay to Maria Jay Banyer, 19 July 1813, JJH; also available at JJCU.

[107] Peter Augustus Jay to Maria Jay Banyer, 8 July 1813, JJCU.

[108] John Jay to Maria Jay Banyer and Ann (Nancy) Jay, 14 April 1818, JJCU.

[109] Peter Augustus Jay to John Jay, 22 April 1818, JJH.

[110] John Jay to Samuel Farmer Jarvis, 4 May 1818, JJCU.

[111] John Jay to Maria Jay Banyer, 2 November 1804, JJCU.

[112] Ibid.

[113] John Jay to Maria Jay Banyer, 19 December 1805, JJCU.

[114] Ibid.

[115] John Jay to Maria Jay Banyer, 27 March 1806, JJH; also available at JJCU.

[116] John Jay to Peter Augustus Jay, 4 June 1806, JJCU.

[117] John Jay to Ann (Nancy) Jay, 6 June 1806, JJCU.

[118] John Jay to Goldsborough, Sr., 7 June 1806, JJCU.

[119] Ibid.

[120] John Jay to Peter Augustus Jay, 12 June 1805, JJH.

[121] Maria Jay Banyer to Mrs. Bell, 1 April 1808, JJH.

[122] Susan L. Ridley to Maria Jay Banyer, 6 April, 1808, JJH.

[123] Peter Augustus Jay to Ann (Nancy) Jay, 13 October 1808, JJH.

[124] Ibid.

[125] Peter Augustus Jay to John Jay, 12 October 1808, JJCU.

[126] Ibid.

[127] John Jay to Maria Jay Banyer, 10 October 1808, JJCU.

[128] Maria Jay Banyer to John Jay, 15 November 1808, JJCU.

[129] McVickar. *A Christian Memorial of Two Sisters,* 3-4.

[130] Ibid, 3.

[131] *The Jay Cemetery Rye New York,* (Privately published, October, 1947), 6.

[132] Ibid.

[133] John Jay to Lindley Murray, Jun. 18 October 1805, HPJ IV: 301-02.

Let Us Be Resigned

A Pleasant Situation

CHAPTER 3

The first few years of John Jay's retirement were plagued with illness and death in his immediate family. With resignation, patience and piety he was able to accept the circumstances and carry on without bitterness or resentment at his fate "Sickness and Death are Visitors who cannot be excluded by a 'Not at Home'."[1] Jay strove to maintain his composure, especially during difficult times, and to be circumspect as well. His daughter Maria noted these qualities in her father's behavior on the death of Polly Jay, blind Peter's wife. Maria observed that while her father was deeply moved by Polly's death, he appeared 'calm'.[2]

Jay wrote to his good friend, Richard Peters, about his views on being retired which afford great insight into how well Jay was coping with his retirement:

> As to what you have heard of my being very retired - it is to a certain Degree true. The Fact is, that I live very much as I have long wished to do. I have a pleasant Situation, and very good neighbours - I enjoy Peace and a Competency proportionate to my Comforts and moderate Desires; with such a Residue of Health, as which it constantly whispers *'memento mori'* still permits me to see my friends with cheerfulness and Pleasure. The Burden of Time I have not experienced. Attention to little Improvements occasional visits - the History which my Recollections furnish - and frequent Conversations with the 'mighty dead' who in a certain

A Pleasant Situation

> Sense live in their Work to
> further with the Succession of
> ordinary occurrences preserve
> me from, 'Ennui.'[3]

Jay fervently wished for the companionship of his family when he wrote to his daughter Maria "...among the Pleasures which have the most attraction, that of again seeing you and the rest of my children around me excites the most fervent wishes, my Dear Daughter,...."[4] Yet Jay received many visitors to his home. Peter Augustus and his family visited often as did Jay's Livingston, McVickar and other Jay relations. Peter Jay Munro and his wife Peggy who lived in Mamaroneck, were also visitors to Jay's farm. Peter Jay Munro was the son of John Jay's sister Eve Jay Munro and acted as John Jay's agent until he relinquished the position to Peter Augustus Jay. The relationship between Jay and his nephew was not always smooth. In discussing his nephew's handling of a financial matter, Jay expressed his displeasure and did not hesitate to pass along a bit of advice to the young man "You are riding a High Horse and I do not feel it to be my Duty to beg the Favor of you to dismount."[5] However, in terminating Munro's agency, Jay wrote succinctly but politely in thanking Munro for his 'Time and Trouble'.

Since travel was difficult, it was not uncommon for guests to stay for weeks, months and sometimes an entire season when visiting Jay at Bedford. Jay preferred small gatherings at the farm " Small select parties please me better - large ones may sometimes be proper, but they seldom afford much of that pleasure which is found in conversing with those whom we like."[6]

Before retirement, Jay had often attended the theatre. While in London in 1795, he and his son Peter saw the great Mrs. Siddons perform in *Measure for Measure* and *The Merchant of Venice*. Jay's opinion of the theater changed over the years when he wrote to his daughter Maria "You know my opinion of Theatre - from me they neither have recd nor will receive Encouragement."[7]

Jay now preferred the simple pleasures of conversation, music and cards, such as 'quadrille playing'. He also enjoyed

A Pleasant Situation

reading and his library included books on history, religion and ethics. The reading of a book was a common pastime and it is known that John Jay took particular pleasure in one book that his niece, Susan Ridley, was reading aloud "I am reading aloud *Don Quixote* and no one appears more entertained at his absurdities or the humors of the renowned Sancho Panza than Uncle;...."[8] Jay was also an avid and expert chess player and he often played with Peter's wife, Mary, who was also an expert chess player "I have played chess with Papa every day after dinner since I last wrote to you, and one afternoon I counted 12 games, tho' Papa thought we could not have played so many, but I believe I am correct."[9] On one occasion Mary achieved the distinction of besting Jay "Papa when after a long fought battle in which victory was often doubtful I had the pleasure of giving him check-mate."[10]

    Not all visits were pleasant as when a Livingston relative was staying at the farm. He had a cough but went for a swim in the Mill Pond which aggravated his cough. He was bled, a blister applied and laudanum was prescribed by the doctor. That evening Livingston tore off the blister and became delirious and so violent that it was difficult to keep him in his room.[11] For several days his health increased and then to Jay's surprise "a <u>violent</u> Fit of Delerium came on early in the Evening" and some of the men from the farm were, "<u>constantly</u> with him."[12] By morning matters became worse with Livingston's 'delerium' continuing and twice he escaped from his room.[13] Arrangements were made for Livingston to be accompanied to New York and returned to his family for care. Jay was much concerned about the health of his Livingston relative and for the restoration of normality to the Jay house "Our situation has for some time past, been that of anxiety and Sollicitude about J.L. and our Tranquility by Day and Night been not a little interrupted - Sally and Caty have managed with great Discretion under Circumstances very unfavorable to Health."[14] Clearly Jay believed that proper deportment was to be maintained in all circumstances, realizing the adverse effect such circumstances could have on one's health.

    Health issues frequently disrupted the normal pace of life and the Jays had the financial means to call upon some of the best

A Pleasant Situation

doctors available. Medicine in the early nineteenth century was influenced by Galen, a Greek doctor who lived during the second century A.D. and rose to prominence with his theory of 'humors' or body fluids. His theories influenced Western medicine well into the nineteenth century. Galen believed that there were four fluids in the body - blood, phlegm, bile and black bile. Any imbalance in the body fluids resulted in illness. Most trained doctors during Jay's lifetime believed in the theory of humors and subscribed to the notion that illness should be treated by depleting a patient's excess fluids. This was done through bleeding, blistering, purging and the inducement of vomiting which the Jay family doctors practiced.[15] Bleeding was performed with a lancet to open the patient's vein and the blood was allowed to flow into a basin. The amount of blood taken was determined solely by the doctor. Blistering was used for localized injuries where a caustic substance was applied to the skin to allow a blister to form and produce a discharge, as in J. Livingston's case. Purging involved the use of large doses of cathartics and laxatives and vomiting employed emetics. Maria's little daughter suffered these last two treatments along with bleeding before expiring. When there was fluid emission in the form of salivation, sweating, frequent urination, blood, pus, vomit, feces, and urine, this indicated to the doctor that the treatment was beneficial. Needless to say, these treatments were dangerous and uncomfortable for the patients, sometimes resulting in death.[16]

Since there were no trained nurses at the time, the family would nurse the patient. Nancy and Maria not only nursed members of their family but spent time administering to the needy in the Bedford area as was noted by a townsperson "Frequently might they be seen entering the abode of some poor widow, or suffering orphan, to administer spiritual comfort, or provide for their physical wants."[17] Maria belonged to the Bedford Female Charitable Society a non-denominational organization devoted to nursing.[18]

There were a number of commonly prescribed drugs by doctors. Calomel, derived from quinine, was a cathartic. Another cathartic, Mercurous chloride, was toxic in large doses and often

A Pleasant Situation

led to the patient developing gum damage and loss of teeth. The Jay family correspondence is replete with descriptions of illness and medical treatments prescribed by a doctor.

When a doctor was needed, the Jays usually relied on two local doctors, Dr. Walter Keeler and Dr. William H. Sackett. Dr. Keeler moved to Bedford from Ridgefield, Connecticut, where his family ran a tavern which stands in the center of Ridgefield to this day. He died in 1871 at the age of 94.[19] Dr. Sackett was born in Bedford and married Rebecca Holly, daughter of Col. Jesse Holly of Bedford. He received his training at Yale and very soon became one of the most accomplished physicians in Westchester County. He was commissioned as Surgeon of Regiment of State Troops and in 1818 became the Hospital Surgeon of the Eleventh Division of Infantry.[20] He has been described as man of excellent breeding and an avid doctor of the new scientific studies of medicine.[21]

Jay expressed no preference for either doctor when medical treatment was needed On one occasion though, Jay took the unusual step of calling for a doctor from New York City. In 1820, Nancy had developed a cold with a cough and fever which was not unusual for her as she suffered these ailments practically every winter. Dr. Keeler was sent for and applied a blister to Nancy's breast but Nancy had a restless night with a high fever and pain in her chest. Her condition worsened and the next day Dr. Keeler arrived and stayed with Nancy most of the day until her severe pains abated. Nancy seemed to improve and Dr. Keeler visited her twice the next day. Jay was so concerned about Nancy that his letter to Peter Augustus was written over several days in which he noted the day and time the doctor arrived, Nancy's condition and the prescribed treatment.[22] Although Nancy seemed to be recovering, Jay sent for Dr. John Watts who was a leading physician in New York City. He consulted with Dr. Keeler and over the course of several days, blisters were applied with effect and they also bled Nancy until she was pronounced convalescent.

Dr. Watts was so highly regarded that Maria wrote to him for a second opinion concerning a poor woman in Bedford who was being treated by a local physician, Dr. Henry Van Kleick. Dr.

A Pleasant Situation

Van Kleick had written to Dr. Watts about the woman and her 'pneumonic symptoms' and the appearance of blood, among other symptoms.[23] In her letter to Dr. Watts, Maria stated that Dr. Van Kliek had done everything for the woman and would Dr. Watts please write to Dr. Van Kliek with his diagnosis and prescription, which Maria generously offered to pay for.[24] It is clear that both Nancy and Maria, and most likely their younger sister, Sarah Louisa, were instilled with a sense of charity and compassion for the sick and those less fortunate, which was no doubt the result of their schooling, religious training and parental guidance.

Jay was never in the best of health and his letters are replete with references to his problems with bile and his bilious attacks and the remedies prescribed by his doctors and family alike. He complained to his son Peter Augustus reminding him to order some medicine "My Complaints are seldom of short Duration - I think myself less unwell than I have been, but my Stomach is still disturbed both by Bile and acidity. For the latter, I find Magnesia the remedy which agrees best with me. This reminds me of requesting you to purchase four or five Bottles of calcinated magnesia - ...."[25] Jay also ate ripe peaches as an antidote for his bile and gave his daughter Maria a precise account of his treatment "So far as respects Bile I have found ripe Peaches useful - but they should not be so very ripe or soft, as to afford Reason to suspect that an acid fermentation had begun in them - such are apt to sour the Stomach - as was the case with me last Week."[26] Dr. Bard, a leading physician in New York City, prescribed a tea for Jay's ailment made from hoarhound and plaintain that should be fresh, dried but not green.[27]

Jay also suffered from pains in his side and rheumatism in his shoulder to which essence of hemlock was applied among other remedies. By 1809 Jay had been diagnosed with a liver ailment "My retirement has not disappointed me, as to my Health - a complaint in the Liver has for several years been impairing it - medical Prescriptions failing to relieve it, relief could only be sought from Palliatives, and among those I find Temperance, Patience and Resignation to be the best."[28] Patience and resignation continued to be excellent remedies for Jay. Although

A Pleasant Situation

he never traveled far from Bedford after this diagnosis, Jay continued to be plagued by his liver, rheumatism and bilious complaints for the rest of his life. He declined invitations to celebrations using his poor health as an excuse, as when Rufus King invited Jay to a reception in New York to celebrate the "...overthrow and Expulsion of Napoleon...."[29] Jay declined on grounds that his health prevented him from attending, "so joyous an occasion."[30]

Gouverneur Morris asked Jay to be godfather to his son in 1813. Jay responded by acknowledging the duties of a godfather and with his own prognosis of his health and prospects of longevity "...whoever consents to be employed as a Shepherd, should recollect that if a Lamb be lost by his negligence, he must answer for it to the owner of the Flock."[31] Jay then advised Morris to find another person "But as I expect to remove at a more early period to a distant country, where I shall not be in a capacity to attend to persons or things here...."[32] Jay would outlive King and Morris and many of his contemporaries despite his view of his 'old age', other 'infirmities' and what he often believed to be his imminent demise.

Jay was as concerned with the health of his family as he was with his own health, writing of Maria's headaches, Sarah Louisa's nervous condition and Nancy's eyes and stomach. Maria found some relief for her headaches with a remedy of "...wearing a flannel cap with sulphur quilted in it...."[33] while Nancy found relief from her disordered stomach by taking bismuth. It was hoped that electric shock treatments would give Sarah Louisa some relief from her nervous disorder. When a tumor and swelling appeared on Augusta's neck, a 'plaister' of Hemlock and Mercury was prescribed. Despite illness and loss of family and friends, Jay never wavered in his desire to have his family with him "Our Fire Side has been warm, and we often have wished to see our dispersed Family collected in a Circle round it."[34]

Yet, on one occasion, Jay advised his family not to travel to Bedford but to stay at home. He feared for their health due to the alarming spread of the 'putrid fever' which had spread to many parts of northern Westchester county and neighboring Fairfield

A Pleasant Situation

county in Connecticut. His letters during the winter of 1812 are mainly concerned with the fever and his usual topics of discussion such as his family and the farm are absent. Only the fever is discussed by Jay. His concern and alarm for the safety of his family and friends was not misplaced. By March Jay wrote of the many people in Bedford who had been stricken with the fever, identifying those who survived and those who died. He advised his nephew, Peter Jay Munro "I am told this morning of several new Cases of the fever. I therefore think it prudent for you to postpone coming here for the present."[35] The local doctors were overwhelmed by the number of patients. Jay reported that in one week Dr. Keeler saw eighty patients and Dr. Sackett tended forty patients. This was a time when country doctors such as Drs. Keeler and Sackett would have ridden to the home of their patients on horseback to administer to them. Jay wrote with the utmost concern to Peter Augustus:

> If (as may be the Case) it [the fever] is generated and spread by something peculiar in the air in these parts, they who live at a Distance had better remain at a distance for the present - it is supposed the mild Weather will check it - our Doctrs say, it is to them a new kind of fever - some think it is a species of the spotted Fever - while it prevails I hope that neither you nor Wm [William Jay broke his journey from New York to Bedford and stayed at Rye with Peter Augustus due to the spreading epidemic] will come here - and I think Mr. Munro had better postpone his intended visit, for the present - If it should come into this family, neither of you could be useful - and your being unnecessarily in Danger would give me more concern than having the Fever - Let us do our Duty at all Risques - but

A Pleasant Situation

> let us not by Rashness <u>tempt Providence</u>.[36]

Several days letter, in another letter to Peter Augustus, Jay wrote that it was the opinion of Dr. Keeler that while the symptoms indicated bleeding, those who had been bled rarely recovered. Dr. Sackett recommended doses of calomel which induced salivation, an indication that the patient would recover. Jay also noted the effectiveness of 'Branches of Hemlock' which proved effective against the fever.[37] Many itinerant workers who entered the area were stricken with the fever and died. By April, the town of Bedford was still a place to be avoided with the fever continuing to spread as Jay noted with great concern "I do not hear that the Fever abates - many are sick and some of them are not expected to recover."[38] By this time, Jay reported that the fever was spreading to the [Long Island] Sound and that sixty deaths have been reported in New Milford, Connecticut. In the neighboring town of Somers, twenty men, all heads of families, died of the fever. In a letter to Maria he still expressed alarm and the danger of being exposed to the fever "I think it right to give the same advice to Sally that I did to William - *viz* not to expose themselves unnecessarily (by a premature Return) to Danger."[39] Jay was adamant about the danger of the fever when he continued "...I therefore cannot approve of their [William and Sarah Louisa] running <u>any</u> Risque by coming here too speedily - on this Subject you shall have Information by every Mail."[40] Jay's letters and his concern for his family are extraordinary and most of his correspondence during this period is devoted exclusively to the fever. By May the fever had begun to subside in Bedford and Jay discussed the possibility of travel among his family to his farm for a visit "The Fever has abated considerably in this Town, but we hear that it prevails in lower parts of the County - It has caused great Distress - We have great Reason to be thankful that our Family has been preserved from it - "[41]

The cause of the fever is not known, but perhaps John Jay may have given a clue about the cause of the epidemic. He wrote earlier that year of the torrential rains and flooding to Peter Augustus "... - we have since had so much Rain, that our Meadow

A Pleasant Situation

looked like a Pond - the Roads have suffered greatly - several Bridges were carried away. I do not remember to have seen so much Water on the Earth at any one time since I lived here-...."[42]. It may have been possible that with the flooding, the privies overflowed and may have contaminated the wells. Many of the cases of the fever occurred among the lower classes and the Jays and other wealthier people seem not to have been stricken as much with the fever. The Jays and other wealthy families would have drunk wine with their lunch and dinner, while the less fortunate would have drunk water that might possibly have been contaminated.

During the first decade of his retirement, Jay devoted a great deal of his time to improvements on the farm, including the construction of a 'Ha-ha'. A Ha-ha was a landscape design, a ditch, to keep the livestock, primarily sheep, from grazing on the lawn and in the gardens. It afforded an uninterrupted view of the property. When strollers on the grounds approached the Ha-ha and suddenly became aware of its presence, it elicited laughter and hence the name. The Ha-ha is still in existence at the John Jay Homestead and continues to delight visitors to the site. By 1818, William and Augusta's ever growing family created the need for more guest rooms in the house and prompted the construction of a new wing for the house.

In 1807, Jay's interests turned to two projects that would impact his family and descendants. The remains of the Jay family members buried in the vault in New York City were brought to Rye and buried in a single grave in the 'East Meadow' of the Jay farm in Rye. Although there is no record of the names of the Jays buried at Rye in 1807, it is known that Jay's wife, Sarah Livingston Jay, was among them. Then in 1809, Maria wrote to her brother Peter Augustus Jay and asked for his assistance in having her husband and children moved to the "family burial ground at Rye."[43] In 1813 when Jay's brother, Peter, died, Jay set aside 82/100ths of land as a family cemetery. He created a Cemetery Trust in 1815 by deed with his son, Peter Augustus, and nephew, Peter Jay Munro, as Trustees. Many members of the Jay family are buried there, including John Jay. It should be noted that

A Pleasant Situation

William Jay chose to be buried in the churchyard of St. Matthew's Church in Bedford along with many of his descendants and some loyal family servants. William gave no explanation for this action and it remains a matter of speculation to this day as to his preference for St. Matthew's burial ground in Bedford.

During his retirement, many of John Jay's projects and interests stemmed from his religious convictions. He performed charitable acts such as maintaining a number of children in various Westchester schools, extending help to the truly needy and when the repayment of a loan he had extended would produce hardship for the debtor, he would cancel the loan.[44]

In 1803 John Jay was elected an honorary member of an Episcopal Society formed for promoting Religion and Learning in the State of New York. In accepting the appointment, Jay stated his "...pleasure to have opportunities of co-operating in the advancement of Religion and Learning - ...."[45] Although Jay's grandfather and other ancestors were Huguenots, the Jays began to attend Episcopalian churches in New York City. One project that consumed Jay's interest and time when he first moved to Bedford was the construction of an Episcopal church in the town. When John Jay moved to Bedford in 1801, there was no Episcopal church and most people in the town were Presbyterian with a few Quakers and Episcopalians. Jay attended the Presbyterian church until plans could be made for the construction of an Episcopalian church in Bedford. As was common practice at the time, Jay often brought his dog, Bob, to Sunday services and there is an account of the dog's behavior in attempting to make friends with the minister to the dismay of the congregation.[46] According to William Jay, John Jay was not of a mind to become a Presbyterian "...nor did he scruple to unite with his fellow-Christians of that persuasion in commemorating the passion of their common Lord."[47] Plans were made for the construction of an Episcopal church in Bedford and John Jay advanced funds for the purchase of forty acres from Jonathan Guion until the funds from a bequest made by St. George Talbot in the mid-eighteenth century were received by the church. Peter Jay Munro and Alexander Hamilton were retained by the Episcopal church to secure the funds due the church.⁴⁸

On one occasion members of St. Matthew's Church, including a man named Jonathan Guion, had tea at John Jay's house to discuss church matters. Later, Mr. Guion, then a Warden of St. Matthew's and a simple farmer, told his family how 'splendid' and 'sumptuous' was the lifestyle of the Jays.⁴⁹

Construction on the church began in 1807. The plans for the construction of a brick church were adopted by a committee that included Peter Augustus Jay and were approved by the vestry. Peter resigned his position on the committee due to his marriage that year and his setting up residence in New York City.

John Jay took more than a casual interest in the construction of the church. As was his nature and approach to any project he chose to undertake, Jay took an active and critical interest in all areas of construction of the new church "I understand that the Brick intended for our church, are not fit for the Purpose. It seems the Inner side of the wall will be of salmon and the outer of hard brick."⁵⁰ Later that year, Jay visited the construction site and expressed displeasure at what he saw "I have been to the Church - The water table is bad. The bricks made for it do not match well."⁵¹ However, the church was completed in 1809 and Nathan Felch was chosen to be the lay leader. Mr. Felch lived in the old glebe house on the property and also worked the glebe as a farm. Then on October 17, 1810, St. Matthew's Church was consecrated by the Rt. Rev. Benjamin Moore, Bishop of New York, who later married William Jay and Augusta McVickar. The Jays were ardent supporters of the church and gave to St. Matthew's in different ways. John Jay donated the pulpit library and purchased a family pew between the windows on the east side of the church for fifty dollars. Nancy and Maria gave a communion service and communion table and Maria donated funds for additional work on the church. William served as a Vestryman for forty-seven years. John Jay was a warden of the church and his warden stick remains on display at St. Matthew's Church. Peter Augustus Jay also served as a Vestryman for two years. Jay had clearly imparted to his family his religious convictions. For many years, the Jays of Bedford were an integral

A Pleasant Situation

part of St. Matthew's Church and gave of their time to religious and charitable endeavors.

John Jay was not actively involved in the administration of the church, except for the episode concerning Nathan Felch, the church's lay leader. Felch was a Methodist preacher in Norwalk, Connecticut, of some repute as Jay himself noted when he wrote that the Episcopal Minister and others who knew Felch in Norwalk "...gave him a good character---that his habits were frugal and industrious, - and that his manners were decent and becoming."[52] When he came to St. Matthew's, Felch settled into the glebe which had been purchased for St. Matthew's. In addition to his duties as a lay leader, Felch also worked the farm and hired two men as boarders who were working on the construction of the church. One of the boarders, John Miller, who was the son of William Miller, a warden of the church and a friend of John Jay, stayed out late one evening returning to the glebe around nine o'clock that evening. Miller was reprimanded by Felch the next morning for having stayed out so late and Miller took offense at Felch's actions. An investigation on the part of the vestry partially absolved Felch but the vestry's original recommendation for Felch's ordination was withdrawn and then reconsidered. Felch was ordained an Episcopal priest later that year.[53] It should be noted that Jay signed the original recommendation for Felch's ordination when he was hired by the vestry.

However, the vestry's investigations into the episode concerning John Miller never were completely settled to Jay's satisfaction, particularly the vestry relenting to Felch's ordination. Calling upon his legal experience, Jay wrote a letter to the Vesty and Bishop Benjamin Moore of New York City concerning Felch. Jay alluded to certain indiscreet behavior on the part of Rev. Felch which originally prompted the investigation into Felch's behavior.[54] Jay attended the meetings and carefully examined the evidence and the resolutions of the vestry. With regard to the statements made by Felch, Jay stated that they "have a Tendency to excite Doubts unfavorable to his Veracity."[55] Jay stated unequivocally that the resolutions, "...do not meet with my approbation."[56] He went on to say that he wanted to state his position on the matter of the ordination:

> I think it proper for me to be explicit. I do not concur in such an opinion, and therefore ought not , by remaining silent, to countenance a Presumption that I do concur in it - Being persuaded that it is better to correct a mistake than to gloss and persist in it, I find myself constrained to retract, and for the present to suspend, my Recommendation of Mr. Felch for ordination.[57]

Jay's statements reveal his ethics and strong commitment to doing what he believed to be the right course of action. He also exhibited humility in admitting that he had made a mistake in endorsing Felch and wanted to set the record straight as to his opposition to the ordination.

Despite the episode, Rev. Felch was rather positive when he commented about the state of St. Matthew's when he wrote that the congregation of the church in Bedford 'flourishes' with a righteous and pious congregation.[58]

In 1811 the old glebe was replaced with a new house and the following year a burial ground was established. The next year, 1813, proved to be anything but peaceful or calm, particularly with the Rev. Felch. Rev. Felch contacted the vestry and stated that he could not possibly continue in his position for less than five hundred dollars a year. The vestry unanimously accepted his resignation. In this action, Jay was in complete agreement with the church body. In a letter to Peter Augustus, Jay discussed Felch's resignation, not overlooking any aspect of Rev. Felch's behavior, and leaving no doubt about his position, adding "…he has cut about 70 fine young oaks -- This has caused much Displeasure and together with his usual Indiscretions, leave no Reason to regret his Departure - the Interest of the church has been injured by him…."[59] In a letter to his daughter Maria, Jay perhaps gave us some insight into why Rev. Felch seemed to be a controversial choice for the congregation "- None of the

A Pleasant Situation

congregation, that I have heard of, oppose his going - He does not find himself at his Ease - and they are not pleased."[60] A new lay leader, George Weller, was selected by the vestry but resigned in 1817 and was replaced by Rev. Samuel Nichols who remained at St. Matthew's for many years.

Jay's reaction to Nathan Felch was in keeping with his character, integrity, discretion and prudence and above all, his belief in God. His letter to the vestry of St. Matthew's and Bishop Moore displays his lawyerly manner with his examination of the 'evidence'.

Many of Jay's letters display this legal approach to problems that confronted him, as well as a very serious nature. The essence of Jay's character also included a precise statement of his position in all matters from religion to politics, his farm and family matters. Jay was usually very emphatic and left no doubt as to his position regarding an issue. He was organized and his actions, whether written or oral, were carefully thought out and presented only when he was certain he had made the correct decision based on the available evidence. He approached the problems of retirement with the same firmness of mind and competence as he had during his public career. In 1804 Jay did not mince words when writing to Bishop Benjamin Moore about some lots that he owned in lower Manhattan which the Bishop and the Vestry of Trinity Church seemed to think Jay had offered for sale to the church "I never Sir ! did offer those Lots directly or indirectly to the Vestry, nor to any other person or persons whatever."[61]

The Jay family attended church regularly and Nancy and Maria, "...took an active part in gathering the children of the neighborhood into the Sunday-school."[62] John Jay continued his support of the church and affiliated groups when he wrote to Eleazor Lord, Secretary of the New York Sunday School Society "I will desire my son [Peter Augustus Jay] to add my name to the List of Life Subscribers to the New York Sunday School Society - "[63] He contributed funds to the American Missionary Society and was elected an honorary member of the American Board of Foreign Missions and the Protestant Episcopal Society for

A Pleasant Situation

promoting Religion and Learning in the State of New York. Jay also supported efforts of the Episcopal Theological Seminary and believed in "...the support of Episcopalians throughout all the states."[64] In 1815 Jay became vice president of the American Bible Society and later became president of the organization.

Jay's religious views were undoubtedly influenced by the persecution of his grandfather and other family members in France at the hands of the Catholics and his family's attempts to escape persecution and find religious freedom. He wrote an essay for his own family, at their urging, which described the travails of his Huguenot ancestors. Jay's account of his Huguenot ancestors is incomplete but he detailed their suffering in France which had a profound influence on Jay's religious beliefs, particularly for his strong support for the Episcopal church. It was England, its American colonies and the Episcopal church that gave sanctuary to his family and so many other Huguenots. His anti-Catholicism often expressed itself during the Revolutionary period and the formation of the federal republic in the restrictions that Jay often sought to mitigate the influence of Catholics. In 1774 in his *Address to the People of Great Britain*, Jay had expressed his strong views against the Catholic church as having "...dispersed impiety, bigotry, persecution, murder, and rebellion through every part of the world."[65]

During his retirement years, Jay's religious beliefs were often expressed in his association with organizations affiliated with the Episcopal church The Bedford Academy was an exception. In 1807 the Bedford Academy was founded under the auspices of the Bedford Presbyterian Church, though it was to be non-denominational in nature. The Academy was built on land facing the Bedford Village green. John Jay was a reluctant subscriber to the Academy at first and doubted if enough funds could be raised when he wrote in a negative tone to his daughter Sarah Louisa, about the adverse influence money can have "...-good Preception cannot be had for trifling Emoluments, especially in this country where money has its full share of Influence - ...."[66] Jay ultimately did become one of the original

A Pleasant Situation

subscribers to the Academy, a preparatory school, which had a distinguished alumni including John Jay's grandson, John Jay II. The building is now the Bedford Free Library.

There was another event that occurred in 1807 that would have an immediate effect on the entire Hudson River Valley when Robert Fulton's steamboat, the *Clermont/North River Steamboat*, made its first journey up the Hudson River. As early as 1801, Robert Fulton partnered with Robert Livingston to build a steamboat. In 1808 the New York State legislature gave Livingston and Fulton a monopoly, for a term of years, to operate boats, moved by fire or steam, on the rivers of New York State with the proviso that the vessel could travel at the rate of four miles an hour. While the vessel was under construction on the East River in Manhattan, passersby often expressed their doubts as to the wisdom of the venture and the boat was ultimately dubbed "*Fulton's Folly*." With invited guests aboard, the *Clermont* made its first voyage in August of 1807 traveling at five miles an hour. The boat docked that evening at Livingston's estate, Clermont, which was about one hundred-ten miles from New York City, for an overnight stay. The *Clermont* reached Albany the next day in eight hours for a total of thirty-two hours for the trip up the Hudson and returned to New York City in thirty hours.

However, this historic event was hardly mentioned in the newspapers but that did not deter the steamboat from becoming a financial success. The boat made regular trips to Albany as a packet boat. Some of the sloops, which had ruled the Hudson since the time of the Dutch settlement, often attempted to ram the *Clermont* and disable or sink her. The sloop owners feared that the success of the steamboat would endanger their property and livelihoods. As a result, the New York legislature passed a law prohibiting the ramming of steamboats under serious penalties.[67] The steamboat ultimately replaced the sloops due to its speed and offered other advantages the sloops could not. The cost of a trip from New York City to West Point was $2.50 and $7 to Albany, which was a very attractive price. The social elite of the area were among the first to use the steamboat which afforded many luxuries.[68] Fulton from the beginning of his venture wanted to

113

offer the passengers comfort. The boats were equipped with ornamental paintings, gildings and polished woods along with three cabins, fifty-four berths, a kitchen, bar and steward's room.[69] Regulations were posted along with fines for improper behavior to protect the furnishings, breakage and injury such as men lying in their berth with their boots on which carried a fine of $1.50.[70]

John Jay did not share the general public's excitement over the innovation when he wrote to his son Peter a month after the *Clermont's* first voyage "Perhaps the Steam Boat may yet be so improved as to be useful and less expensive. In its present State I doubt its proving advantageous to the owners."[71] The steamboat did prove to be profitable and popular. With the monopoly granted to Livingston and Fulton by New York State and later on the lower Mississippi River, they were ultimately challenged in court by other businessmen seeking to operate steamboat lines. This brought the Commerce Clause of the U.S. Constitution into question. The matter resulted in a landmark decision by the United States Supreme Court in 1824, *Gibbons v. Ogden*, in which the court upheld that the power to regulate interstate commerce was granted to Congress by the Commerce Clause of the U.S. Constitution. However, the steamboat became an accepted mode of transportation by members of the Jay family when, in 1817, William Jay, along with his sisters, Maria and Sarah Louisa, made a trip to Niagara Falls. They journeyed up the Hudson River to Albany by steamboat and then on to Niagara Falls via coach.[72]

Jay's simple life on the farm was punctuated with visits from neighbors and fellow jurists, Benjamin Isaacs and William Miller. Jay's expressed his view of the local townspeople when he wrote of them :

> I attend every Election, even for Town officers; and having delivered my Ballots, return home, without having mingled in the crowd or participated in their altercations. In this Town however Elections cannot but little distress - the great majority having been firm Whigs during the War, and

A Pleasant Situation

decided Federalists since the new Constitution.[73]

He disapproved of the fact that the townspeople opposed the ratification of the Constitution. Jay nonetheless had excellent relations with Isaacs and Miller.

During his retirement, Jay was often approached by biographers to comment on a book or to help write a biography. Alexander Hamilton's widow paid Jay a visit at his farm to discuss Jay writing a biography of her late husband. Jay declined her request due to lack of time and interest. On one occasion, Jay had read the fifth volume of the works of Benjamin Franklin which had been published by James Duane, who was a pro-Jefferson editor of the Philadelphia newspaper, *Aurora*. Jay became incensed when Duane asserted that the Journals of Jay and John Adams, written during the Treaty of Paris negotiations, were in his possession. After writing to Adams about the matter, Jay then replied to Duane in a very direct manner "Be pleased Sir! to inform me what are the Papers thus called our [Jay and Adams] Journals and from whence they were derived."[74] Jay then proceeded to instruct Duane on the facts of the subject.

Now that Jay was retired from public office and the legal profession, he steadfastly refused to give legal advice and said so in very strong language when responding to such a request:

> On retiring to this place, it appeared to me not improbable that opportunities of this kind would occasionally be made to me - To give Law opinions to some of my friends, and to deny them to others, would be to make offensive Distinctions- to give them to all, might involve me in more Business than wd be convenient - after considering this Subject in its various Lights, I concluded to give no opinions on the Law Questions.[75]

At times Jay did express a legal opinion but only as a fiduciary, in

A Pleasant Situation

his capacity as Executor or Trustee.

Jay subscribed to newspapers and periodicals keeping abreast of the latest news and advancements. He received pamphlets from acquaintances and sermons from clergy men, some of which were given to the Town Library in Bedford. Other publications he kept in his own library and were given to the New York Historical Society on his death. He also subscribed to a biography of Gen. Henry "Light-Horse Harry" Lee, *Memoirs of the War in the Southern Department of the United States. Eyewitness Accounts of the American Revolution*. Jay had always admired the military campaigns of Gen. Lee and counted the Lee family "…among the Number of my Friends." Jay wrote to the General's brother, Richard Bland Lee "The Subject and the author excite my attention and my Desire to procure a Copy…I wish that my name may be on the List of Subscribers, and that I may use my Endeavours to increase the number of them."[76] Jay was so single-minded in this project that when he his letter to Richard Lee arrived in New York City, Jay instructed his son, Peter Augustus, to "open the packet" to hasten his subscription to the memoir and have his letter published to increase the sale of the book. This latter move by Jay to endorse the biography was extraordinary and not something he did for other authors and indicated his admiration for Gen. Lee and his accomplishments during the Revolutionary War.

A good deal of Jay's time was spent in managing his finances. Jay abandoned a lucrative legal career to take up the cause of American independence. When he retired, he was not a very wealthy man but he was a man of substantial means and he lived comfortably. He was not extravagant but wanted the best quality in everything from building materials to clothing and household items. This included quills for writing when he instructed Peter Augustus "Formerly the best quills were imported from Holland - if any of the first quality are sold in New York, bring fifty of them for me when you come to Bedford - I would rather have excellent ones at a high Price than inferior ones however cheap."[77]

He also loaned money, as his father did, and kept Peter

A Pleasant Situation

Augustus busy collecting the interest and principal on the bonds and mortgages due John Jay. Jay also owned property in lower Manhattan where houses were built and rented out. In his letters to Peter he often complained about falling rents, the taxes due and the future of his stocks. In 1823 Jay wanted some stock in Merchants Bank sold and the proceeds invested in 'Stock of the United States' to avoid a state tax on dividends when he wrote to Peter Augustus "I am apprehensive that the state tax on dividends may eventually, and perhaps soon, diminish the value and price of the one, and increase that of the other."[78] He was often approached to lend money to individuals but Jay was always prudent and in 1805 he wrote to his friend Egbert Benson that he could not 'subscribe' to a loan for Mrs. Alexander Hamilton, who was left heavily in debt after her husband's death. Although Jay was urged by Benson and others to loan the money to Mrs. Hamilton, he refused simply because he did not have the money to loan and needed it for his own purposes. Yet years later, Jay would loan money to Benson and send him a Demijohn of Madeira on occasion.

    During his retirement, Jay's interests also extended to the welfare of the servants in his household and on his farm, nor was he insensitive to their needs. When Jay arrived at the farm in 1801, he wrote to his wife Sarah "The Servants are all well and satisfied - I imagine that they all found things better than they expected."[79] It is not clear how many servants were employed in the house, but census reports indicate that the number of household servants varied from four to twelve. Jay's account book shows entries for a man named Peter Blake, a coachman who lived on the farm with his family. Jay usually indicated the full name of a skilled worker in his account book, as he did with Peter Blake. On more than one occasion, Jay spoke of his concern for his servants as when Peter Blake, his wife and three children were ill with typhus fever. Jay also expressed his concern for the recovery of one of Blake's children as 'doubtful.' The following year, Blake was ill with 'rheumatic pains' which made him unable to work but Jay followed Blake's recovery and noted "...and the Doctr thinks he will not be free from them before we have warm

A Pleasant Situation

weather."[80]

Nor did Jay or his son Peter Augustus Jay forget former servants, such as Tom Rascoe. Rascoe, who at one time worked for Peter Augustus Jay as well as John Jay. Rascoe returned to New York having entered Peter Jay's office in a 'Sailors Dress.' Rascoe told a tale of sailing to the South Seas for acquiring sandal wood and seal skins for the lucrative market in Canton, China. When the vessel reached Manila, the ship was deemed unseaworthy and the crew was paid off and abandoned. He ultimately made his way to Canton where the American consul arranged for his passage home where he sought out Peter Augustus Jay.[81]

It was difficult to hire skilled workers for a farm so remote from an urban center and at times local people were employed. A family named Powell, living in the Cantitoe section of Bedford, which is where Jay had his farm, had sons who worked for Jay. One son was a coachman and the other was a personal attendant.[82]

The Jays certainly employed a cook. There were two kitchens in the house, one at ground level and the other a subterranean, summer kitchen. With open hearth cooking being the norm, it was cooler in the summer to cook in the underground summer kitchen It is said that lobster from New York harbor was a favorite dish of John Jay. He was also known to be partial to oysters and commented on a shipment received from Peter's wife Mary "… - we had some of them at breakfast this morning, and found them excellent.[83] Oysters at this period were commonly eaten at breakfast. The shells were usually pulverized for fertilizer or ground for cover along the paths on the farm.

The Jays raised most of their food on the farm and sent to New York City for items that were unavailable such as tobacco, wine, cloth, and manufactured goods. Jay particularly enjoyed his Madeira wine which was ordered from New York City. His love of Madeira wine and shellfish might well explain the gout that Jay developed in his foot later in life. His gout stool remains on view in the office/library at his farm.

The family took their meals in a spacious dining room. The dining room was a new concept and one that Jay had employed when remodeling his house for retirement. The idea for a separate room for meals originated in England and France in the late eighteenth century. This trend in dining rooms may possibly have been noted by the Jays in the course of his diplomatic career. The room contained the dining room furniture made for John and Sarah, complete with three tables and twenty-four chairs in the mandarin style. With twenty-four chairs, the Jays could accommodate the large family and numerous guests at the house.

Jay also kept a thermometer in the dining room commenting on several occasions about the weather "...the thermometer in our dining room, having been up to 84°,...."[84]. Being a farm, it would be natural that a discussion of the weather would be deemed appropriate by those in attendance. On several occasions, Jay wrote of the effects of the weather on the house and the reading of another thermometer on the piazza "We have had severe cold Weather. On Friday Evening last the mercury fell, on our north Piazza, down to 0!--a good deal of our Wine in the Store Room Froze."[85] He also commented on the unusually mild weather one December when he wrote to his daughter, Maria "...-as yet there has been no Frost in the House and very little of it."[86] and the effect of an early frost on the crops, "The severe late frosts have diminished our Prospect of Fruit - The greater part of the young Peaches have dropped from the Trees - ...we had a few Pears and Quinces, but they are all gone."[87]

The table would be set with the Jay's Chinese porcelain dinnerware with the initials "JJ" in the center. The dinner service and other serving needs were kept in a pantry located between the dining room and kitchen. The table was set for each meal and served by a waiter. A waiter was considered a skilled position and in 1813, William Jay wrote to his father about hiring a new waiter who would become a devoted servant of the Jay family:

> I have however engaged for you a Mulatto Man who will I hope prove a good Servant. He was born in Sicily & when 8 years old was brought over to this Country 12 years ago by Lieut. Izard of Philadelphia & has

A Pleasant Situation

> remained until lately in Mr. Izard's family as a waiter...His price is $10pr month or $100 pr year. He has agreed to do whatever you please & to sleep with whoever you please....His name is John.[88]

John's full name was Joseph Cusno and in February of 1813 when he started to work for John Jay as a waiter, he began a remarkable journey in which he embraced the opportunities available to him in America made possible by the generosity and assistance of the Jay family. When Joseph came to Bedford, John Jay loaned him seventy-one dollars as part of an agreement written in Jay's hand to buy "a small Stone Dwelling House at Cantitoe". Joseph purchased the house on what is now Girdle Ridge Road which was a short walk to the Jay farm. The loan was repaid in two years. Since Joseph was not naturalized, he could not legally own land. Jay assisted him by drawing up a document stating all the facts and extending a covenant to Joseph whereby Jay retained title in the property until such time as Joseph became a naturalized citizen.

Jay also granted another loan to Joseph of seven hundred fifty dollars which Joseph repaid in 1818 - "Cusno's bond for $750 was paid off last week."[89] Period maps show the location of Joseph's home with a dot and the notation "J.Cusno" It is not known whether the two loans were part of Joseph's employment terms, but he must have impressed John Jay with his character and work ethic for Jay to take such extraordinary and generous actions. Joseph's wages were noted by Jay in his account book usually at the rate of five dollars per month, then ten dollars per month or one hundred dollars per year. Since Joseph was a skilled worker, Jay noted his full name and underlined his name in the journal he kept "To <u>Joseph Cusno</u> ...on account of Wages 5 Dolr."[90] As with Peter Blake and Joseph Cusno, Jay always wrote in the full name of all skilled workers in his account book and underlined it. Other workers were identified by their Christian name only.

Census records indicate that Joseph married a woman named Millicent and by 1818, they had a son named Edward and a

A Pleasant Situation

daughter, Sally. In that year Joseph tried to contact his family in Sicily where he was born. John Jay wrote a letter about Joseph's life for Peter Augustus to take to the American or British Consul on Sicily for his impending trip to Europe. Joseph wanted his family to know that he was alive and well. According to Joseph, his given name was Carmello. He was born in the Kingdom of the Two Sicilies in a town called Gergenti [now Argento] around 1796. Joseph was an only child and ran away from home because of his step-mother's mistreatment of him. He worked as a logger and then acted as a guide for a blind musician, finally arriving in the city of Syracuse where part of the American navy was stationed. This was around the time of the First Barbary War (1801-1805) when the United States was involved in a conflict with the nations on the northern coast of Africa, known as the Barbary Coast. Joseph did not explain how he came into the employ of Midshipman Ralph Izard, Jr. who was stationed on a U.S. gunboat. This association would dramatically alter the course of Joseph's life. Ralph Izard, Jr.'s father was a member of the Continental Congress and later a U.S. Senator. He was part of the American peace contingent living at Passy, France during Jay's employment in the Treaty of Paris negotiations. Sarah Jay spoke of socializing with Mrs. Izard at Passy.

It was during the First Barbary War that Midshipman Izard became a naval and national hero by volunteering to scuttle and burn the *USS Philadelphia*, an American warship, which had run aground in the harbor of Tripoli and was seized by the Tripolitans and her crew held for ransom. Rather than let the ship be re-fitted and used in combat against the American navy, Lt. Stephen Decatur led nineteen volunteers who entered the harbor of Tripoli by boat and in disguise for the purpose of scuttling the ship. Izard later wrote of the raid that the *Philadelphia* was boarded and fifteen minutes later she was engulfed in flames.[91] The raid was a total success and Izard and the others returned to Syracuse as national heroes, the first American military heroes since the American Revolution. When word of the attack reached British Admiral Horatio Nelson on board his flagship, *HMS Victory*, he called the raid, "...the most bold and daring act of the

A Pleasant Situation

age."[92]

Izard returned to America with Joseph in 1806. Izard had resigned his commission in 1810 when he established himself as the owner of a large Izard family plantation in South Carolina with three hundred slaves. Joseph worked in the Izard house where he learned the trade of a waiter. The Izard family had business interests in Pennsylvania where Ralph Izard was living with his family in 1813 when Joseph was hired by William Jay. Presumably, Joseph's skills as a waiter while in the Izard household and his association with that family no doubt held him in good stead with the Jay family and secured his employment with the Jays.

While working in the Jay household, Joseph, as well as other Jay servants, was treated with respect, kindness and attention to his needs. By 1825 it was legally possible for Joseph, still an alien, to own property, but he had to become a naturalized citizen within six years. Despite an injury to his hand, John Jay prepared the deed for Joseph to take title to the property he bought in 1815. William Jay and Maria Jay Banyer were witnesses to the signing of the deed, now in Joseph's name. In 1834 Joseph became an American citizen when he took the Oath of Citizenship in the Court of Common Pleas before Judge William Jay and Judge Benjamin Isaacs. The name on the document was "Joseph Cozzino" which may have been Joseph's real name.

When John Jay died in 1829, he left a small house to Joseph, even though Joseph never took title to the property or lived there. Joseph continued working as a waiter for William Jay. When William died in 1858, he left Joseph an annuity of "$100 dollars per annum" in recognition of Joseph's "faithful and honest" service to the Jays for more than forty years. William's Will also provided for Joseph's burial in the churchyard at St. Matthew's Church in William's family plot and that a grave stone be placed over Joseph's grave. Joseph continued working for John Jay II who was now the owner of the farm. When Joseph died on September 10, 1880 at the age of eighty-three, he was buried in the churchyard of St. Matthew's Church not far from William's family plot. He is buried alongside his wife, Millicent, who died in 1877.

A Pleasant Situation

As executor of William's Will, John Jay II had the following inscribed on Joseph's gravestone:

> Joseph Cozzino
> Born at Gergenti Sicily
> Died September 10, 1880
> Aged 83 Years
> This stone is erected by
> The Executors of
> Judge William Jay in
> pursuance of a provision
> in his Will to commemorate
> Joseph Cozzino's
> faithful service to the family
> of Chief Justice John Jay
> and his descendants
> at Bedford for more
> than 60 years[93]

The gravestone still stands and the dedication, though somewhat worn with age, is still legible. Joseph found the better life he had been seeking when he ran away from Sicily, and through the beneficence of the Jays, he was able to find that life in Bedford. He was highly regarded by the Jay family as evidenced by all that they did for him and the many kindnesses they extended to him. Peter Augustus Jay was unable to locate any of Joseph's family in Sicily and Joseph never saw or heard from any of his Sicilian relatives for the rest of his life. John Jay and his family did not hesitate to extend to Joseph every opportunity to make a better life for himself in Bedford, nor did Joseph refrain from accepting the generosity of the Jay family for helping him partake of the American experience. Although John Jay never expressed himself about Joseph, perhaps it gave Jay a great sense of satisfaction to help Joseph become an American citizen and enjoy the liberties which Jay had worked for many years before.

There were other workers on the farm who may not have considered life at Bedford "a pleasant situation" - the slaves owned by John Jay. Jay came from a slaveholding family as did other Founding Fathers. As the cause for independence from

A Pleasant Situation

Great Britain began to gain support, so did the abolitionist movement gain momentum in the colonies. Jay and other abolitionists were fighting for liberty and justice, which included a person's right to property such as slaves, while following the tradition of owning slaves. While this seemed to be hypocritical, Jay was resolute in his efforts for the abolition of slavery and he favored a gradual emancipation:

> In my opinion every man, of every colour and description, has a natural right to freedom, and I shall ever acknowledge myself to be an advocate for the manumission of slaves, in such a way as may be consistent with the justice due them, with the justice due to their masters, and with regard due the actual state of society. These considerations unite in convincing me that the abolition of slavery must necessarily be gradual.[94]

Jay realized that slavery had become an established practice and was an integral part of the economic system. Views of those supporting slavery would have to be changed and this Jay believed could not be accomplished without 'gradual' efforts.

In 1785, Jay corresponded with Dr. Richard Price, a British moral philosopher he met while in London. Price had sent Jay a copy of a pamphlet he wrote about the American Revolution. He reprimanded Jay and other Founders in his denunciation of the continuation of slavery in America "…it will appear that the people who have struggled so bravely against being enslaved themselves are ready enough to enslave others;"[95] Jay's response to Price's statements was measured and bespoke his support for "gradualism" in eliminating slavery in America "The cause of liberty, like most other good causes, will have its difficulties and sometimes its persecutions to struggle with. It has advanced more rapidly in this nation than in other countries, but all its objects are not yet attained."[96]. Jay argued that the "wise and the good" usually do not constitute a majority in any society. Yet he admitted to Price "That men should pray and fight for their own

A Pleasant Situation

freedom, and yet keep others in slavery, is certainly acting a very inconsistent as well as unjust, and perhaps impious part."[97] Jay then asserted that it would be wise, given the circumstances in America "to be patient" and "All that the best men can do is, to persevere in doing their duty to their country…"[98] Jay invoked God by leaving the consequences to Him and abolitionists, like himself should persevere "…being neither elated by success, however great, nor discouraged by disappointments however frequent and mortifying."[99] Jay's response to Price reveals his frustrations with ending slavery but he never doubted that with time and patience and changing attitudes, the goal of emancipation could be accomplished.

    Jay also stated these sentiments unequivocally in a letter to Dr. Benjamin Rush, who was a noted abolitionist, having founded the Pennsylvania Society for Promoting the Abolition of Slavery and a signer of the Declaration of Independence. Jay wrote to Rush in 1785 "I wish to see all unjust and all unnecessary discriminations everywhere abolished, and that the time may soon come when all our inhabitants of every colour and denomination shall be free and equal partakers of our political liberty."[100] Despite the embarrassing situation he found himself in with regard to desiring the abolition of slavery, Jay was in fact still a slave owner. Yet, his desire to end the practice of slavery manifested itself when in January of 1785, Jay, along with Alexander Hamilton and many Quakers, founded the New York Society for Promoting the Manumission of Slaves and Protecting Such of Them as Have Been or May Be Liberated. Jay was elected first president of the Society which would work for the manumission of slaves in New York; protect freedmen against kidnappers and ensure their rights in New York; and educate the 'Negro children of all classes'. In 1785, the Society worked for and gained passage of a law in New York prohibiting the sale of slaves imported into the state.

    Jay was Minister of Foreign Affairs under the Articles of Confederation from 1784 to 1789, which took up a great deal of his time. Yet, he always found time to work for the Manumission Society. Jay served on a committee to oversee the appropriation

A Pleasant Situation

of donations and chaired the Correspondence Committee which included welcoming foreign abolitionists to the Society, among whom was General Lafayette. In 1787, the Society founded the African Free School to provide education to children of slaves and freedmen. Jay felt strongly about this project "I consider education to be the soul of the republic,....."[101] Jay served as a trustee of the School which began with forty students in a one-room school and grew to seven schools with more than one thousand students in New York City. The African Free School and its facilities were ultimately integrated into the New York City public school system in 1835.

During his retirement, Jay resumed corresponding with William Wilberforce, a leading abolitionist and member of Parliament who worked tirelessly to end the slave trade in the British empire. The two had met while Jay was in London negotiating the Jay Treaty. For several years the two men wrote to each other concerning slavery and the international slave trade. Both believed that abolishing the slave trade would weaken the institution of slavery. In 1805 Wilberforce wrote to Jay and expressed, in the words of 'my favorite poet', his admiration for Jay having attained "domestic life in rural leisure passed."[102] Wilberforce hoped that the two countries would enact a convention to have warships of both nations seize slave ships and bring them to adjudication. Jay responded by agreeing with Wilberforce that the two nations should work in concert to end the slave trade "...and I believe that a convention for the purpose would be approved by all who think and feel as you and I do respecting that base and cruel traffic."[103] Jay went on to state the virtues of such action and his feelings of being unable to offer help, but with a determination to do whatever he could do "They who offer to do what is fit and right to be done, cannot be losers by it. I can do little - that little shall be done."[104] Jay also wisely advised Wilberforce to be patient and learn from past experiences, whether they be successful or not "To see things as they are, to estimate them aright, and to act accordingly, is to be wise. But you know, my dear sir, that most men, in order to become wise, have much to unlearn as well as to learn, much to undo as well as

A Pleasant Situation

to do."[105] Jay was no doubt referring to his gradual approach to abolition of slavery and the need to change the way people think. By 1810 Jay and Wilberforce were still bemoaning the fact that both countries were still engaged in the slave trade.

In 1817 the New York State Legislature passed a law that all slaves born before 1799 would be free on July 4, 1827. The passage of this law must have pleased Jay, to see New York State closer to emancipation. He no doubt took pride in the knowledge that his sons William and Peter Augustus were actively involved in working for the passage of the law by gaining public support. Peter Augustus, a former state representative, was active in Federalist party politics and organized rallies in support of passage of the bill.[106] William was also active in obtaining support for the bill through his tireless work with manumission and religious organizations.[107]

Jay's somewhat passive role in the fight to abolish slavery during his retirement years was interrupted when in 1819 he once again took a public stand for the abolition of slavery. The catalyst was the Missouri Compromise. The Missouri Compromise was an attempt to maintain the balance of power in Congress between free and slave states. When the bill became law in 1820, Maine was to enter the union as a free state and Missouri would enter as a slave state. It also abolished slavery in the Louisiana Territory north of the 36° 30' latitude line. Anti-slavery activists had sought to stop passage of the bill to prevent Missouri from entering the Union as a slave state.

In 1819 Jay received a circular letter from abolitionist, Elias Boudinot. Both men served together in the Continental Congress and Boudinot was now acting in his capacity as chair of the Trenton Committee on Slavery. Boudinot was not only seeking Jay's support for the campaign against the spread of slavery, but more importantly, Jay's signature on the circular letter. Jay's response was strong and unequivocal in his support for the gradual abolition of slavery. He argued, as the jurist he once was, about his belief that Congress had the power to prohibit the migration and importation of slaves "I concur in the opinion that it ought not to be introduced nor permitted in any of the new

A Pleasant Situation

States; and that it ought to be gradually diminished and finally abolished in all of them."[108] Jay then reasoned that Article One, Section 9 of the Constitution, which enumerates the powers given to Congress, *does* give Congress the power to limit the importation and migration of 'persons' after 1808:

> ...but that Congress were at liberty to make such prohibition as to any new State which might, in the mean time, be established, and further, that from and after that period, they were authorized to make such prohibition , as to all the States, whether new or old.[109]

While the word 'slaves' is not used in Article One, Jay argued that the word was '*intended*'. He believed that the word '*slaves*' was not used at the time of the drafting of the Constitution with good reason:

> The word slaves was avoided, probably on account of the existing toleration of slavery, and of its discordancy with the principles of the Revolution; and from a consciousness of its being repugnant to the following positions in the Declaration of Independence, *viz*.: 'We hold these truths to be self-evident: that all men are created by their Creator with certain unalienable rights; that among them are life, liberty and the pursuit of happiness.[110]

Jay declined any active role in 'organizing a plan of cooperation' due to the state of his health. However, Jay's background and his enduring credibility, as well as his position as former Chief Justice proved to be a strong inducement for the publication of his remarks. Elias Boudinot released Jay's response to the press and it was published. in many newspapers throughout the country. His letter received great acceptance in the North and was attacked in the South. Jay was even accused by Pres. James Monroe of trying to establish control of power in the eastern states

A Pleasant Situation

for inappropriate motives.[111] Jay's son, Peter, spoke forcefully at a meeting in New York City on the Missouri question of the detrimental terms of the Compromise.[112] The meeting, held at the City Hotel, was attended by two thousand people as well as prominent Federalists such as Timothy Dwight and Gen. Matthew Clarkson.[113]

Jay received another pamphlet from Daniel Raymond, a noted economist, that year regarding the "Missouri Question". The pamphlet outlined the detrimental effects slavery had on the welfare of the country. Jay responded strongly saying "The obvious dictates both of morality and policy teach us , that our free nation cannot encourage the extension of slavery, nor the multiplication of slaves, without doing violence to their principles, and without depressing their power and prosperity."[114] Jay urged Raymond to have the pamphlet circulated since the views contained in it "…will have a strong tendency to render public opinion on this very important subject correct and settled."[115] Jay never hesitated to express his revulsion of slavery on moral and legal grounds. During his retirement he tended to not actively participate in political causes, although he retained an active interest in them. The abolition movement proved to be too vital a cause for Jay to remain silent. Taking direct action, Jay did what he thought he could do despite his physical limitations.

Jay was brought up in a household where there were slaves. His family's treatment of their slaves no doubt made a lasting impression on him for he strove to treat his slaves fairly and to provide them with an opportunity for manumission. His father Peter owned slaves and in 1781 when John was in Europe, his brother, Frederick, wrote to Jay about their father's slaves. Owning slaves was costly due to maintenance and in an effort to reduce expenses at the Rye farm, Frederick hoped that John might be able to convince their father to sell some of the slaves particularly the older ones who could no longer work in the fields "A hint from you to Papa, might perhaps be of service.[116] Jay's father refused to sell any slaves without any explanation. However, in his Will, Peter Jay took a benevolent approach to his slaves. Unlike many slave owners of the time, Peter directed in

A Pleasant Situation

his Will that two slaves, Mary and Zilpha, were "...to have their choice of masters among my sons."[117] Peter Jay did this out of consideration for their long service to him. He also gave another slave, Plato, his choice of masters from among the Jay family. This was a very unusual practice for the time, since many slaves with families were given to different owners and families were broken up to the distress of the slaves.

Peter's daughter, Anna Marika Jay, treated her slaves with even greater respect when she directed in her Will, that her slave, Hannah, was to be freed on Anna Marika's death. If Hannah had any children, they too were to be freed and were to remain in the care of Hannah. Hannah was also given £10 per year in two payments. In a Codicil, Anna Marika also left Hanna "...one feather bed with a bolster and two pillows, four strong sheets, four pillow cases and four blankets and also ten pounds of new wearing apparel such as they [the executors] think most proper and purposeful."[118] Such kindness and generosity no doubt had an effect on John Jay. In 1798 when responding to the property assessors in Albany, Jay stated his handling of his slaves "I have three male and three female slaves.... I purchase slaves and manumit them at proper ages and when their faithful services shall have afforded a reasonable retribution."[119] Jay also taught his slaves a trade which may have accounted for Jay's use of the term "faithful services." This was Jay's pragmatic approach to gradual manumission of slaves and by 1820, the Federal census reported no slaves in Jay's household.[120] In this, Jay stood apart from other Founders who continued to own slaves. On the death of James Madison, the abolitionist William Lloyd Garrison wrote of Madison that on his death, Madison left one hundred slaves in bondage and bemoaned Madison's lack of enough integrity or charity to free any of his slaves on his death.[121] When Lafayette returned to America for a triumphal two-year tour from 1824-1825, he visited Thomas Jefferson and James Madison at their plantations and lectured the two former presidents and their guests about the exceptional rule of liberty for all.[122]

Jay strove to treat his slaves fairly and imparted this view to his children. A slave, named Phillis, was giving Jay's son,

A Pleasant Situation

Peter, difficulty. Jay wrote to his son advising him that emancipation for the woman was unwise in that it would set a bad example for the other slaves considering Phillis's unacceptable behavior and 'bad habits'. Jay then advised his son to sell Phillis for not more than two years with the guarantee of manumission at the end of the term. He thought that fifteen to twenty pounds would be a good price.[123] Here again, Jay linked manumission to a period of time served for the slave and he usually dealt with difficult slaves by selling them. The period of time for the services of the slave was usually the amount of time to work off the slave's purchase price. After manumission, it was not uncommon for Jay to offer the former slave a position in his household or on the farm.

Yet, with many slaves and former slaves, Jay exhibited generosity as was the case with Old Mary. Old Mary was probably the Mary who was mentioned in the Will of Jay's father when he gave a slave named Mary her choice of a new owner from among his sons. As she was in old age and a poor woman, Jay desired "...to have Old Mary comfortably provided for in every respect, at my expense."[124]

Of particular interest are two other slaves, Clarinda and Zilpha. Clarinda had been in the service of the Jay family for many years in New York City. She had married and given birth to several children. It was not uncommon for slaves to marry, with both spouses being from different households and seeing each other whenever the situation allowed. Clarinda's only surviving child was Zilpha, a/k/a Zelpha and Clarinda was anxious to have her daughter with her. By 1811 Zilpha was working for John Jay at Bedford. It was suggested that Zilpha work for the Jay family in New York City until she was twenty-five years old for three dollars per month.[125] At age twenty-five, she would be free. As Zilpha approached her twenty-fifth birthday in 1817, John Jay honored his pledge when he wrote to his son Peter Augustus "She will be of that age in May next...Zelpha will then be free, and we shall engage her in our service and at the same wages."[126] Zilpha remained in the employ of the Jay family at Bedford and took the surname of Montgomery. When she died on January 13, 1872, the

A Pleasant Situation

terms of William Jay's Will stipulated that she was to be buried in the Jay family plot at St. Matthew's church in Bedford. William's Will also provided for a grave stone to be erected and he acknowledged her as a faithful domestic servant for more than sixty years. Zilpha is buried alongside two other servants from the Jay household - Ann McFarland who was a nurse for John Jay II and another woman named Agnes who worked for William Jay and died in 1913.[127]

John Jay also remembered Zilpha's mother, Clarinda, in his Will "Clarinda had for a long course of years been in my service. She was born in my father's family. She is too far advanced in years to be long able to provide for herself. The proportion of my estate given to my son William, induces me to commit her to his care, to be by him comfortably maintained during her life."[128]

Jay's treatment of his slaves no doubt stemmed from his religious beliefs of civil and religious liberty. He was influenced by his family's kind treatment of slaves. Jay grew up during the Age of Enlightenment which may have influenced his concern for human rights and the ethics of slavery. Jay realized that the abolition of slavery would be a 'gradual' process. Slaves were regarded as property and slavery was part of the economic system. Throughout his life, he corresponded with leaders of the abolition movement including William Wilberforce, Elias Boudinot, Anthony Benezet and John Woolman. Benezet and Woolman were Quakers and were prominent in the Quaker movement to abolish slavery, believing slavery to be a sin. Jay's correspondence with these men had influenced Jay's views on slavery and its gradual abolition.

Jay lived in New York City almost forty years at a time when slavery was an established and accepted practice. Even with the Revolutionary War, the adoption of the Constitution, the efforts of the Manumission Society and the establishment of the African Free School, the need for slaves did not abate in the city. Between 1790 and 1800, the slave population of New York City increased by twenty-five percent to 2,500 slaves. The economy was booming and there was a particular need by the wealthy to

A Pleasant Situation

have female slaves for domestic work. By 1800 three-fourths of New York City's slaveholders had not owned slaves ten years before. Yet, by 1800, the number of slaves in the African American community had declined due to a sharp rise in the population of free blacks. Half of New York's African American community was comprised of free blacks. Many slaves were aided by free blacks and escaped from New York City to other states.[129] However, most free blacks found themselves unequal to the challenges of a wage-labor market and were employed in low-paying jobs, illiterate and without skills. Many free slaves were reduced to pauperism. Many continued in the same type of labor when they were slaves, earned a wage, and lived in the same sub-standard cellars or outbuildings of their employers.[130] With the introduction of the 'gradual' abolition of slavery in New York State, the number of manumissions had increased and by 1810, eighty-four per cent of New York City's African American population were free blacks.[131] Jay and his two sons who lived in New York City at one time or traveled there, were aware of these developments and the plight of many free blacks. This must have had an influence on these men to work to alleviate the plight of freed slaves, fight for their civil liberties and end slavery in America.

    Slavery existed in Bedford with the first United States census of 1790 reporting that thirty-eight slaves lived in Bedford.[132] However, attention was paid to slaves' ability to provide for themselves, when in 1795, there is a record of the freeing of a slave named, "Sarah", under the age of fifty and belonging to Caleb Sands. She is described as having "Sufficient ability to provide for herself."[133] In 1802 a Negro boy was purchased from Benjamin Hays of Bedford for $200.00. His new masters from Scarsdale agreed to give him his freedom in ten years.[134] The papers for both transactions for Sarah and the Negro boy were recorded in the County Bureau of Land Records, under Mortgages, since slaves were still considered property. When the 1817 New York law providing that every "Negro, mulatto or mustee" within the state born after July 4, 1799 shall be free, the number of manumissions became a "general practice" but with the

A Pleasant Situation

proviso that the owner was liable for the former slave's support unless the owner was relieved of this responsibility.[135]

During retirement, John Jay played a more passive role in the struggle for emancipation while his sons, William and Peter, persevered in their efforts. This legacy was also imparted to Jay's grandson, John Jay II, who distinguished himself in the abolition movement as well. Jay's approach to his slaves was unique and it did result in emancipation for many of his slaves. He also believed in treating all workers on his farm with dignity and respect, as when all members of the household staff assembled in the rear parlor for morning and evening prayers. Jay wanted justice to be done for all in the gradual abolition of slavery including the masters, society and the slaves. In 1824, the last slaves in Bedford were owned by a man named Samuel Pine. He had John Jay draw up the manumission papers which must have given Jay a good deal of satisfaction.[136] John Jay ultimately lived to see the end of slavery in his home, in the village of Bedford and in New York State.

A Pleasant Situation

[1] John Jay to Maria Jay Banyer, 1 February 1808, JJCU.

[2] Maria Jay Banyer to Ann Jay, 26 April 1824, McVickar, *A Christian Memorial to Two Sisters,* 21.

[3] John Jay to Richard Peters, 30 August 1808, JJCU.
"*Memento mori*" A Latin phrase for "Remember your mortality.".

[4] John Jay to Maria Jay Banyer, 22 February 1814, JJCU.

[5] John Jay to Peter Jay Munro, 31 March 1803, JJCU.

[6] John Jay to Maria Jay Banyer, 28 March 1814, JJCU.

[7] John Jay to Maria Jay Banyer, 2 February, 1813, JJCU.

[8] Susan L. Ridley to Maria Jay Banyer, 6 April 1808, JJH.

[9] Mary Clarkson Jay to Maria Jay Banyer, 6 June 1811, JJH.

[10] Mary Clarkson Jay to Peter Augustus Jay, 8 June, 1809, JJH.

[11] John Jay to Peter Augustus Jay, 20 June 1817, JJCU.

[12] Ibid.

[13] Ibid.

[14] John Jay to Maria Jay Banyer, 25 June 1817, JJCU.

[15] Jack Larkin. *The Reshaping of Everyday Life 1790-1840,* (New York, 1989), 88.

[16] Ibid, 88-90.

[17] George Warner Nichols. *Fragments from the study of a pastor,* (New York, 1860), 127.

[18] McVickar, *A Christian Memorial to Two Sisters,* 15.

[19] The Keeler Tavern Museum, Ridgefield, CT.

[20] Charles H. Weyant. *The Sacketts of America: Their Ancestors and Descendants 1630-1907,* (Newburgh, NY, 1907), 190.

[21] J.Thomas Scharf. *History of Westchester County I-II*, (Camden, ME, 1992) I: 574.

[22] John Jay to Peter Augustus Jay, 22 May, 1820, JJH.

[23] Dr. Henry Van Kliek to Dr. John Watts, 27 April 1822, Watts Special Miscellaneous Collection, Butler Library, Rare Book and Manuscript Collection, Columbia University, New York, NY.

[24] Maria Jay Banyer to Dr. John Watts, 20 April 1822, Watts Special Miscellaneous Collection, Columbia University.

[25] John Jay to Peter Augustus Jay, 27 January 1808, JJCU.

[26] John Jay to Maria Jay Banyer, 27 August 1811, JJCU.

[27] Peter Augustus Jay to Mary Clarkson Jay, 8 September, 1815, JJH

[28] John Jay to Jedediah Morse, 1 January 1813, JJCU.

[29] Rufus King to John Jay, 20 June, 1814, JJCU.

A Pleasant Situation

[30] John Jay to Rufus King, 23 June 1814, JJCU.

[31] John Jay to Gouverneur Morris, 22 February 1813, JJCU.

[32] Ibid.

[33] Maria Jay Banyer to John Jay, 17 April 1810, JJH; also available at JJCU.

[34] John Jay to Peter Augustus Jay, 2 August 1814, JJH.

[35] John Jay to Peter Jay Munro, 17-18 March 1812, JJCU.

[36] John Jay to Peter Augustus Jay, 18 March 1812, JJCU.

[37] John Jay to Peter Augustus Jay, 24 March 1812, JJCU.

[38] John Jay to William Jay, 13 April 1812, JJCU.

[39] John Jay to Maria Jay Banyer, 15 April 1812, JJCU.

[40] Ibid.

[41] John Jay to Maria Jay Banyer, 12 May 1812, JJCU.

[42] John Jay to Peter Peter Augustus Jay, 11 February, 1812, JJCU.

[43] Peter Augustus Jay to John Jay, 13 January 1809, JJCU.

[44] JJFM 429.

[45] John Jay to Rev. John Henry Hobart, 21 January 1803, JJCU.

[46] Jay. *Memorials of Peter A. Jay Compiled for his Descendants by his Great Grandson,* 35.

[47] JJWJ I:243.

[48] Barbara S. Massi. *The Story of Mary Guion Brown from her Diary of 1800-1852,* (North Castle, NY, 2000), Footnote, 15.

[49] Ibid, 94.

[50] John Jay to Peter Augustus Jay, 22 June 1807, JJH; also available at JJCU.

[51] John Jay to Peter Augustus Jay, 12 September 1807, JJH; also available at JJCU.

[52] John Jay to Bishop Benjamin Moore, 8 February 1810 and John Jay to the Vestry of the Episcopal Church of Bedford 14 February, 1810, JJCU.

[53] Thatcher T.P. Luquer. *An Historical Sketch of St. Matthew's Church, Bedford, NY 1634-1938,* (Bedford, NY 1938), 11.

[54] John Jay to Bishop Benjamin Moore, 8 February 1810 and John Jay to the Vestry of the Episcopal Church of Bedford 14 February, 1810, JJCU.

[55] Ibid.

[56] Ibid.

[57] Ibid.

[58] Members of the Parish Family. *A Sesquicentennial History of St. Matthew's Protestant Episcopal Church, Bedford, NY,* (Bedford, NY 1960), 28.

A Pleasant Situation

[59] John Jay to Peter Augustus Jay, 22 March 1813, JJCU.

[60] John Jay to Maria Jay Banyer, 30 March 1813, JJCU.

[61] John Jay to Bishop Benjamin Moore, 22 April 1804, JJCU.

[62] Nichols, *Fragments from the Study of a Pastor,* 126-27.

[63] John Jay to Eleazor Lord, 22 April 1816, JJCU.

[64] John Jay to Bishop Thomas Church Brownell, 4 September 1820, JJCU.

[65] *Address to the People of Great Britain,* HPJ I: 28.

[66] John Jay to Sarah Louisa Jay, 8 February 1807, JJCU.

[67] Shonnard and Spooner. *The History of Westchester County New York From Its Earliest Settlement to the Year 1900,* 538.

[68] Allen Keller. *Life Along the Hudson,* (Tarrytown, NY 1985), 103, 108; Tom Lewis. *The Hudson A History,* (New Haven CT and London 2005), 161.

[69] James Thomas Flexner. *Steamboats Come True American Inventors in Action,* (Boston and Toronto 1944), 328.

[70] Ibid.

[71] John Jay to Peter Augustus Jay, 2 September 1807, JJCU.

[72] John Jay to Peter Augustus, 2 September, 1817, JJCU.

[73] John Jay to Timothy Pickering, 24 December 1808, JJCU.

[74] John Jay to James Duane, 3 March 1821, JJH.

[75] .John Jay to Thomas Stoutenburgh, 12 November 1804, JJCU.

[76] John Jay to Richard Bland Lee, 7 September 1812, JJCU.

[77] John Jay to Peter Augustus Jay, 25 November 1823, JJCU.

[78] John Jay to Peter Augustus Jay, 12 June 1823, JJCU.

[79] John Jay to Sarah Livingston Jay, 17 May 1801, JJCU.

[80] John Jay to Peter Augustus Jay, 3 April 1820, JJCU.

[81] John Jay to Maria Jay Banyer, 4 May 1812, JJCU.

[82] Alva P. French, ed.. *History of Westchester County, New York I-V,* (New York and Chicago 1925) IV: 656.

[83] John Jay to Peter Augustus Jay, 7 December 1824, JJCU.

[84] John Jay to Maria Jay Banyer, 3 July 1808, JJCU.

[85] John Jay to Peter Augustus Jay, 23 January 1810, JJCU.

[86] John Jay to Maria Jay Banyer, 19 December 1805, JJCU.

[87] John Jay to Sarah Louisa Jay, 19 May 1807, JJCU.

[88] William Jay to John Jay, 29 January 1813, JJCU.

[89] John Jay to Peter Augustus Jay, 16 November 1818, JJCU.

A Pleasant Situation

[90] John Jay's Account Book 1813-1829, JJH.

[91] Robert W. Love. *History of the US Navy 1775-1941* (Harrisburg, PA 1992), 80

[92] Brier. *Joseph Cusno: the Sicilian Immigrant and the Jays of Bedford*.87: 2, 8.

[93] Ibid, 51.

[94] JJWJ I:161-62.

[95] Dr. Richard Price to John Jay 9 July, 1785, HPJ III: 159.

[96] Ibid, 168.

[97] Ibid.

[98] Ibid, 168-69.

[99] Ibid, 169.

[100] John Jay to Benjamin Rush, 24 March 1785, JJCU.

[101] John Jay to Dr. Benjamin Rush, 24 March 1785, JJCU.

[102] William Wilberforce to John Jay, 1 August 1809, HPJ IV: 319.

[103] Ibid, 324.

[104] Ibid.

[105] Ibid, 325.

[106] Jay. *Memorials of Peter A. Jay,* 94.

[107] Stephen P. Budney. *William Jay Abolitionist and Anticolonialist,* (Westport CT and London 2005), 25.

[108] John Jay to Elias Boudinot, 17 November 1819, HPJ IV 430-31: JJCU.

[109] Ibid.

[110] Ibid.

[111] Ibid.

[112] Moore. *The Missouri Controversy, 1819-1821,* 79.

[113] Ibid, 78.

[114] John Jay to Daniel Raymond, 25 November, 1820, JJWJ II: 224.

[115] Ibid.

[116] Frederick Jay to John Jay, 10 April 1781 JJCU.

[117] Last Will and Testament of Peter Jay, proved 28 May 1782, JJH.

[118] Last Will and Testament of Anna Marika Jay dated 4 February 1790; Codicil dated 1 March 1791, JJH.

[119] JJGP, 293-94.

[120] United States Census Reports: Populations Schedules of the Fourth Census of the United States, 1820, No.33, Roll 75, Vol. 14, Washington D.C.; National Archives, 1958, 410.

¹²¹ Elizabeth Dowling Taylor. *A Slave in the White House: Paul Jennings and the Madisons (*New York 2012), 139.

¹²² Ibid.

¹²³ John Jay to Peter Augustus Jay, 26 January 1799, JJH; also available at JJCU.

¹²⁴ John Jay to Peter Augustus Jay, 4 November 1824, JJH; also available at JJCU.

¹²⁵ John Jay to Peter Augustus Jay, 8 May 1811, JJCU.

¹²⁶ John Jay to Peter Augustus Jay, 12 March 1817, JJCU.

¹²⁷ Brier. *Joseph Cusno: The Sicilian Immigrant and the Jays of Bedford.:* 50.

¹²⁸ Last Will and Testament of William Jay, dated May 15, 1858, JJH.

¹²⁹ Edwin G. Burrows and Mike Wallace. *Gotham A History of New York City to 1898* (New York and Oxford 1999), 347.

¹³⁰ Ibid 349-50.

¹³¹ Ibid 349.

¹³² Duncombe et al. *Katonah.* 76; Bedford (New York) Town Book IV, 1784-1841 (unpaged). MS (At Bedford Town House).

¹³³ Westchester County. Division of Land Records. Mortgages. Liber G, pp 120. MS. (At the County Office Building, White Plains, N.Y.)

[134] Duncombe et al. *Katonah.* 76; Westchester County. Division of Land Records. Mortgages. Liber G, pp 213. MS. (At the County Office Building, White Plains, N.Y.)

[135] Duncombe et al. *Katonah.* 94.

[136] Wood. *The History of the Town of Bedford to 1917,* 622.

Just and Necessary Wars

CHAPTER 4

John Jay was essentially a peacemaker. In the *Address to the People of Great Britain* and *The Olive Branch Petition,* Jay sought reconciliation with Great Britain in trying to avert war. As events proved reconciliation impossible, Jay came down on the side of American independence as the only course possible. He was a delegate from New York to the Continental Congress in 1776 and when the Declaration of Independence was signed, Jay was in New York at the New York Provincial Congress exerting his considerable influence in the formation of a new state government. When news arrived about the Declaration of Independence, Jay drafted the *Resolutions of New York Convention Approving Declaration of Independence,* which was unanimously approved by the New York Congress. *The Resolutions,* in Jay's own handwriting, also called for the publication and reading of the Declaration of Independence throughout the State, along with the Resolutions unanimously adopted by the New York Convention in White Plains on July 9, 1776.

Jay was now committed to the cause of American independence and the war that ensued. In the Treaty of Paris and later with the Jay Treaty, he strove to attain a lasting peace with Great Britain. Jay used his powers of reasoning and his debating skills in a lawyerly manner to argue his points and obtain results. In the cases of the Treaty of Paris and the Jay Treaty, he achieved political results that were not only as favorable to America as could be negotiated, but also contributed to a lasting Anglo-American alliance.

In a moral approach to peace, Jay also believed that through the Gospel, mankind could attain universal peace. He had very strong views on waging war. During his retirement, Jay exchanged several letters with John Murray, Jr. which shed light on Jay's moral view of war. Their correspondence on the subject of just and necessary wars spanned three years, 1816-1819, and reveals much about Jay's religious and ethical views on the subject. They shared similar interests and both men were among the founding members of the New York Manumission Society and were actively involved in the African Free School. Murray was a Quaker and a member of the New York Monthly Meeting. His brother, Lindley, and John Jay were law clerks in Benjamin Kissam's firm. Not much is known about John Murray, Jr. except that he came from a prosperous Quaker family of merchants in New York City. The Murray home, Inclenberg, was one of the most elegant estates in the city during the late eighteenth century, located at what is now Park Avenue and 36th Street in the Murray Hill section of Manhattan.[1] It was at the Murray wharf at the corner of Pearl and Beekman Streets that George Washington debarked the day of his inauguration as President of the United States.[2]

In September of 1816, Murray wrote to John Jay about Jay's retirement availing him of the opportunity to "prepare his spirit for eternity" and for "…the all important work of promoting the spiritual good, and the temporal welfare of men. - "[3] Murray, a pacifist, quickly pursued his belief "…wars and fightings are inconsistent with the doctrines of the Gospel,…."[4] Murray reflected on John Jay's early participation in the movement to abolish the slave trade and the institution of slavery and hoped that Jay would be equally committed to "the cause of universal Peace" believing that to work for peace is righteous and results in, "joy and assurance for ever". Murray's beliefs are clearly based on moral and ethical considerations. Utilizing his considerable debating skills and powers of reasoning, Jay's reply the following month is interesting and reveals much about Jay's strong religious views, his literal interpretation of the Bible and his reasoning of the subject "Whether war of *every* description is prohibited by the gospel, is one of those questions on which the excitement of any of the passions can produce no light. An answer to it can result only from careful investigation and fair reasoning."[5]

Jay was at the beginning of a lengthy pursuit over the next two and a half years, in drafting a response to Murray's letter and proving to Murray that the moral law is not only inherent in the gospel but that the gospel promotes mankind to observe the moral law which is "exactly the same now as it was before the flood."[6] Jay then stated "If *every* war is sinful, how did it happen that the *sin* of waging *any* war is not specified among the numerous sins and offences which are mentioned and reproved in both the Testaments?"[7] Furthering his argument, Jay reasoned that while war and peace are in the hands of rulers in many nations where rulers are unelected, in America,

Just and Necessary Wars

Providence has given the people a choice to elect their rulers and that people should strive to elect Christians.

Murray responded to Jay's assertions by challenging Jay's statement that the moral law is immutable. Murray was of the opposite opinion that the New Testament offered to enlighten people and bring them to the "<u>divine principle,</u> of peace "...- hence I infer that no man can arrive to the perfection of the Christian system, while he is in the spirit of War, and under the dominions of those Lusts from whence it hath its origin."[8] It was Murray's contention that the Old Testament prophets believed that a Messiah would come and usher in an age of peace. Murray then stated " - ...I think I am not insensible to the weight of character of the man I am addressing, and for whom I entertain a sincere friendship - to whom I feel a proper and due deference,..."[9] but Murray was resolute in his beliefs and said that he made no apologies to Jay for them.

True to Jay's cautious and guarded nature, he expounded on his ideas as to whether "War of every kind was forbidden by the Gospel" in a twelve page letter to Murray dated April 15, 1818. Jay asserted "The Moral or Natural Law was given by the Sovereign of the Universe to all mankind." He believed that this law was immutable "Being founded on infinite Wisdom and Goodness or eternal Right, which never varies, it can require no amendment nor alteration."[10] He then expounded on the distinction of "Divine positive ordinances and institutions" which being founded on 'expediency', are not absolute and therefore subject to change "There were several Divine *positive* ordinances and Institutions at very early Periods - Some of them were of limited obligation; such as circumcision, - others of them were of universal obligation - as the Sabbath - Marriage, Sacrifices - the particular Punishment for Murder - "[11] Jay reasoned that Christ had come not to destroy the Old Testament laws and prophets, but to fulfill them "The law is *holy*, and the commandments *holy, just,* and *good.*"[12] Jay then discussed revenge in the Scriptures and Mosaic Laws believing that Solomon understood the Law by advocating loving and forgiving your Enemy and Christ "...removed all doubts on this point". Jay reasoned:

> As, therefore, Divine ordinances did
> authorize just war, as those ordinances

were necessarily consistent with the moral law, and as the moral law incorporated in the Christian dispensation, I think it follows that the right to wage *just* and *necessary* war is admitted, and not abolished by the gospel.[13]

To further prove his point and to convince Murray that war is sanctioned in the Bible he quoted what Christ said at the conclusion of the Last Supper when he said to his disciples "He that hath no sword, let him now sell his garment and buy one." They answered: 'Lord, here are two swords.' He replied: 'It is enough.'"[14]

Jay then turned to the justification for war in that Christians are bound to dutifully 'sustain and fulfill' their *spiritual* and *worldly* obligations. He spoke of Christians fighting with spiritual weapons against all enemies and also fighting in a 'temporal' world "...they are in that capacity bound, whenever lawfully required, to fight with weapons in just and necessary war, against the *worldly* enemies of that state or kingdom."[15] He then expounded on 'another view' of the subject by stating that every nation had the right to protect itself against domestic and foreign aggressions "Thus two kinds of justifiable warfare arose: one against domestic malefactors; the other against foreign aggressors. The first being regulated by the law of nations; and both consistently with the moral law.[16] Jay considered the '*first* species' to be universally 'just and indispensable' and "it commands us to obey the higher powers or ruler." As to the '*second species*' Jay considered it the right of every nation to defend itself from outside aggression. As much as Jay desired the abolition of war, he wrote to Murray "...yet until the morals and manners of mankind are greatly changed, it will be found impractible."[17] In writing to Murray optimistically Jay stated "I nevertheless believe, and have perfect faith in the prophecy, that the time will come when 'the nations will beat their swords into ploughshares, and their spears into pruning-hooks."[18] Jay stated that '*meanwhile* and *until*' such peace is attained, he believed that there would be wars "...I think mankind must be prepared and fitted for the reception, enjoyment, and preservation of universal permanent peace, before they will be blessed with it."[19] He questioned the wisdom of disarming peaceful nations while aggressors are still in a position to wage war:

> By what other means than arms and military force can unoffending rulers and nations protect their rights against unprovoked aggressions from within and without? Are there any other means to which they could recur, and on the efficacy of which they could rely? To this question I have not as yet heard, nor seen, a direct and precise answer[20]

This was the end of the Jay/Murray correspondence. In 1819 Murray slipped on the ice and became lame and died. He is buried in the cemetery of the Flushing Monthly Meeting in Flushing, New York. Yet the correspondence is illuminating with regard to Jay's distinction between 'domestic' and 'foreign' wars when considering Jay's own efforts as a public official in the *Address to the People of Great Britain* and the *Olive Branch Petition* to avert war with England. Reluctantly, Jay had become an ardent supporter of American independence and even held the rank of colonel in the Second Regiment of the New York City militia during the war.[21] He played an important role in the negotiations of the Treaty of Paris, a treaty that he hoped would establish a lasting peace between the two nations. Later, in the Jay Treaty, he was faced with the reality that militarily, American was in no position to wage war with England. Fearful that such a war might cost America its independence, he negotiated a treaty rejected and damned by many Americans because Jay had not obtained certain hoped-for economic concessions from England. The Jay Treaty secured peace with England, and forestalled the outbreak of another war until such time as America was in a position to defend itself. Reflecting upon this in his retirement, it is not difficult to understand why Jay thought that war was sometimes *just and necessary,* until such time as universal peace became a reality.

Jay's first reactions to the French Revolution were initially positive but changed dramatically as the revolution evolved. In 1796 Jay reflected on the effect of "…the long Reign of such a monarch as

Just and Necessary Wars

Louis the fifteenth, have to debase and corrupt their Subjects,...."[22] He clearly believed at the outset of the Revolution, that the people of France were justified in rebelling against a 'domestic malefactor.' Jay's views continued to be altered by the downward course of the revolution and the curtailment of liberties by the National Assembly "In the Revolution which just put a Period to it, I did cordially rejoice, I meant the one which limited the Power of the King & restored Liberty to the People."[23] Reflecting on the next phase of the revolution under the National Convention with the execution of Louis XVI and the Reign of Terror, Jay commented:

> They abolished the Constitution and Government which had been just established, and brought the King to the Scaffold. This Revolution did not give me Pleasure. I derived no Satisfaction from the disastrous Fate of a Prince who (from whatever motives) had done us essential Services, and to whom we had frequently presented the strongest assurances of our attachment and Affection. This Revolution had in my Eye more the appearance of a War than of a Blessing- It has caused Torrents of Blood and Tears, and been marked in its Progress by atrocities very injurious to the Cause of Liberty, and offensive to Morality and Humanity.[24]

With the rise of Napoleon, Jay had lost all faith in the French Republic "There must be in the Republic an unprecedented & unparalleled want of virtue.[25]

By 1803, Jay had definitely turned against the revolution when he wrote to his good friend, Rufus King "Viewing the French Revolution as a Tragedy, I am inclined to think that we have only seen the <u>first</u> act concluded."[26] "Tragedy" was the word Jay used most often in his correspondence when describing the French Revolution. In an almost prescient state, he predicted the outbreak of the Napoleonic Wars when, in the same letter to King, he stated "It would not surprise me if future Eruptions from that Volcano should again desolate some of the neighboring countries."[27] Three years later his perspective on the French Revolution bore out his concerns when Jay wrote to Wilberforce about the signing of the Treaty of Amiens, which ended hostilities between France and England "We have seen concluded, with the Treaty of Amiens, the <u>first</u> act of the astonishing Tragedy which the French Revolution has introduced on the Theatre of the World."[28] It was his opinion that in this 'prodigious Drama', Great Britain had an important role yet to play. By 1810 Jay's views of the Revolution and Napoleon, whom he referred to in one of his letters as a "demagogue", and "the Nebuchadnezzar of the day"[29] left no doubt as to his decidedly negative opinions on the subject "There came forth with the French Revolution a Spirit of Delusion which like an Influenza passed over and infested all Europe."[30] He also expressed his fear of America becoming 'involved in war unnecessarily'.

Jay had initially viewed the French Revolution favorably as people rising up against 'domestic malefactors' and considered it 'just and necessary.' Many Americans rejoiced at the news of the revolution celebrating with cannon salutes. *La Marseilles* was sung in theaters, Liberty Poles were erected throughout America and people adorned their hats with tri-colored cockades People were openly addressed as Citizen or Citizeness. In Philadelphia the execution of Louis XVI was exhibited in the waxworks before cheering crowds. John Adams characterized America's reactions as 'sound and fury' and Jefferson likened it to 'music.'[31]

Jay was never a monarchist and was always true to his Huguenot heritage, but he recognized the help that Louis XVI had given America during its own revolution and pitied the fate of the French monarch. However, with the corruptioin of the lofty goals of 'Liberty, Equality, Fraternity', Jay later rejoiced at the fall of Napoleon calling it a 'joyful event.' He reached the conclusion "The French Revolution has so discredited democracy, and it has so few influential advocates in Europe,…. Without a portion of it there can be no free government."[32] He was no doubt reflecting on the reactionary movement of the victorious powers of England, Russia, Austria, Prussia and the many German princes, who, at the Congress of Vienna, agreed to maintain the status quo and restore the balance of power in Europe which Napoleon had disrupted with his imperialism. In the end, the Bourbons were returned to the throne of France. Jay reflected at one point during the Reign of Terror about the legacy England bequeathed to America and its effect on the course of American independence "It certainly is chiefly owing to Institutions Laws and Principles of Policy & Government originally derived to us as british colonials, that with the Favor of Heaven the People of this Country are what they are."[33]

While Jay had initially viewed the French Revolution as justifiable he later altered his opinion after the lofty goals of the revolution had been corrupted by the Reign of Terror and Napoleon.

With regard to his own country, Jay was strongly opposed to the War of 1812. Prior to the outbreak of the war, the United States was concerned with England's violation of America's neutrality. In 1807, England and France were at war and England impressed thousands of American seamen into service on British warships and confiscated American merchant ships. The British rationalized that these actions were war related and necessary for England's survival. The British also issued a series of Orders in Council to restrict America's trade with France.

By 1807, the American merchant marine was the world's largest neutral fleet and Britain was its largest trading partner. Jefferson tried restraint but with England's increasing violation of American neutrality there was growing public support for some form of action against England. Upon the recommendation of Jefferson, Congress enacted the Embargo Act on December 22, 1807. The goal of the embargo on American trade with France and England was to end the belligerent actions of those nations against America by prohibiting all American ships to sail to or from a foreign port. Instead, it had the opposite effect by inflicting economic hardships on the American economy and people. In February of 1808, a few months after the Embargo was enacted, Peter Augustus Jay wrote to John Jay about the effects of the Embargo in New York City:

> The Embargo presses very heavily on
> the class of people who were
> accustomed to maintain themselves by

Just and Necessary Wars

daily labour along the wharves, & to consume their Wages as soon as they receive them. I was informed today that the persons maintained in the Almshouse, & those who receive daily rations from it, amounted altogether to more than <u>five thousand</u>.[34]

Peter then described the devastating effects of the Embargo on the "Irish Laborers" over a thousand of whom left New York City searching for work "…over the Country and in all Directions - "[35]

As a result of the Embargo, England began trading with South America to offset the loss of trade with America. England had normally purchased 80% of America's cotton and half of other American exports. Loopholes in the law and outright evasion by Americans weakened the effect of the embargo. Foreign trade continued among American merchant ships with much trade and smuggling being done across the Canadian border. American ships rotted on the wharves and farmers, particularly from the South, could not sell their crops on the international market. Protests broke out in America against the embargo. Federal officials were viewed as exercising regional favoritism in administering the embargo. Foreign nations viewed the United States as inept and unable to enforce its own laws. This resulted in huge gains at the polls for the Federalists in Congress. John Jay's correspondence at this time reflects his strong support of the Federalists and the results of the elections for them. During his retirement, Jay had maintained an active interest in politics but eschewed any participation "The Properties attached to a situation like mine, assign certain limits to achieve Interferences in political concerns - …"[36]

Timothy Pickering, a leading Federalist, Senator and friend of John Jay wrote to Jay in December of 1808 about the growing debate in Congress over the Embargo and the lack of debate over Jefferson's reasons for it. He noted that most of Jefferson's support was along party lines.[37] In January of 1809, Pickering again wrote to Jay about the controversy in Congress over the Embargo and expressed his wish that Jefferson would be exposed as "an imposter of no ordinary size."[38] American's faith in the Jefferson administration was

Just and Necessary Wars

undermined and before he left office in March of 1809, Jefferson signed the repeal of the Embargo Act. Congress passed the Non-Intercourse Act in April which gave Pres. James Madison the power to resume trade with England or France should either of those nations remove its trade restrictions against America. The new law proved to be just as ineffectual as the Embargo. However, the Embargo did have a positive effect on manufacturing which resulted in increased textile production in New England, lessening America's reliance on England for such goods.

While Jay maintained a respectful distance from active participation in politics and refrained from any direct statement about the Embargo Act, he was nonetheless, a loyal Federalist. The events of the next few years would alter Jay's stance and his respectful discretion for any form of 'Interferences in political concerns'.

During Pres. Madison's first term of office, British trade restrictions against American ships trading with France continued as well as British impressment of American sailors and merchantmen into the Royal Navy. This and another issue troubling Americans was the British obstruction of American expansion into the Northwest Territory of what now comprises the states of Ohio, Indiana, Illinois, Michigan and Wisconsin. The British supported raids by Native Americans, particularly under the leadership of the Native American, Tecumseh, against American settlers in the area in the hope of creating a neutral, Native American state. The perception that America should uphold its national honor in the face of continuing British violations of American neutrality resulted in a declaration of war against Britain on June 18, 1812. Madison had sent a message to Congress outlining America's grievances against Britain, without calling for a declaration of war. The vote for declaring war was very close with the measure passing the Senate by a vote of 19 to 13 and in the House of Representatives by a vote of 79 to 49. Not one of the thirty-nine Federalists in Congress voted for a declaration of war. The declaration of war and the perception that Britain continued to violate America's neutrality became the central issue in the coming general election. Madison would be opposed by New York City Mayor and a fellow Democratic-Republican, DeWitt Clinton, who was opposed to the war.

Just and Necessary Wars

Jay's reaction to the Declaration of War was swift, decisive and prescient when he wrote in June to his son Peter "The Stillness which followed the Declaration of War, does not surprise me - how long it will last, or what will be its Results, Time only can discover."[39] Jay's concern was not only for the nation but for his family and his own comforts, when he wrote in the same letter "The war makes it prudent to purchase more articles for Family use, than may be convenient or immediately necessary - I shall want a Cask of Lisbon wine - it will not be cheaper - if to be had, get the best - when Nancy arrives I shall be informed of such other articles as should be obtained without Delay."[40]

Jay realized that Clinton's supporters, who were themselves Democratic-Republicans from the same party as Madison and represented a small minority favoring peace, would want to unite with the Federalists in opposition to the war. Jay spoke of the need for a joint meeting and the adoption of joint resolutions and offered his 'Sketch' to Peter Augustus to be presented for discussion and adoption at a planned meeting:

> We the Freeholders and the Free Citizens of the City of New York, who are now Convened to express our Sentiments respecting the War recently declared for the People of the U.S. against G. Britain together with such of the Reasons for the same as have been published by the Govt, think it proper to come to the following Resolutions
>
> Resolved that as the said War hath been constitutionally declared, it is the constitutional Duty of the People, faithfully to do their part in carrying it on vigorously, until a satisfactory peace shall be obtained -
>
> Resolved that notwithstanding the Reason alleged for it, the said

Just and Necessary Wars

> Declaration of War is in our opinion, unnecessary and unwise; and will produce more injury than advantage to our Nation -
>
> Resolved, that we have no Confidence in the Fitness of James Maddison for the very important Station to which he has been elevated - and that the People can in no other Way recover and secure their natural Prosperity, than by committing the managemt of their affairs to Men whose attributes and Principles afford ample Ground for Trust and Reliance
>
> Resolved that we for our parts will unite in promoting the Election of Men of that Description; and by that and other constitutional and lawful Means will do our best Endeavours to rescue our Country from the Dangers and Distresses to which she has become exposed by this unseasonable and ill advised War and by the neglect of competent Supplies and Preparations for it - [41]

Jay's comments reflect his thoughts on 'just and necessary war' to John Murray, Jr., in which Jay wrote that every nation had the right to defend itself from foreign aggressions but Jay saw no justification for this war on those grounds. Jay referred to the war as 'unjustified' and he severely criticized Madison's conduct. Without stating it, Jay obviously thought that negotiations and not war would lead to a peaceful resolution. However, he did recognize the war was 'constitutionally declared' and on that basis, he urged Americans to strive to bring the war to a peaceful conclusion and elect people to office who would work to 'rescue' America from this 'ill advised

Just and Necessary Wars

War' and the lack of preparations for it, thereby upholding the rule of law. Yet, he was still of the opinion that he did not want to become actively involved in the general election or 'public affairs' "...I have no Desire to meddle with public affairs, further than as a private citizen to promote public good; and without being unnecessarily implicated in this or that Measure -...."[42] He advised his son Peter to consult with his brother William 'without Reserve' since Jay had confided his thoughts to William. The 'Stillness' that Jay spoke of after the Declaration of War was shattered that summer when riots broke out in Baltimore, and Jay's friend, General Richard Henry Lee, the American Revolution hero known to the public as Lighthorse Harry Lee, died of wounds received in the riot while trying to defend the editor of the Baltimore newspaper, *The Federal Republican.* Jay was outraged at the treatment and lack of respect for Lee and wrote Lee's "...claims to public Gratitude have so long and so justly been acknowledged throughout the United States."[43]

At the time of the Baltimore riots, Jay began to relinquish his veil of discretion when he wrote to Peter Van Schaack "No event that is highly interesting to our Country, can be viewed with Indifference by good citizens; and there are certain occasions when it is not only their Right, but also their Duty to express their Sentiments relative to public Measures."[44] Jay then wrote of how opposition to the war should be carried out since:

> As the War has been <u>constitutionally</u> declared, the People are evidently bound to support it , in the manner which constitutional Laws do or shall prescribe. In my opinion the Declaration of War was neither necessary, nor expedient, nor seasonable - and I think that they who entertain this opinion, do well in expressing it, both individually and collectively, on this very singular and important occasion - [45]

Here again, Jay is stressing the 'constitutionality' of the war and the rule of law but he has taken a further step in his call to action.

Just and Necessary Wars

Jay noted that 'irascible Passions' should be countered with a change "A change of Measures would result from a change of Rulers; and public opinion is the proper means of effecting it."[46] He ended his letter with his usual circumspection "I do not hesitate to express these Sentiments on proper occasions - but it would not be pleasant to be quoted in newspapers, or hand Bills. or public Speeches."[47]

Jay was clearly becoming more outspoken with his trusted friends about the war but was not yet ready to commit himself to action. When Jay was a public official, he had not hesitated in his actions to avoid war with Great Britain and to effect a peaceful reconciliation. He advocated a break with Great Britain only when no other recourse was available. Now retired, he was faced with the dilemma of accepting the war being 'constitutionally' declared. He opposed the war at the polls and advocated voting the current government out of power. To that end, Jay, Rufus King and other Federalists attended a meeting at Morrisania, the home of Jay's friend, Gouverneur Morris, in what is now part of the Bronx. De Witt Clinton was also there and solicited the support of the Federalists in the coming election and in the formation of a peace party. Jay had believed shortly after the Declaration of War that the Clintonians might join with the Federalists in working for peace. Yet after this meeting, Jay and King were uncertain of their support of Clinton and the small group of anti-war Democratic-Republicans who backed Clinton, while Morris actively worked for Clinton's election.

Jay would prove to be in the minority when the Federalists held a three-day national convention at Kent's Tavern on Broad Street in Manhattan and through the efforts of Morris, endorsed Clinton for president.[48] Jay did not support Clinton and he declined to be a delegate to the convention in New York on the grounds of his poor health "Since my return from Morrisania I have lost ground...."[49] He wrote to Gouveneur Morris "The last is the only Week, since I set out from Morrisania, in which I have not had Effusions of Bile, a pain in the side and a slight fever."[50] Jay discussed with Morris his hopes and some of his advice for the convention with the hope that either Morris or Rufus King should preside over the convention. Jay, in true diplomatic style but with circumspection, urged, "Moderation but no Timidity -Wisdom but not cunning, should mark their Proceeding -

Just and Necessary Wars

"51

Jay also favored Friends of Peace conventions in all the states with a correspondence set up among the various state presidents of the parties. This was similar to a tactic employed by the colonies prior to the outbreak of the Revolutionary War and one which Jay had participated in as a member of the New York Committee of Fifty-One. Jay was pragmatic and resigned in his support of Clinton, which was lukewarm, when he wrote to Peter Augustus "…if we must have either Mr. Madison or Mr. Clinton, I prefer the latter, for Reasons which have less Relation to his personal Qualifications, than to the existing state of things."[52]

The Federalists convened a state convention in Westchester to choose a slate of state and local candidates. Jay was appointed a delegate to the convention but he declined to attend on grounds of poor health. Yet, Jay's reputation and views on the war had an effect on the convention. Jay and others opposed the nomination of a candidate for state office due to his questionable character, and withheld support which resulted in the defeat of the candidate while all other candidates were returned to office. Jay was censured by the party and he published anonymously his reply stating "Adherence to party has its limits, and they are prescribed and marked by that Supreme Wisdom which has united and associated true policy with rectitude, and honour, and self-respect."[53]

Clinton lost in the general election to Madison but it was the strongest showing of a Federalist candidate since 1800. Madison had won the support of the southern and western states while Clinton's support was from New England, New York, New Jersey and some mid-Atlantic states. New York generally favored peace since their highly profitable trade with Great Britain was being stifled by the blockade of the Atlantic coast by the British fleet. John Jay commented on the corn crop and the demand for it which had been created by the British blockade of the Atlantic coast, in December of 1812 "The Demand for it is great and the Price of all country produce is high, and probably will continue so, unless our navigation should be more interrupted by ourselves or others."[54] Jay continued to view the war as unnecessary when he expressed grave doubts in early 1813 about the wars in Europe and America "A deep tragedy is now

Just and Necessary Wars

exhibiting in the European Theatre - and the United States have begun to exhibit another - these are sufficient for <u>Tragedy</u> - ...."[55]

The war was essentially fought in three theaters; at sea with warships and privateers attacking each other; merchant ships and warships attacking each other; and on the frontier along the Great Lakes and the St. Lawrence River. The war at first did not go well for the United States, but on September 10, 1813, Commodore Oliver Hazard Perry gained a major victory when he led the Americans in action against the British fleet in the Battle of Lake Erie. Perry's victory gave the United States control of the West and earned him numerous awards. At Albany, Sarah Louisa Jay wrote of the reception given in Perry's honor with the presentation of a sword and gold box containing the Freedom of the City. There was a ball which was attended by three to four hundred people and how 'diffident and unassuming' Perry was.[56] Despite Perry's victory, Jay remained opposed to the war and reflected on George Washington's policy of foreign neutrality and domestic growth of which he had been an instrument " - That great man's System of Policy was founded on Wisdom and Virtue, and therefore naturally provided Peace and Prosperity - Had his Examples and Precepts been followed, Peace and Prosperity would doubtless have Still continued to Bless our Country."[57]

By 1814 the British had defeated Napoleon and were able to train all their resources on the war with the United States. The Federalists celebrated the news of Napoleon's defeat with a dinner in New York City, to which John Jay declined an invitation due to ill health. The British then established a blockade of Chesapeake Bay and proceeded north and burned Washington D.C.. Jay, like many Americans, was concerned about the course of the war since the British were now threatening New York City which affected Bedford as Jay noted:

> The recent events at Washington, and the various Reports respecting danger to New York and other places excite uneasiness among the People here. Portions of the Militia have been ordered to New York, and it is expected

Just and Necessary Wars

that further Detachments will be required - Heartfelt inconveniences from leaving their Homes; and we hear that their accommodations at New York have not been satisfactory. Unpleasant rumors Daily reach us, we can seldom ascertain whether any and what degree of Credit is due them.[58]

Jay also expressed his concern that Congress will issue 'Paper Money' as legal tender and that the banks "have ceased to pay in Specie,...."[59] He stated that the public is 'agitated,' "but we know that they are under the control of Him who governs all - Let us think and act accordingly --- "[60]

There were two uniformed companies, cavalry and artillery, in Bedford and both were sent to New York City and stationed at Brooklyn for several months. Militiamen could serve for a period of only six months each year, according to the law and no militia could be ordered to serve outside the United States.[61] Peter Augustus Jay was in New York City and two days after his father had expressed grave concern about the war, Peter wrote to his sister, Maria, "the British have been defeated at Baltimore" and he expressed his belief that New York would be safe until next year.[62] Yet American victories along the Canadian border by the Great Lakes in September of 1814, the British withdrawal from Baltimore and the Battle of New Orleans in January of 1815 effectively ended the war. By August of 1814, Great Britain sued for peace. It should be noted that the Battle of New Orleans was fought after the Treaty of Ghent was signed by the United States and Great Britain on December 24, 1814, ending the war between the two countries.

While the nation awaited news of the treaty negotiations, John Jay reflected on the course of the war when he wrote to Timothy Pickering and once again expounded on the 'Delusion' which had gripped the country leading it to war but that it was the right of every nation to defend itself. With reference to the negotiations in Ghent, Jay expounded on how he thought the negotiations should proceed "...to dictate such propositions and to tell us that we must accede to them as the Price of Peace, is to assume a Language rarely used

Just and Necessary Wars

unless by the victorious to the vanquished."[63] Jay was uncertain whether or not Great Britain expected the war to end as soon as it did but he clearly thought that the affairs in Europe and the desire for peace on all fronts may have had an effect in ending the war. The British were tired of war taxation and their merchants wanted a restoration of trade with the United States. Jay still believed that only with a change of leaders in the United States, would there be a chance for peace "If we should change our Rulers, and fill their places with men free from Blame; the Restoration of peace might be more easily accomplished - "[64] Jay was resolute in his belief that we should not be, "too vigilant" in examining the administration of the war "in all its departments" and called for a thorough investigation and report of expenditures during the war, "…and that the Results be authenticated and published in such a Manner as to obviate Doubt and Disbelief."[65] Jay no doubt recalled all the accounts that he kept as a diplomat in Spain, France and Great Britain which had to be reviewed and approved by Congress, at times with debate.

Jay had not changed his views about the war and held to the notion that the leaders of this country had misled the people into an unnecessary war. As an experienced diplomat, Jay clearly believed that negotiations would have been preferable to war. In January of 1815 as the country awaited news of a treaty, Jay continued to express his doubts to his friend Richard Peters that the coming year would be a good one for the country "I should rejoice to find myself mistaken but I cannot be persuaded that general Prosperity will be so restored while our nation continues to be mislead by the Delusions which caused and prolong our Calamities."[66] In another letter to his friend and former neighbor, William Miller, Jay stated that while he is anxiously awaiting 'the fate of New Orleans' he hoped for an American victory so as not to prolong the war. Jay discussed his pessimistic view of the future "- Our political prospects are gloomy - we have Rulers without Wisdom, officers without Soldiers & a Treasury without Money - [67]" Jay thought that to expect future prosperity would be 'to expect a Miracle' because 'the people shut their Eyes and are willingly ignorant of their Situation'. Despite his misgivings, Jay rejoiced when the news of peace arrived in February and he wrote to his son Peter Augustus "It was Yesterday reported

Just and Necessary Wars

that a Treaty of Peace had arrived, and this afternoon we found the Report was confirmed - this Event will cause great and universal Joy - God grant that the Delusion which caused the War, may terminate with it."[68] The terms of the Treaty of Ghent called for no territorial changes, prisoners were exchanged, captured ships were restored, captured slaves were returned to their American owners and both countries agreed to work for the abolition of the slave trade.

With the restoration of peace, Jay still had much to say about the war and the future of his country. He continued to comment on the war and its causes and his hopes for peace in writing to Richard Peters "Peace will terminate the Delusion which caused the war - the Peace will diminish it."[69] Jay believed that with the defeat of Napoleon, France would no longer agitate in this country against Great Britain which he thought contributed to the 'Delusion' the country was suffering from. He also noted that the conscription and the war debt accumulated by the government will diminish confidence in the current government. Jay also commented about the belief that people mean well is not true and that people do not adhere to the dictates of their conscience. In these statements, Jay was certainly speaking as a Federalist. The Federalists opposed not only the Embargo of 1807 but the War of 1812. Businessmen and merchants from the large cities dominated the party, favored support for industrial development and held to Alexander Hamilton's financial policy of a national bank. In foreign affairs, the Federalists opposed the French Revolution, favored good relations with Great Britain and supported a strong army and navy.

There was an inherent mistrust of the public by the Federalists and they were often regarded as elitists. The War of 1812 was extremely unpopular in New England where the Federalists were the majority party. The region's economy was dependent on trade and the British blockade of the New England coast threatened to ruin the area's economy. Late in 1814, the New England Federalists sent delegates to the Hartford Convention. The Convention discussed secession from the Union and advocated amendments to the Constitution, including financial compensation from Washington for trade lost during the war, a two-thirds vote in Congress to impose an embargo, standards for admission of a state to the Union and guidelines for a declaration of war. They also proposed that the presidency should be limited to one term and no candidate for president from the same state could be elected in succession. The latter was a reference to the state of Virginia with Madison having succeeded Jefferson, two unpopular presidents with the Federalists. During the war, the Federalists had voted as a bloc in Congress and the Hartford Convention was an attempt by the Federalists to regain political power lost during the war. While Jay was not a delegate to the Convention, Roger M. Sherman, a delegate from Connecticut, sent Jay a copy of the Convention's Report. Jay thought that the Report displayed "Temper and Wisdom" and he concluded by stating "In my opinion it is well calculated to be precursory to such ulterior measures in case future Events should render them necessary and advisable."[70] Jay was undoubtedly referring to what seems like an implied threat by the Convention, that should the war continue and the defense of New England also continue to be neglected as the delegates believed it was from the outset of the war, then the delegates to another convention in Boston should do what may be required in any perceived crisis.[71] Jay did not expound on his statement so it is unclear what action, if any, Jay thought would be advisable for the Federalists to take. The vagueness of secession in the Report appeared to many as a call for secession and a separate alliance with England. Events overtook the Federalists with the signing of the Treaty of Ghent in December of 1814 and the major victory achieved by Gen. Andrew Jackson at the Battle of New Orleans in January of 1815.

    The Federalists had opposed the war and did not support conscription or funding for the war and voted that way in Congress during the course of the war. The patriotic feelings that swept the nation with the news of peace left the Federalists with no national support. After the War of 1812, Chief Justice John Marshall remained the highest ranking Federalist in office. The Hartford Convention was the death knell for the Federalists. Their support weakened with each election due to their image of being disloyal as a result of the Hartford Convention. The party was further undermined by the commencement of the Era of Good Feelings between America and Great Britain immediately following the end of the war. The

Just and Necessary Wars

collapse of the Federalist party resulted in a lack of political partisanship, accentuated by the decisive victory of James Monroe for president in 1816 and his overwhelming reelection in 1820. The period was marked by a renewed sense of nationalism as America turned its interests to building turnpikes, canals, steamboats and railroads as it participated fully in the Industrial Revolution. Cotton was transforming the South as the Industrial Revolution had transformed the North. Jay's friend, Rufus King, was the Federalist's last presidential candidate in 1816 and Richard Stockton was the last Federalist candidate in 1820. By 1826, the Federalist party was no longer a force in American politics.

However much Jay opposed the war, Westchester County was affected with the population declining by 4,000 people due to the war.[72] However, there were some beneficial side effects for the county that can be attributed to the war. Marble quarries in the towns of Tuckahoe, Sing Sing, Hastings and Thornwood became the major suppliers of marble for the reconstruction of federal buildings destroyed by the British in Washington D.C. during the war.[73] The British blockade of American ports resulted in a lack of foreign competition for trade and as a result, Westchester county's farm and mill production increased with state aid. The products were shipped to New York City via the Hudson River and new turnpikes.

In 1812, the state was working to build a strong, educated population. The state offered financial aid to any township that would put up an equal amount of money for the establishment of a public school system. The town of Bedford participated in this program and in 1813 Benjamin Isaacs, Aaron Read and David Olmsted were elected education commissioners. The commissioners promptly set up eleven public school districts for Bedford.[74] Perhaps it was Peter's wife, Mary Clarkson Jay, who best expressed the sentiments of the public in New York City about the end of the war when she wrote to her sister, Maria Jay Banyer, that people were jubilant, smiling faces everywhere, about the peace and congratulating one another.[75] The war that John Jay had bitterly opposed was over and peace was restored to a jubilant America.

Jay was rigid, yet implacable, in his views of what constituted a 'just and necessary war' and believed in his views utterly. He recognized the 'cruel necessity' for the break with England by the American colonies and the establishment of free and independent states as 'unavoidable'. He further proclaimed in the Resolutions of the New York Convention that the reasons for the steps taken by the colonies as stated in the Declaration of Independence were 'cogent and conclusive'. He also believed, having grown up during the Age of Enlightenment, that England had broken the contract with the colonies and the colonies were therefore freed from their bond with the mother country as England. With regard to moral justifications, the Bible, he believed, sanctioned and authorized a just war against 'domestic malefactors' such as Great Britain. However, with regard to subsequent foreign and domestic wars, Jay could not justify any of them. His views on this subject remained constant throughout his life as he worked to further the cause of 'just and necessary wars'.

Just and Necessary Wars

---

[1] Charles Monaghan. *The Murrays of Murrary Hill*. (New York, 1998), 20.

[2] Ibid. 17.

[3] John R. Murray, Jr. to John Jay, 22 September 1816, JJCU.

[4] Ibid.

[5] John Jay to John R. Murray, Jr., 12 October 1816, JJCU.

[6] Ibid.

[7] Ibid.

[8] John Murray, Jr. to John Jay, 28 August 1817, JJCU.

[9] Ibid.

[10] John Jay to John Murray, Jr., 15 April 1818, JJCU.

[11] Ibid.

[12] Ibid.

[13] Ibid.

[14] Ibid.

[15] Ibid.

[16] Ibid.

[17] Ibid.

[18] Ibid.

[19] Ibid.

[20] Ibid.

[21] JJFM, 74.

[22] John Jay to Robert Harper Goodloe, 7 January 1796, JJCU.

[23] Ibid.

[24] Ibid.

[25] John Jay to Peter Augustus Jay, 23 August 1797, JJH.

[26] John Jay to Rufus King, 20 January 1803, JJCU.

[27] Ibid.

[28] John Jay to William Wilberforce, 14 April 1806, JJCU.

[29] John Jay to Richard Peters, 24 July 1809, JJCU.

[30] John Jay to Richard Peters, 26 February 1810, JJCU.

[31] JJFM 49.

[32] John Jay to William Wilberforce, 25 October 1810, JJCU.

[33] John Jay to Robert Harper Goodloe, 7 January 1796, JJCU.

34 Peter Augustus Jay to John Jay, 19 February 1808, JJCU.

35 Ibid.

36 John Jay to Timothy Pickering, 24 December 1808, JJCU.

37 Timothy Pickering to John Jay, 10 December 1808, JJCU.

38 Timothy Pickering to John Jay, 13 January 1809, JJCU.

39 John Jay to Peter Augustus Jay, 29 June 1812, JJH.

40 Ibid.

41 Ibid.

42 Ibid.

43 John Jay to Richard Bland Lee, 7 September 1812, JJCU.

44 John Jay to Peter Van Schaack, 28 July, 1812, JJCU.

45 Ibid.

46 Ibid.

47 Ibid.

48 Burroughs and Wallace. *Gotham A History of New York City to 1898,* 425.

49 John Jay to Jacob Radcliff, 16 September 1812, JJCU.

[50] John Jay to Gouveneur Morris, 21 September 1812, JJCU.

[51] Ibid.

[52] John Jay to Peter Augustus Jay, 23 September 1812, JJCU.

[53] JJWJ I: 249-51; JJGP 310-11.

[54] John Jay to William Miller, 30 December 1812, JJCU.

[55] John Jay to Maria Jay Banyer, 2 February 1813, JJCU.

[56] Sarah Louisa Jay to William Jay, 9 November 1813, JJCU.

[57] John Jay to Ebenezer Russell White, 26, January 1814, JJCU.

[58] John Jay to Maria Jay Banyer, 13 September 1814, JJCU.

[59] Ibid.

[60] Ibid.

[61] David M. Ellis and James A. Frost, Harold C. Syrett and Harry J. Carman. *A History of New York State.* (Ithaca and London 1957), 139.

[62] Peter Augustus Jay to Maria Jay Banyer, 15 September 1814, JJH.

[63] John Jay to Timothy Pickering, 1 November, 1814, JJCU.

[64] Ibid.

[65] Ibid.

[66] John Jay to Richard Peters, 9 January 1815, JJCU.

Just and Necessary Wars

---

[67] John Jay to William Miller, 20 January 1815, JJH.

[68] John Jay to Peter Augustus Jay 14 February 1815, JJCU.

[69] John Jay to Richard Peters, 14 March 1815, JJCU.

[70] John Jay to Roger M. Sherman, 31 January 1815, JJCU.

[71] James M. Banner, Jr.. *To the Hartford Convention: The Federalists and the Origins of Party Politics in Massachusetts 1789-1815.* (New York 1969), 312-16.

[72] Shonnard and Spooner. *History of Westchester County,* 539.

[73] Susan Cochran Swanson and Elizabeth Green Fuller. *Westchester County* (Westchester County Historical Society 1989), 52.

[74] Duncombe et al. *Katonah - The History of a New York Village and its People,* 84.

[75] Jay. *Memorials of Peter Jay Compiled by His Descendants,* 76.

1. *John Jay*,
by John Trumbull
John Jay Homestead State Historic Site, Katonah, New York
New York State Office of Parks, Recreation
and Historic Preservation.

2. *Sarah Livingston Jay,*
by Daniel Huntington after Alexandre Roslin
John Jay Homestead State Historic Site, Katonah, New York
New York State Office of Parks, Recreation
and Historic Preservation.

3. *William Jay*,
by Henry Antonio Wenzler
John Jay Homestead State Historic Site, Katonah, New York
New York State Office of Parks, Recreation
and Historic Preservation.

4. *Peter Augustus Jay*,
by Henry Bryan Hall
New York Public Library Digital Collections, New York, N.Y.

5. *Ann (Nancy) Jay*,
by Gideon Fairman
John Jay Homestead State Historic Site, Katonah, New York
New York State Office of Parks, Recreation
and Historic Preservation.

6. *Maria Jay Banyer*,
by Charles Balthazar Julien Ferret de Saint Memin
John Jay Homestead State Historic Site, Katonah, New York
New York State Office of Parks, Recreation
and Historic Preservation.

7. *John Jay II*,
by Daniel Huntington
John Jay Homestead State Historic Site, Katonah, New York
New York State Office of Parks, Recreation
and Historic Preservation.

8. *John Jay Residence, Bedford, New York,*
by J. W. Barber and Henry Howe
Westchester County Historical Society.

9. John Jay: Twenty Pounds Reward, 17 September, 1802
Westchester County Historical Society.

10. *Village of Sing Sing and the Hudson River*,
by W. H. Bartlett and R. Wallis
Westchester County Historical Society.

11. *The Clermont on the Hudson*,
by Charles Pensee
New York Public Library Digital Collections, New York, N.Y.

12. *Lindley Murray*,
by E. Westoby
New York Public Library Digital Collections, New York, N.Y.

13. *Richard Peters*,
unknown (scan from 1904 book by Nellie Peters Black:
Richard Peters: His Ancestors and Descendents)
New York Public Library Digital Collections, New York, N.Y.

14. *Napoleon Bonaparte, Premier Consul,*
by Francois Delpech
New York Public Library Digital Collections, New York, N.Y.

15. *The War of 1812, MacDonough's victory on Lake Champlain, and defeat of the British Army at Plattsburg by Genl. Macomb, Septr. 11th, 1814,*
by Benjamin Tanner
New York Public Library Digital Collections, New York, N.Y.

16. *James Fenimore Cooper*,
by Edward Scriven after Wesley Jarvis
New York Public Library Digital Collections, New York, N.Y.

17. *Gilbert du Motier, Marquis de Lafayette*
by Ary Scheffer
New York Public Library Digital Collections, New York, N.Y.

18. *Landing of Gen. Lafayette
at Castle Garden, New York, 16th August 1824*
by Sam Maverick Set
New York Public Library Digital Collections, New York, N.Y.

19. *DeWitt Clinton Mingling the Waters
of Lake Erie with the Atlantic*
by Philip Meeder
New York Public Library Digital Collections, New York, N.Y.

20. *View on the Erie Canal, 1829*,
by J. W. Hill
New York Public Library Digital Collections, New York, N.Y.

21. *Benjamin Vaughan*,
attributed to Thomas Badger
Vaughan Homestead Foundation.

Our Mutual Esteem and Regard

CHAPTER 5

John Jay had strong views on the nature of just and necessary wars. For him, the Revolutionary War was both just and necessary. Jay also came to realize the effects of war, regardless of their nature, could be unjust to people with regard to friends and families. People were often forced to make decisions for a particular cause, ultimately straining and ending relationships. In many ways, the American Revolution was a civil war and most people had to chose between Great Britain or the new nation, the United State of America.

John Jay was no exception and some of his closest friends chose a course that interrupted, but never ended their friendship. Jay wrote to his good friend, Peter Van Schaack, that he vowed to remain loyal to his friends no matter what their opinions.[1] This was evident in the friendship that Jay shared with Peter Van Schaack, a friendship that lasted for seventy years. There were many common threads in the lives of Jay and Van Schaack. Van Schaack was born in Kinderhook, New York, near Albany, the son of a wealthy merchant family of Dutch origin. In 1762, at the age of sixteen, he entered Kings College where he met and became life-long friends with John Jay, Gouveneur Morris and Robert R. Livingston, Jr. He graduated first in his class and studied law with Robert R. Livingston, Jr. under William Smith, Jr., who was one of the leading attorneys in New York City. Smith said of Van Schaack that he was a 'genius' of all the young men in New York.[2]

Van Schaack established lucrative law practices in New York City and Albany. As the movement towards a break with Great Britain began to develop, Van Schaack was a member of the Committee of Fifty, served on its committee of correspondence and along with John Jay and James Duane, drew up the rules of the committee. He supported the First Continental Congress and believed that the resistance in Massachusetts Bay Colony was a 'common cause' and that there would be no peace until Great Britain repealed the repressive acts against the colonies.[3] He was convinced there would be no peace with Great Britain and did not support reconciliation.[4] He maintained 'a gloomy prospect' for the colonies fearing that the bond with England 'may perhaps forever be destroyed'. He wrote in January of 1776 in terms of the Enlightenment philosophy and the contract that existed between the rulers and the populace.[5] Van Schaack did not want to use force against Great Britain and thought the Continental Congress would reject that option. However, personal considerations would enter into Van Schaack's thinking and the position he would take in the coming war.

In 1775 Van Schaack moved his family to Kinderhook, New York. His wife and son were ill, and four of his infant children had died recently. Van Schaack suffered from cataracts and had lost his sight in one eye. He had hoped to seek medical treatment for his wife in New York City and journey to London for his own medical needs but his requests were denied. By 1776 Van Schaack had wanted reconciliation with England but he refused to sign a pledge to take up arms against Britain. The New York Provincial Congress considered Van Schaack an 'equivocal character' and in 1777 when he refused to sign another oath of allegiance, he was exiled to New England. At Jay's intercession, Van Schaack returned to Kinderhook and he signed a 'parole' "not to prejudice the American Cause." He was now *de jure* neutral but still thought of himself as a British subject. When his wife died in 1778, Van Schaack and his three children were exiled to Great Britain where he received medical treatment. Jay wrote to his good friend and pledged the two would remain friends.

This must have been a difficult decision for Van Schaack. He had read works by the leaders of the Enlightenment, John Locke and Montesquieu among others, and believed in natural law and the compact between a ruler and the people. He further believed that the compact could only be broken by the tyranny of the ruler. He drew a fine line of distinction in his belief that Great Britain had not broken the compact but the nation was misguided. He expressed his Enlightenment views asserting that the Declaration of Independence was based on the belief that the constitution under which the colonies were governed had been dissolved. As a result, the colonists were in a state of nature with the government vested in them along with the right to create a new form of government.⁶ When he left for London, a citizen of the world, Van Schaack believed that America would ultimately win its independence. During his stay in London, he visited the debates in the House of Lords and Commons thanks to his brother-in-law, Henry Cruger, who was a member of Parliament. By 1780 he was convinced that Great Britain's only interest in America was for revenue and he was 'determined to return to America.' To Van Schaack's thinking, Great Britain had broken the contract with the American colonies and he had returned to a 'state of nature'. He renewed his correspondence with Jay, which had been suspended during the Revolution and in 1782 he stated 'he hardly knew what to say' and that he was 'embarrassed' by their former and present situations 'but that nothing that has occurred during the war had altered his thinking between 'right and wrong.' Van Schaack was a Latin scholar and quoted Homer to Jay *"Caeelum non animum"*⁷ Jay responded with understanding and did not blame Van Schaack for his choice and then assured Van Schaack of his friendship "…as an independent American, I considered all who were not for us, and you among the rest, as against us; be assured that John Jay did not cease to be a friend to Peter Van Schaack."⁸

    At this time, Jay was living in Passy, outside Paris, and was a member of the American Commission to negotiate a peace treaty with Great Britain. Jay had asked Van Schaack to handle some legal matters in London regarding the estate of his late father. Jay still regarded Van Schaack 'as a good old friend' and reiterating his belief that no one should be blamed for choosing sides since it was a person's duty to choose. Van Schaack wrote to Jay in 1783 recognizing Jay's strict distinction of impartiality knowing that Jay always judged matters on their merit "The line you have drawn between your political character and your private friendships is so strongly marked, and will be so strictly attended by me, that I hope our correspondence will not end here."⁹ In that letter Van Schaack revealed his true allegiance, when he referred to America as "our country" and how he had suffered from his decision to leave America "I have dragged at each remove a lengthening chain."[10] Van Schaack then paid homage to his friend "I have always considered you as one of the most formidable enemies of this country, but since what has happened, has happened, there is no man I more cordially wish the glory of the achievement."[11] On October 14, 1783 Jay arrived in London after the signing of the Treaty of Paris and was reunited with his old friend. Jay wrote in his diary that they met affectionately as old friends would after a long absence.[12]

When Jay returned to America, he met with Gov. Clinton on behalf of Van Schaack. By 1784 the New York Legislature restored to Van Schaack and several others "all rights, privileges and immunities, as citizens" upon taking an oath of allegiance. Van Schaack returned to New York City on July 20, 1785 and John Jay was at the dock to welcome his friend 'home' as Van Schaack noted that Jay came on board Van Schaack's ship and when on shore, introduced Van Schaack to the local officials, as an old friend would do.[13] Van Schaack discovered that his estates and properties had not been confiscated, no doubt aided by his strong ties to many important leaders in New York. He was readmitted to the bar and returned to Kinderhook to practice law. He wrote to John Jay of his return:

> As a Friend I love and esteem you, as a Citizen (and permit me to add as a <u>Patriot</u>), I consider your Abilities as an Ornament, and your integrity as a Blessing to your Country. May She long continue to enjoy and to set a proper Value on so rare an Assemblage of great and good Qualities! These are the sincere Dictates of my Heart.[14]

Van Schaack resumed his law practice, acting on behalf of John Jay on occasion, and opened a law school which he ran until his death in 1826. He was warmly received into society. After his return to America, Jay and Van Schaack exchanged letters and in 1809, Jay visited his friend in Kinderhook. This was not Jay's first visit with his friend in Kinderhook. In 1780 when riding circuit as Chief Justice, Jay noted in his diary that he broke his

Our Mutual Esteem and Regard

circuit and had breakfast with his old friend.[15] It was the hope of both men that they would meet again and there were prospects of a visit by Van Schaack to Bedford, but the visit never took place. Jay's children, Peter Augustus, William and Maria apparently made visits to Kinderhook to pay their respects to Van Schaack over the years. It must have given both men great pleasure when Van Schaack's son took a position in the law firm of Peter Augustus Jay.

The bond of friendship between the two men seemed to strengthen with the passing of time. In 1827, Jay reflected on their friendship which he considered to have been interrupted by war, but never ended "It gives me pleasure to reflect that our mutual Esteem and Regard have from an early period been constantly productive of Cordiality and Gratification - "[16] This feeling between Jay and Van Schaack sustained them throughout their lives despite urgent family pressures and matters of conscience for both men.

Yet the friendship between John Jay and Lindley Murray took a far different course in which the Revolutionary War caused both men to make different lifetime choices. Lindley Murray, the son of a successful Quaker merchant named Robert Murray, was born in in 1745 in Lebanon County, Pennsylvania. He was educated in Pennsylvania at the Benjamin Franklin Academy and Charitable School. In 1753 the wealthy Murray family moved to New York City where Lindley received a proper education for the son of a wealthy merchant which would prepare him to one day enter the merchant trade like his father. It was here that Lindley discovered his love of penmanship, after reviewing a sample of his writing, which would one day gain him international prominence.[17]

It is difficult not to realize the joy of discovery in Murray's reaction to a simple school assignment. Murray would retain his exquisite penmanship throughout his life and wrote books on the subject in later years. Yet this was an age when penmanship was a serious matter and was highly regarded as an accomplishment. Penmanship was part of the course of study for children of the upper classes. This may be difficult for some contemporary readers to comprehend in an age where cursive writing is regrettably disappearing from the school curriculum and as an established part of contemporary life.

    Murray was brought up among wealth and privilege due to his father's great fortune. The Murrays were known as great hosts at their estate in Manhattan. To attest to the environment Murray was raised in, consider the family coach with an interior decorated with lace, silk, tassels and tufting at a cost of £153.14.[18]

    Murray was sent to his father's counting house to learn the merchant profession but as Lindley soon discovered, he did not want to become a merchant.[19] Lindley studied at the Quaker Academy in Burlington, New Jersey where he learned French and read Voltaire and other Philosophes who greatly influenced his thinking. He was tutored in classical studies as well as science but he was attracted to the law. He attended Kings College and his father relented on Lindley's desire to practice law and saw to it that his son was placed in the best possible law firm for his clerkship. Murray began his studies under the tutelage of Benjamin Kissam, one of New York City's leading attorneys. It was here that Murray met fellow clerk, John Jay, of whom he wrote in his *Memoirs* that Jay's talents and virtues boded well for future renown along with his reasoning and determination.[20] Murray also thought that Jay's handwriting was 'crabbed' and 'hard to read'. Lindley was not the only member of his family to establish a friendship with John Jay. His brother, John, Jr. corresponded with John Jay on the subject of 'just and necessary wars.'

    After his tenure as a clerk in Kissam's office, Murray set up a law practice of his own. He joined The Debating Club, whose members included John Jay and Peter Van Schaack, among many other distinguished attorneys. The Club met at the establishment of Mrs. Brass in the evening, continuing debate until midnight.[21] On one occasion, Murray, John Jay, Egbert Benson, Benjamin Kissam and Peter Van Schaack, were among the debaters on the following subjects: "Whether the laws ought to compel a subject to accept of a public employment?"; "Whether in an absolute monarchy it is better that the Crown should be elective than heredity?"; "Whether a people are more happy under an elective or hereditary monarchy?"; "Was Virginius morally justified in putting his daughter Virginia to death to preserve her from violation by Appius?".[22] It is interesting to note that at this early date, topics relating to an elective rather than hereditary monarchy were debated, albeit in an abstract form.

    Murray went to London with his brother, Robert, to set up a branch of the family's business along with his wife, Hannah Dobson of the Flushing Monthly Meeting and their two daughters. The Murrays, being Quakers, attracted the attention of royalty, since the English Queen liked the Friends and treated them with a smile.[23] He and his family returned to America in 1768 where Lindley acted as the attorney for the Murray family business earning a great fortune for himself. He and his family settled in Manhattan and in that same year, Lindley became a founding member of the New York Chamber of Commerce. In 1775, as the colonies became more resolved to travel the road that would lead to independence, Murray became a member of the New York Committee of Sixty along with his friend John Jay who noted the zeal of the public for their cause.[24] Although Murray was a member of the Committee, an episode occurred that altered the reputation of the Murray family and cast doubt on their loyalties.

    The colonies had enacted a non-importation law regarding ships from Great Britain. When one of the Murray family's ships, *Beaulah*, was blocked from unloading its cargo in Manhattan, the ship was unloaded under cover of darkness on Staten Island. The attempt by the Murray family to cover up the incident became fodder for the public and the press. The *Beaulah* affair was widely reported in newspapers along the east coast and the Murray family was labeled 'Loyalists'. Lindley and his family retreated to Islip on Long Island to weather the political climate in New York.[25] Lindley and his family returned to New York City in 1779 and he resumed work in the family business. When the British occupied New York, they were welcomed by the Murray family who gave their loyalty to the British ostensibly to protect their business interests. However, there is an account of an incident during the early days of the revolution that has become part of New York

Our Mutual Esteem and Regard

City folklore. After the Battle of Manhattan in 1776, Lindley's mother, Mary Lindley Murray, entertained the British General, Sir William Howe and his staff at the family's Manhattan estate, Iclenberg. This enabled Gen. George Washington, Gen. Putnam and the American troops to retreat safely from the city. Only the day before, Washington had used Iclenberg as his headquarters. Today a plaque at Park Avenue and Thirty-Seventh Street in New York City where Iclenberg once stood, commemorates the incident. Whether true or not, the allegiance of the Murray family appeared to be Loyalist as the Murray Hill section of New York became a gathering place for the British during their occupation of the city. It should be noted that Mary Murray's family was decidedly patriotic with members of her family serving in the military during the Revolution.

Lindley and his family settled at an estate three miles from Manhattan near the East River and 25th Street, Bellevue, which is today the site of Bellevue Hospital. At this time, Lindley's health began to decline shortly before the move to Bellevue that left him debilitated, unable to walk, along with chills and fever.[26] Upon the advice of his doctors, Lindley was advised that exercise and travel would be beneficial to his health. He then moved his family to Bethlehem, Pennsylvania and lived among the Moravians who were pacifists. Murray delighted in the beauty of the countryside and the tranquility of its people.[27] Murray was joined by his father and sister, and when his father thought it 'prudent' to return to New York City, Lindley accompanied his father on the journey. Murray consulted a leading physician in the city who advised him to settle in York, England due to the climate.[28] There is some difference in the interpretation of Murray's motives to remove to England. The author, Charles Monaghan, (*The Murrays of Murray Hill*) asserts that Murray moved to England to protect his own and his family's reputation having been branded as Loyalists in the colonies. Monaghan points out that Yorkshire is hardly noted for its healthy climate and that Murray and his wife constantly suffered from colds and developed symptoms related to rheumatism or arthritis. In addition, Murray's appearance later in his life was described by a visitor as "ruddy and animated" and he

Our Mutual Esteem and Regard

lived to the then advanced age of eighty-one. However, new research by Lyda Fens-de Zeeuw (*Lindley Murray (1745-1826) Quaker and Grammarian*) asserts that Murray did journey to England for his health having expressed his intent to return to America within two years after the anticipated restoration of his health.[29] Murray's health continued to decline and travel was made almost impossible and he spoke of 'the weakness of my Limbs and Voice continues' and that 'small Exertions, long in recovering from them' and that he was 'more susceptible of taking cold' and 'a day or two of giddiness or swimming in the head'.[30] Visitors to Murray's house in York confirm his disabilities of not being able to walk more than a few yards at a time, speaking only in a whisper and having to be wheeled to his carriage. Fens de-Zeeuw suggests his illness may have been myasthenia gravis, an autoimmune neuromuscular disease, or post-polio syndrome, neither of which would have deprived Murray of his intellectual capacity. Yet, Murray being a Quaker, bore his ailments without complaint seeing in pain and suffering a path to immortality.[31] It should be noted that when Murray sailed for England in 1784, he retained his U.S. citizenship and never applied for compensation for lost property. Whatever the true nature of Murray's disability, he was able to write eleven school textbooks. His *English Grammar* focused on penmanship, and the *English Reader* contained selections from liberal prose and poetry to improve language, piety and virtue. Both books were popular sellers and became the standards of the time in English and American schools, selling more than twenty million copies.

  Jay and Murray seemed to have continued their friendship with Murray sending Jay a copy of a book he had written, presumably *The Power of Religion on the Mind in Retirement, Sickness and Death* which Jay replied had given him much satisfaction. In 1794 when Jay was named Envoy Extraordinary to the Court of London to renegotiate certain terms of the Treaty of Paris, Murray wrote a cordial letter to Jay congratulating him on his appointment and expressed his hope for:

> …a speedy and happy dispersion of those clouds of hostility, which have

> been for some time gathering, and
> which seemed of late ready to involve
> the two Countries in confusion and
> distress. I hope I shall be excused when
> I say, that I do not know any other
> person in America, whose appointment
> to this High Office would have given
> me so much satisfaction and promised
> so successful an issue:....[32]

Murray's confidence in Jay's abilities also extended to the European theater. Murray hoped Jay would be able to exert his influence to avert an unnecessary war in Europe. Murray also expressed his wish that Jay might come to York to visit Murray since he was too feeble to travel. Jay responded to Murray's letter from the Royal Hotel, Pall-Mall, where Jay was staying in London during the treaty negotiations and referred to Murray as 'my good friend' and stated "It really would give me great pleasure to visit you before I return;...."[33] Jay realized that the duties of his mission might not allow such a visit, as was to be the case. Jay also expounded on Christianity:

> I perceive that we concur in thinking
> that we must go home to be happy, and
> that our home is not in this world. Here,
> we have nothing to do but our duty, and
> to regulate our business and our
> pleasures;...The theory of prudence is
> sublime and in many respects simple.
> The practice is difficult; and it
> necessarily must be so, or this would
> cease to be a state of probation.[34]

In commenting on Murray's revisions to *The Power of Religion on the Mind in Retirement, Sickness and Death*, Jay wrote:

> The sentiments diffused through your
> book are just, striking, and useful; but,
> my good friend, our opinions are oftener
> right than our conduct. Among the
> strange things of this world, nothing

> seems more strange than that men pursuing happiness should knowingly quit the right road and take a wrong road, and frequently do what their judgments neither approve nor prefer. Yet so is the fact; and this fact points strongly to the necessity of our being healed, or restored, or regenerated by a power more energetic than any of those which properly belong to the human mind.[35]

Jay then stated very clearly "For this purpose only one adequate plan has ever appeared in this world, and that is the Christian dispensation. In this plan I have full faith."[36] It is then that Jay made a very interesting statement to Murray "I mention these things that you may see the state of my mind relative to these interesting subjects, and to relieve yours from doubts which your friendship for me might render disagreeable."[37] Jay's remarks have been interpreted by Charles Monaghan and by Lyda Fens-de Zeeuw in decidedly different ways. Monaghan believed that Jay's remarks are a strong rebuke of Murray's past actions and Loyalist sentiments when Jay discussed the wrong road often taken by right thinking men. Until the *Beaulah* affair, Murray had been active in the patriot cause. Murray made the wrong choice according to Monaghan when he participated in his family's defiance of the non-importation agreement which almost caused the family's expulsion from New York City. Monaghan points to Jay's remarks about his wanting to relieve any doubt that Murray had on the subject. Fens-de Zeeuw accurately points out in disagreement with Monaghan that nowhere does Jay specifically indict Murray for making the wrong decision during the Revolution. One characteristic of Jay's writings is the force and clarity of his views particularly on religion and politics. One is never left in doubt about Jay's views which he expresses through reasoning and in lawyerly terms. It seems that Jay was commenting on the present state of morality when he wrote to Murray "Man, in his present state, appears to be a degraded creature;...."[38] After this passage in which Jay wished to relieve any doubts about his present 'state of mind' and expressing his continuing friendship for Murray, he then discussed his views about the current state of affairs leading from his comment about the degraded state man is in at the present. Jay intuitively wrote about the current political climate and its long range effects:

> As to the wars now waging, they appear to me to be of a different description from ordinary ones. I think we are just entering on the age of revolutions, and that the impurities of our moral *atmosphere* (if I may use the expression) are about to be purified by a succession of political storms. I sincerely wish for general peace and good-will among men, but I shall be mistaken if (short intervals excepted) the season for those blessings is not at some distance. If any country escapes, I am inclined to think it will be our own; and I am led to this opinion by general principles and reasonings, and not by particular facts or occurrences, some of which so strongly favour a contrary idea as to produce in my mind much doubt and apprehension.[39]

Jay was prescient in his view that the American Revolution was a spark and catalyst that would produce other revolutions, *just and necessary,* in their ideals but going astray for 'a contrary idea'. He also wrote that if any country was to escape the impending calamities, he referred to America by using the words 'our own' recognizing Murray's status as an American citizen. Jay's hope in this letter was to enlighten Murray on Jay's 'state of mind' regarding his affirmation that Christianity is the 'dispensation' for all the inadequacies. It is not clear what Jay thought about Murray's motives for leaving America, but it is clear that he still considered Murray a friend, whatever his beliefs.

Our Mutual Esteem and Regard

Jay and Murray never met after Murray left for England but their friendship and correspondence continued throughout their lives with Murray sending books to Jay on occasion. In 1805 Jay wrote to Murray of his retirement "Being retired from the fatigues and constraints of public life, I enjoy with real satisfaction the freedom and leisure which has at length fallen to my lot For a long course of years I had been looking forward with desire to the tranquil retirement in which I now live, and my expectations from it have not been disappointed."[40]

Murray, like Jay, opposed the War of 1812 and earnestly hoped for a peaceful settlement of differences between America and Great Britain. He was also concerned about his properties in New York City when he wrote to his brother, John, in 1807 that he feared another war between the two countries; he was concerned for his property and that he should be considered an American.[41] Murray's situation was not unlike a number of American expatriates at this time, who, for their own reasons fled America during the Revolution never to return.

By 1821 both men were in their seventies and Jay commented to Murray "we have both experienced afflicting dispensations. Your portion of health has for a long time been diminished; and I have not had a well day for the last twelve years."[42] Jay once again expressed his fondness for Murray

> We have both passed the usual term of life, or (as the lawyers say) our leases have expired, and we are now holding over. To be thus circumstanced, is not very important to those who expect to remove from their present abodes to better habitations, and to enjoy them in perpetuity. That we may both be, and continue to be, numbered with these, is the sincere desire of - Your affectionate friend, JOHN JAY.[43]

While 'just and necessary wars' continued to interrupt some of John Jay's relationships, the Revolutionary War made possible his friendship with Benjamin Vaughan which led to an extraordinary turn of events. Vaughan was born to Samuel Vaughan, a West India merchant, and to Sarah Hallowell. Sarah was the daughter of a Boston merchant, Benjamin Hallowell, who was also the King's Commissioner and later an American sympathizer. Vaughan was raised a Unitarian and attended a school in Liverpool specifically for Quakers and Unitarians where he was tutored by the scientist, Joseph Priestly. Unitarians, Baptists, Methodists and Presbyterians were labeled 'Dissenters' in England and were restricted by law from becoming officers in the Army and Navy, holding a seat in Parliament or becoming judges or heads of corporations. He later attended Cambridge with William Petty, the Earl of Shelburne, but being Unitarian, he was denied a full degree. Shelburne was a liberal who wanted political and social changes in England.

Over the years, Vaughan sent Shelburne papers he had written concerning social and political reforms, especially for Parliament. Shelburne became Prime Minister during the waning days of the American Revolution, 1782-1783, while the Treaty of Paris negotiations were continuing. Shelburne sent Vaughan to Paris as a minister without portfolio. Some peace commissioners thought Vaughan was an unofficial agent of Shelburne. Vaughan's mission was to reconcile differences between Franklin and the other American peace commissioners and to conclude a timely treaty with the Americans. Vaughan was already a friend of Benjamin Franklin, dating back to Vaughan's childhood. He was also known to the Jay family since Vaughan's brother, John, had recently applied for American citizenship while in Madrid. Jay and Vaughan struck up a lasting friendship upon meeting. Vaughan described Jay as friendly, honest and having a forthrightness that did him credit.[44] Vaughan and Shelburne thought that the American Revolution was hopeless if Britain continued to deny America independence. Vaughan's new friendship with Jay was used to advantage by Jay. Jay discovered that the French Foreign Secretary, Comte de Vergennes, sent his undersecretary, de Reyneval, to talk to Shelburne about a separate and bilateral treaty for England and France. Jay cleverly sent Vaughan back to London with a message for Shelburne concerning the recognition of American independence and French interests "That it hence appeared to be the obvious interest of Britain immediately to cut the cords which tied us to France, for that, though we were determined to fulfill our treaty and engagements with this Court, *yet it was a different thing to be guided by their or our construction of it.*"[45] Jay was mistrustful of French intentions during the negotiations and made comments to Vaughan that if Britain would sever its relations with France, the negotiations would proceed more rapidly. Jay had made similar comments to Vaughan before Vaughan's departure with a message for Shelburne wondering why Britain did not break with France.[46] Jay also argued before Vaughan that the best way England could bargain with France was to make a good bargain with America.[47]

    Jay's use of Vaughan as an American intermediary succeeded in gaining America the recognition it desired when Vaughan urged Shelburne to concede this point. Shelburne granted the "Act of Independence under the Great Seal" in which Britain recognized American independence. Jay said of Vaughan's mission that he is deserving of America's commendation.[48] Vaughan played a definitive role in hastening the conclusion of the negotiations with British recognition of American independence and by assisting with the drafting of the Preliminary Articles of Peace. Vaughan had from the start of the Revolution advocated reconciliation and realized the enormous trade potential for Britain with America when he commented with great foresight that within forty years America's population will equal that of Great Britain and in eighty years America will have eighty million citizens.[49]

    Before retuning to America after the signing of the Treaty of Paris, Jay and his wife journeyed to London where they were entertained by the Vaughans and the two families became friends. Jay bid farewell to Vaughan at Dover for the voyage to America but this would not be the last time the paths of these two men would cross as their friendship continued through the years.

    In one final comment about the British and their approach to the negotiations with America, Jay wrote to Vaughan "The policy of Britain respecting this country is so repugnant to common sense that I am sometimes tempted to think *it must be so;* and the old adage of *quos Deus,* etc., always occurs to me when I reflect on the subject."[50] In that same letter, Jay gave some advice to Vaughan about India, the British treatment of the Indians and the sovereignty of the Indian states "The India business never appeared to me a difficult one. Do justice, and all is easy. Cease to treat those unhappy natives as slaves, and be content to trade with them as with other independent kingdoms."[51]

Several years later, while Minister of Foreign Affairs under the Confederacy, Jay wrote to Vaughan about life in America in exceedingly flourishing terms:

> I begin to flatter myself that if you and Mrs. Vaughan could enjoy this country in only half the degree that I do you would not greatly regret leaving Old England. I am more contented here than I expected. Some things, it is true, are wrong, but more are right. Justice is well administered, offences are rare, and I have never known more public tranquility or private security. Resentments subside very sensibly, though gradually. I have met with whigs and tories at the same table. The spirit of industry throughout the country was never greater. The productions of the earth abound.[52]

Jay's remark about 'resentments' subsiding and in a sensible and gradual manner are insightful and help to explain why some of Jay's friendships weathered the storm of the American Revolution, despite different beliefs about the cause of American independence. This approach coincided with Jay's circumspection. The 'spirit of industry' that Jay also referred to could very possibly be attributed to the new found freedom that America now enjoyed which resulted in great economic expansion.

Our Mutual Esteem and Regard

In 1794 Vaughan went on to become a member of Parliament. His Republican attitudes and sympathy with the French Revolution caused a stir in Parliament. When war broke out between the two countries, it caused a republican backlash against the French Revolution and republicanism in England. He was summoned before the Privy Council in May, 1794, which absolved Vaughan but he fled the country to France fearing for his safety as well as for his family and friends. Vaughan's goal was to emigrate to America.

In a previous trip to Paris in 1790, Vaughan's initial impression of the revolutionary spirit in Paris was positive and he met with French officials Vaughan commented to John Jay about the "…family feeling" among the military and that "the seed has fallen upon the best soil…that could be found in Europe." with the coming of the revolution to France.[53] In that same letter he refers to the American Revolution as "…little more than a separation of partnership accounts." adding that "I trust our friends in America will not be jealous at hearing, that the French Revolution is thought by much the most instructive of any upon record, and as agitating the greatest assemblage of principles respecting human and even domestic society"[54] Vaughan suggested that when British law is eliminated from the American courts, that will result in furthering the cause of the American Revolution.

Paris in 1794 was in the midst of the Reign of Terror as the French Revolution took a radical turn. As a foreign national, Vaughan was now viewed with suspicion in France. He was imprisoned in Carme Prison in Paris for a while and then journeyed to Switzerland and spent several years there where his past experiences in France led to a change of views about the French Revolutioin. Jay was contacted by Vaughan concerning his settling in America. Jay did not hesitate to write to James Monroe, the new American Ambassador to France, for support, stating that Vaughan's "character and attachmt to our Country are known…." Jay expressed concern that there may be some doubt that Vaughan's recent actions have caused him to be viewed unfavorably by the current American government "It is possible that circumstances may occur to render the good offices of his

Our Mutual Esteem and Regard

Friends expedient. Considering the Zeal of his family for the welfare of our Country, and that he has been particularly useful, I think he has a just Claim to our Friendship, and to such marks of it, as may be requisite and proper."[55]

Vaughn was in a difficult position trying to obtain an American passport since he was neither native born nor a naturalized citizen living in America for five continuous years. James Monroe and Thomas Paine both wrote letters to the French authorities on behalf of Vaughan. By 1797 Jay was expecting Vaughan's arrival in America when he wrote to Vaughan's brother, John, now in America, about "...a portrait of the late President, engraved from a painting of Stewart...." that Benjamin Vaughan was presenting to Jay. Jay then went on to say "I am impatient to hear of Benj - and the more as we had Reason to expect he would this time have arrived in America - "[56] The next month, Benjamin Vaughan wrote to John Jay from Little Cambridge, near Boston, where he had settled temporarily after receiving a passport to join his wife and children in America. Vaughan stated "...I have the pleasure to inform you that we have resolved <u>immediately</u> to pitch our tent in the township of Hallowell, so named after our grandfather."[57]

Vaughan's new home was to be on the banks of the Kennebec River in Maine on land received from the Plymouth Company by members of his family. Vaughan expressed his intent:

> I shall little incline to any public situation during the remainder of a life apparently to be destined to be spent on a continent with which I have long had so many ties. As a private citizen, I shall zealously labor for the public good; and my first essay will be the making known by the way of the press, the <u>life of a peasant</u>, who was alike memorable for his industry, senses, knowledge in farming, & virtue, & whose example may be essentially

useful to this country.[58]

Jay immediately replied to Vaughan by congratulating him and his family on their arrival in America "may your expectations of happiness be fully realized." Jay expanded on political policy and the American government to his friend:

> I presume that our political sentiments do not differ essentially. To me it appears that the American government be preserved as it is, until mature experience shall very plainly point out very useful amendments to our constitution; that we steadily repel all foreign influence and interference, and with good faith and liberality treat all nations as friends in peace, and as enemies in war; neither meddling with their affairs nor permitting them to meddle with ours. These are the primary object of my policy. The the secondary ones are more numerous, such as to be always prepared for war, to cultivate peace, to promote religion, industry, tranquility, and useful knowledge, and to secure to all the quiet enjoyment of their rights, by wise and equal laws irresistibly executed. I do not expect mankind will, before the millennium, be what they ought to be; and therefore, in my opinion, every political theory which does not regard them as being what *they are,* will prove delusive.[59]

When Vaughan settled in Hallowell, Maine, he brought with him his private library which became one of the largest private libraries in New England with nearly 12,000 volumes. He was interested in promoting higher education and he received honorary degrees of LL.D from Harvard and Bowdoin College in

Our Mutual Esteem and Regard

1807 and 1812 respectively. Vaughan was active in the development of Bowdoin College which opened in 1802 and in organizing its curriculum and library. He and other members of his family made many donations to the College's library. He practiced his trained profession, medical doctor, attending only to the poor and provided for their medications at his own expense, while remaining a consultant to the local doctor in Hallowell. He became active in encouraging the settlement of the Kennebec region building houses, mills, stores, a distillery, and a printing office. He also helped to establish the seaport at Jones's Eddy, near the Kennebec river. Vaughan was a prolific writer on political and economic subjects some of which were published anonymously. At the request of Pres. Adams, Vaughan prepared an historical report on the northeast boundary of America.

    Vaughan continued his friendship with Thomas Jefferson and James Madison, visiting both men at their respective estates, Monticello and Montpelier. His correspondence with both men focused on their mutual interests in agriculture, science and politics. He also stopped at Mount Vernon especially to view the marble mantelpiece given to Washington by his father, Samuel, and to visit the gardens described in his father's diary during his visit to Mount Vernon in 1787.[60] He was a staunch Federalist, and like Jay, promoted good relations between Great Britain and America and openly opposed the War of 1812. In time, Vaughan had earned a highly respected place in America with his numerous interests and efforts. When Lafayette visited America in 1824-25, Vaughn met with Lafayette at a reception in Portland given by the governor of Maine who referred to Vaughan as a revered man and as an old and intimate friend of the Marquis.[61]

    Vaughan paid a visit to John Jay at Bedford in 1819 along with his son, Robert Hallowell, his cousin, Robert H. Gardiner and the Rev. Dr. Kirkland, President of Harvard College. Vaughan wrote to Jay of the impending visit that he and his companions should be treated like relatives.[62] Jay responded with great anticipation of Vaughan's impending visit:

> The prospect of receiving a visit from
> you and your Son and Mr. Gardiner

gives me Pleasure. There is not the least Probability of my being absent from Home - The state of my health not having admitted of it for several years past. The expectations of soon having an opportunity of conversing with you renders this letter more concise than it would otherwise be.[63]

After Vaughan's visit to Bedford, Jay noted in returning a book to Vaughan via his son Peter Augustus, Coe's treatise on billary concretions which Vaughan had loaned to Jay, "Mr. Vaughan when here spoke much in favor of a Book on <u>bilious</u> Complaints - "[64] a condition that plagued Jay throughout his adult life. It must have given Jay a great deal of personal satisfaction to welcome Benjamin Vaughan to America and to his farm in Bedford, as Jay so often referred to his place of retirement. It is ironic that while Jay initially worked for reconciliation with England, he realized that the American Revolution was a 'just and necessary' war. It was in the waning days of this conflict, that Jay found a lasting friendship with Benjamin Vaughan. Their friendship began under unusual circumstances, almost as adversaries, but with a common goal. The friendship resulted in Vaughan settling in America and embracing the ideals of the American republic. Jay was steadfast to his commitment that he remain loyal to his friends, whatever their beliefs and those friendships seemed to have enriched all.

While John Jay had pledged his fidelity to many of his friends who chose to be Loyalists during the Revolutionary War, his relationship with one person was strained and severed for many years - his brother, Sir James Jay. James Jay was John's older brother, born in 1732. He received his medical degree from one of the premier medical schools of the time, the University of Edinburgh. Upon graduation, James returned to the colonies and set up a practice in New York City. He later settled in England to practice medicine. His other goals were to raise funds for Kings College and to promote higher education in the colonies. While in England, James met the Rev. William Smith who traveled to England on behalf of the College of Philadelphia. The two men

Our Mutual Esteem and Regard

worked jointly to raise funds for both institutions and divide the proceeds. With the aid of the King, they raised £10,000. On March 25, 1763, after reading an address from the Governors of Kings College, James Jay was knighted by King George III. A premature attempt to collect the funds due Kings College resulted in a law suit instigated by the Governors of Kings College against Sir James but was subsequently dropped. This resulted in a rift between Sir James and the Governors as they did not acknowledge Sir James' efforts on behalf of the College. Peter Jay, the father of Sir James Jay, was not pleased with the dishonor brought on his son's character and urged his other son, John, to make the best of the situation so as to redeem his brother's reputation which had been tarnished undeservedly.[65] Sir James remained in England and distinguished himself with the publication of a pamphlet, *Reflections and Observations on the Gout,* while establishing a successful medical practice. In his travels through Great Britain prior to the outbreak of the Revolution, Sir James observed first hand what he considered to be the oppression of the Irish people by the British. This may have made him reconsider England's treatment of the colonies. His apprehension for the colonies drove him to journey to a cannon foundry to learn about munitions production, since the colonies lacked weapons. In January of 1776, John Jay wrote to Sir James who was then residing at Bath, advising him of the situation in America:

> Everything with us is in a good Way, and tho We desire Reconciliation, are well prepared for contrary Measures. This is an unnatural Quarrel & God knows why the British Empire should be torn to Pieces by unjust Attempts to subjugate us. Some say a great Number of Foreign Troops are coming over, but I think it somewhat uncertain whose Battles they will fight.[66]

When the Revolution broke out, Sir James returned to America in July, 1778, and his zeal for American independence caused him to loan $20,000 in colonial currency to a Boston clothier, James Mease, to outfit American troops. Only a small portion of the loan was repaid due to depreciation of the colonial currency, and Sir James would spend many years seeking compensation for his loss.

The sympathies of Sir James at the outset of the war seemed to be on the side of the American cause. He was a member of the New York State Senate from 1778-1782 and in 1779, he proposed and voted for the passage of the Act of Attainder which led to the confiscation of the property of prominent New York Loyalists. His brother John, did not agree with the Act of Attainder and John wrote a scathing letter to Gov. Clinton attacking the unfairness of the law and the dishonor brought on the country.[67] Jay viewed the Act of Attainder as a form of persecution for the beliefs held by some people. He was deeply committed to the cause of American independence and for the principle of justice. This was a view that John Jay held throughout the Revolution that people were entitled to their opinions without persecution and was the basis of his continued friendship with Loyalists throughout the Revolution and years later. His views may have been shaped by the persecution of his Huguenot ancestors by French Catholics, and he did not wish to see his fellow Americans persecuted for their views.

During this period, Sir James concocted many schemes to aid the Americans, such as experimenting with cannons at Fishkill, New York where he was staying with members of the Jay family. He also proposed a plan to the Naval Committee of Congress for two rowboats and troops which he would lead into New York harbor to burn British ships and storehouses. His plan was rejected by the Committee as being too dangerous. Sir James also experimented, unsuccessfully, with fireworks on the frozen Hudson River near West Point.

The plan that Sir James is probably most associated with and for its success, is 'Sympathetic Inks' or invisible ink. In 1775 Sir James conducted experiments that led to the development of invisible ink. By 1776, Sir James had furnished his brother, John, with a supply of the ink. John was obviously impressed with his brother's invention and realized its importance in secret correspondence, being a member of the Committee for Secret Correspondence for the Continental Congress along with Robert Morris and Silas Deane. John Jay gave a supply of the ink to Silas Deane before his departure to France and the invisible ink was known only to Jay and the inventor.[68] The 'Inventor' was no doubt his brother, Sir James Jay. Sir James had been unsuccessful in aiding the Revolution in the past but he realized the significance that invisible ink might have. While the history of invisible ink dates to ancient Greece and Rome, Sir James described his vision for the use of invisible ink as being a curiosity at first but a benefit for politics and war time.[69] John Jay was not the only person who received a supply of invisible ink from Sir James. Sir James sent a supply of the 'medicine', invisible ink, to George Washington. Washington fully realized the benefits of Sir James' experiments and made full use of the supply of ink sent to him and asked Sir James for additional supplies.[70] Washington was so impressed with the invisible ink that he sent a supply to Maj. Benjamin Tallmadge of the Continental Army who was one of Washington's master spies. Tallmadge also furnished the ink to other individuals engaged in secret correspondence. Sir James had developed his invisible ink in London and described his experiments with the ink when he sent a letter to his brother John about family matters and included secret intelligence written in invisible ink which passed through the post office and arrived in New York, undetected.[71]

It should be noted that the intelligence that Sir James transmitted to Congress was the plan of the British to send Gen. Burgoyne from Canada with an army down the Hudson River to subjugate the colonies and end the Revolution. Sir James Jay was no doubt committed to the cause of American independence and his 'Sympathetic inks' aided in the secret correspondence of the Americans.

As the Revolution progressed, Sir James seemed to change his views and he favored reconciliation as his access to important personages and his lack of further accomplishments waned. He decided to go to New Jersey and his safety was vouched for by New York Gov. George Clinton. In April of 1782,

Our Mutual Esteem and Regard

Sarah Jay's mother, Susannah French Livingston, wrote to her daughter from Elizabeth Town, New Jersey, believing that Sir James was a Revolutionary "Sir James Jay has been one of my family since the first of February. I often told him that he was in a very unsafe place, & that my house was in danger by him to be situated."[72] Susannah later reported that Sir James left several days later and was "carried into the king's lines." Was Sir James 'captured' by what seemed to be a pre-arrangement with the British in New Jersey?

    At this point, Sir James' loyalty to the Revolution came under suspicion by a number of Americans. Sir James was imprisoned in New York City but was released. Letters to John Jay and his wife, Sarah, about Sir James and his loyalties proliferated among the Jays' friends and colleagues. A month later, Gouveneur Morris wrote to John Jay "James is at large in New York."[73] That same month Robert R. Livingston, Jr. said of Sir James in a letter to John Jay "Sir James was taken to New York. It is said that he has gone to England, but it is not known whether he has gone as a prisoner or of his own accord."[74] By July, Alice Izard, wife of American Peace Commissioner Ralph Izard, wrote to Sarah Jay "Sir James has arrived in London."[75] Alice Izard's husband, Ralph, wasted no time in writing to Mrs. Jay as well in July of 1782 about Sir James "When I came home last evening I found a letter from a friend of mine in London, which confirms the information I saw in the Newspapers with regard to your brother, and to Sir James Jay, and adds farther, that Sir James was arrived in London, and that he came over in the last Packet from New York."[76]

    Newly arrived in London, Sir James wasted no time in writing to George Washington about his being exchanged for a certain Captain Eld of the British Guards who was attached to Lord Cornwallis and that Eld's father had been friendly to the American cause from the outset of hostilities.[77] At this point in time, Sir James seemed to consider himself a British prisoner and not a spy or Loyalist.

    Many of John Jay's relatives, friends and associates were concerned about the Sir James Jay episode, and did not hesitate to write to John Jay with every bit of information at hand. Robert R. Livingston, Jr. expressed his view of Sir James in a letter to John Jay "I for my part acquit him of everything but from imprudence - His going to England has given some credit to the assertions of his enemies - The State of New York has made on the ground of a resolution for vacating his seat."[78] At this time Gouverneur Morris again wrote to John Jay and expressed his views in no uncertain terms on the subject of Sir James "His political race like a new market horse has run round in a circle and brought him back to where he started."[79] Whatever effect these letters about Sir James had on John Jay, he still harbored no ill feelings towards his brother and remained reticent about his brother's loyalties when he wrote discreetly to Egbert Benson "Sir James is in England, but I know not in what capacity. I have not had a letter from him since I left Philadelphia."[80] Yet, Jay was not so discrete in a letter to his friend Peter Van Schaack. Jay did not mince words in commenting about what he considered to be his brother's defection "You mention my brother. If after having made so much Bustle in and for America, he has (as is surmised) improperly made his Peace with Britain, I shall endeavour to forget that my Father had such a Son."[81] John Jay had 'crossed the Rubicon' regarding his brother and his views would change very little over the coming years.

      Sir James, on the other hand, wrote to Benjamin Franklin about his "parole" and his "captivity" as well as his "exchange". Sir James spoke of "…some persons in London, in converting me into a Messenger of peace from Congress…."[82] and gave the impression that he was a prisoner and possible agent of the British and not a defector. Sir James spoke of his possible exchange for a Lieutenant Colonel, such as Col. Tarleton [the very colonel whose troops participated in the burning of Bedford] or Col. Dundee both of whom were taken prisoner at Yorktown. Sir James also wrote to John Adams about the suspicion that he was disloyal to America and claimed that it was not so.[83] What is known about Sir James is that he did not succeed in his plans to negotiate a reconciliation between America and England. Undaunted, he journeyed to the Hague before going to Paris with schemes that he

Our Mutual Esteem and Regard

hoped would interest the French. While in Holland, he wrote to his brother John but all that John Jay would say on the subject to his brother Frederick was "Sir James is in Holland and has written to me."[84] Once in Paris, Sir James contacted the French about a naval operation to disrupt British merchant ships and trade to embarrass the British government. Edmund Genet, a French Minister to America, recalled years later how Sir James would visit the house of Genet's father in Versailles and denounce his brother John claiming that John had opposed American independence, hated the French because of their treatment of his Huguenot ancestors and would negotiate a treaty with England establishing an alliance between the two countries.[85]
Nothing came of Sir James and his schemes and his doubtful change of mind. Some Americans considered him a spy. Others thought he was committing treason by attempting to negotiate a separate peace without portfolio or official sanction from Congress. One thing is certain, the two brothers never met while in Paris during the peace negotiations. However, not all Americans considered him to be a spy or traitor, otherwise why did Sir James attend to John Adams who had been stricken with a fever in September of 1783? Sir James bled Adams and cured him of his illness.[86] Even after the conclusion of the Treaty of Paris negotiations, John Jay returned to England but made no attempt to see or communicate with Sir James who had also returned to England. From London, Jay wrote to his nephew, Peter Jay Munro "Sir James Jay I am told is here, but I have not seen him."[87]

After his failed attempts in London and Paris, Sir James settled in England and practiced medicine until his return to America around 1784-85. He settled in New Jersey in the Tenafly, Hackensack area on land inherited from his aunt, Anne Chambers, which adjoined land owned by his brother Peter. Sir James lived with his children and his "companion", Nancy Erwin, who it is said declined to marry Sir James because of her adherence to the social philosophy of Mary Wollstonecraft for women's rights.[88]

Sir James continued to press Congress for payment of the $20,000 he loaned to James Mease at the outset of the

Revolutionary War. He traveled to Washington D.C. and petitioned Congress for repayment of his loan - *To the Honorable the Senate and House of Representatives in Congress Assembled (1813).* He also wrote a lengthy letter to Thomas Jefferson in 1806 in which he outlined in detail his contributions to the American cause as justification for repayment of the loan. As a result of these efforts, a settlement ultimately was made to him. It should be noted that some difference of opinion regarding Sir James and his war-time activities existed and may explain the settlement of the loan and why his property was never confiscated during the war.

Throughout John Jay's retirement, his son Peter Augustus acted as agent for his father. Peter had established a lucrative legal practice in New York City and performed many services for his father including that as an intermediary for his father and Sir James Jay. In March of 1809 Peter Augustus visited Sir James Jay at his office in New York City for the express purpose of settling the estate of Peter Jay, the father of John and Sir James. Sir James was a residuary legatee of the estate and when Peter Augustus offered Sir James a 'Receipt' 'Recd. New York 25 Feby 1809 of James Jay £226 8 Shlgs & 7 pence in full of the Balance due from him to me as of the Residuary Devises of our Father Peter Jay decd."[89] Sir James objected on the grounds that the settlement was in "<u>full</u>". Peter Augustus argued "…it was time a final Settlement shd take place…."[90] Sir James countered that he too thought it time for a settlement but also said "…he did not want the money and I [Peter Augustus Jay] might pay it or not as I pleased---"[91] The two exchanged words on the settlement due Sir James until Sir James changed the subject and inquired about John Jay's health and could John give Sir James an account of the history of their ancestors in France and other family matters. Several days later, Sir James and Peter Augustus met again and discussed the settlement of the estate. Sir James wanted to review John Jay's Account of the estate because Sir James harbored the notion that John had received more money from the estate than he was entitled to. After several days, Peter Augustus spoke with Sir James again and Sir James, after reviewing the Account, had agreed to settle the matter. After discussions back and forth, Sir James did sign a Receipt "Recd in New York March 2, 1809 of James Jay Esq. by the hands of Peter Augustus Jay £226 8/7 in full of my share of the Balance of the above account. JAMES JAY"[92] It is interesting to note that James did not use his title of 'Sir' when signing the agreement. However, the estate of Peter Jay was now settled with regard to James Jay's interest but not without rancor and personal observations and continued discussions about other family estates.

Several years later, Peter Augustus would conduct the final business concerning James Jay. On July 16, 1815 John Jay wrote to his son about his brother Sir James, "You did well to visit Sir James on hearing that he had been struck with the Palsy - I am glad that Report proved to be unfounded - as to Debility - it is to be expected by Persons of his age."[93] This was the first mention by John Jay of his brother in many years. Then on October 16th Peter Augustus wrote to his father from the Jay farm in Rye about events that had occurred in New Jersey, New York City and Rye the last few days:

>...I heard of the Death of Sir James, & as I was going to bed found a Note in the entry had been sent during my Absence from Sir James's son requesting to see me. The next morning I called on him. He told me of the loss of his Father & requested permission to bury him in the family burial ground. He was brought to town in the afternoon, & the burial service was read over him in Trinity Church by the Ep., nobody being present except his son & son in law, Mr. Munro, his two sons & myself. He had desired that his funeral be private. Yesterday he was brought here & interred. His son, Mr. O'Kelly & myself followed the Carriage. Mr. Munro had come on before & had the

> grave prepared. His son & son in law
> dined here & returned in the afternoon
> to town. Sir James since I saw him
> last summer had continued to grow
> weaker. For a fortnight past, it was
> perceived that he could not live long, &
> on Thursday last he expired. His
> son expressed great Regret at the
> Differences which subsisted between his
> father & son, & said that Sir James had
> declared to him, that he felt no sort of
> Resentment or Enmity towards you....[94]

Knowing that his father would want to receive this news as soon as possible, Peter Augustus had a servant deliver his note to John Jay at his farm in Bedford. When John Jay received his son's letter he replied:

> I have recd your Letter of this morning
> informing me of the Death of Sir James.
> This Event excites Feelings and
> Reflections too natural to be obvious.
> The Temper respecting me in which he
> died should extinguish Resentments on
> our part, and lead us to conciliatory
> Deportment towards his Family.[95]

John Jay saw to it that his letter was delivered to Peter Augustus by hand the next morning.

After so many years of rejecting his brother, John Jay finally realized that the proper and perhaps Christian thing to do was to relinquish the past and move on to normalize relations with his other family members. It is not difficult to realize why Jay felt as he did about his brother. Sir James was an intelligent man and gifted doctor of medicine but he was also proud and vain. His actions at times were precipitous, misguided and extreme, with dubious allegiance. During the Revolution, he took on the roles of inventor, would-be spy and diplomat. His attempts at negotiating a treaty of peace with England were nothing less than treason since he was not acting with the consent of Congress. Sir James succeeded only as an inventor. While John Jay was reserved and acted with circumspection and a sense of purpose, Sir James was the exact opposite. His clumsy and sometimes outrageous and treasonous attempts at diplomacy certainly did nothing to aid his fellow Americans who were the delegated peace commissioners. The tension between the two brothers dated back to John Jay's days as a student at Kings College when Sir James was embroiled in the controversy regarding the funds he had raised for Kings College with John's father urging his son John to 'vindicate' the reputation of his brother. In the end, John Jay was obviously overcome with emotion but moved on towards a normalization of relations with the family of Sir James.

    War, whether it was 'just and necessary' affected John Jay's public and private life. He never condemned the Loyalists for siding with the British during the Revolutionary War, realizing that people should be free to make their own decisions. Jay often came to the assistance of Loyalists, such as Col. James De Lancey, who received a royal commission and was imprisoned in a Hartford, Connecticut jail. Jay wrote about their early friendship "How far your situation may be comfortable and easy, I know not; it is my wish and shall be my endeavour that it be as much so as may be consistent with the interest of the great cause to which I have devoted everything I hold dear in the world;..."[96] The Phillipses, who were relatives of Jay, were Tories who emigrated but were not condemned by Jay. Many people struggled with their loyalties as did Dr. Beverly Robinson, who asked Jay to look after his family while contemplating his decision. Perhaps the knowledge of what his Huguenot ancestors had to endure convinced John Jay to pursue his course of action by not persecuting people for their beliefs. This view may also have arisen from Jay's commitment to one of the principal themes of the Revolution, in justice for all. When the war ended, Jay renewed many of his friendships with Loyalists who had made their choice based on principle. This enlightened and broadminded approach enabled Jay to maintain friendships throughout his life, including those who did not support American independence. He also worked for the return of some of his

Our Mutual Esteem and Regard

Loyalist friends to America. He never begrudged them for their decision to remain loyal to the Crown, as he fought what he considered a 'just and necessary war' for the cause of American independence. Jay always treasured and wanted to preserve the 'mutual esteem and regard' he had for his friends and the reciprocal feelings his friends had for John Jay.

Our Mutual Esteem and Regard

---

[1] Robert A. East and Jacob Judd eds. *The Loyalists of America: A Focus on Greater New York*. (Tarrytown, NY 1975), 49.

[2] Henry Cruger Van Schaack. *Memoirs of the Life of Henry Van Schaack.* (Chicago 1892), 15.

[3] Ibid, 38.

[4] Ibid, 46.

[5] Ibid, 50.

[6] Ibid, 73.

[7] Horace. *The Odes of Horace.* The entire line is *Caelum non animum qui trans mare currunt.* They change their sky, not their soul, who rush across the sea.

[8] JJWJ I: 93.

[9] Ibid, 94.

[10] Ibid.

[11] Ibid, 95

[12] Van Schaack. *Memoirs of the Life of Henry Van Schaack,* 313.

[13] East and Judd eds. *The Loyalists of America: A Focus on Greater New York,* 53.

[14] Peter Van Schaack to John Jay, 21 February 1786, JJCU.

[15] John Jay. *Circuit Court Diary.* 20 October, 1790, JJCU.

[16] John Jay to Peter Van Schaack, 23 January 1827, JJCU.

[17] Monaghan. *The Murrays of Murray Hill*, 25; Elizabeth Frank. *Memoirs of the Life and Writings Lindley Murray: in a Series of Letters, Written by Himself.* (New York, Philadelphia and Boston 1827), 12.

[18] Monaghan. *The Murrays of Murray Hill*, 21; Lyda Fens-de Zeeuw. *Lindley Murray (1745-1826) Quaker and Grammarian.* (Utrecht, Netherlands, 2011), 44.

[19] Monaghan. *The Murrays of Murray Hill*, 21.

[20] Frank. *Memoirs of the Life and Writings Lindley Murray: in a Series of Letters, Written by Himself,* 34.

[21] Monaghan. *The Murrays of Murray Hill*, 32.

[22] The Debating Society of New York, 22 January 1768, JJCU.

[23] Monaghan. *The Murrays of Murray Hill*, 45.

[24] Ibid, 56.

[25] Ibid, 58.

[26] Fens-de Zeeuw. *Lindley Murray (1745-1826) Quaker and Grammarian,* 46.

[27] Ibid, 47.

[28] Frank. *Memoirs of the Life and Writings Lindley Murray: in a Series of Letters, Written by Himself,* 62-3.

[29] Ibid, 88-9.

[30] Fens-de Zeeuw. *Lindley Murray (1745-1826) Quaker and Grammarian.* 54 -5.

[31] Ibid, 55.

[32] Lindley Murray to John Jay, 15 July 1794, JJCU.

[33] John Jay to Lindley Murray 22 August 1794, JJCU.

[34] Ibid.

[35] Ibid

[36] Ibid.

[37] Ibid.

[38] Ibid

[39] Ibid.

[40] HPJ. IV: 301.

[41] Monaghan. *The Murrays of Murray Hill*, 83.

[42] John Jay to Lindley Murray 24 April 1821, JJCU..

[43] Ibid.

[44] JJWS, 149.

[45] HPJ, II: 405.

[46] JJWS, 154.

[47] Ibid, 154-55.

[48] Mary Vaughan Marvin. *Benjamin Vaughan 1751-1835*. (Hallowell, Maine 1979), 19.

[49] JJWS, 161.

[50] John Jay to Benjamin Vaughan 30 November 1784, , *HPJ*, III: 134. Note *"quos deus vult perdere prius dementat"* Those whom a god wishes to destroy he first drives mad.

[51] Ibid.

[52] John Jay to Benjamin Vaughan, 2 September 1784; HPJ, III: 131-32.

[53] Benjamin Vaughan to John Jay, 4 August 1790, JJCU.

[54] Ibid.

[55] John Jay to James Monroe, 31 October 1794, JJCU.

[56] John Jay to John Vaughan, 31 July 1797, JJCU.

[57] Benjamin Vaughan to John Jay, 18 August 1797, JJCU.

[58] Ibid.

[59] John Jay to Benjamin Vaughan, 31 August 1797, JJCU.

[60] Marvin. *Benjamin Vaughan,* 93.

61 Ibid, 96.

62 Ibid, 92.

63 John Jay to Benjamin Vaughan, 4 January 1819, JJCU.

64 John Jay to Peter Augustus Jay, 19 October 1819, JJCU.

65 JJFM, 38.

66 John Jay to Sir James Jay 4 January 1776, JJCU..

67 JJFM, 166.

68 John Jay to Robert Morris 15 September 1776, 1JJRM, 315.

69 Sir James Jay to Thomas Jefferson. 14 April, 1806, *The Thomas Jefferson Papers Series 1. General Correspondence.* Library of Congress, Washington D.C..

70 George Washington to Sir James Jay, 9 April 1780, *The George Washington Papers at the Library of Congress, 1741-1799.* the Library of Congress, Washington, D. C..

71 Sir James Jay to Thomas Jefferson. 14 April, 1806, *The Thomas Jefferson Papers Series 1. General Correspondence.* Library of Congress, Washington D.C..

72 Susannah French Livingston to Sarah Jay, 21 April 1782, JJCU.

73 Gouveneur Morris to John Jay, 21 May 1782, JJCU.

74 Robert R. Livingston to John Jay, 22 May 1782, JJCU.

75 Alice Izard to Sarah Jay, 2 July 1782, JJCU.

76 Ralph Izard to Sarah Jay, 21 July 1782, HPJ, II: 320.

77 Sir James Jay to George Washington, 21 July 1782, *The George Washington Papers at the Library of Congress, 1741-1799*. Library of Congress, Washington, D. C.

78 Robert R. Livingston to John Jay, 17 September 1782, JJCU.

79 Gouveneur Morris to John Jay 6 August 1782, JJCU.

80 John Jay to Egbert Benson, 26 August 1782, JJCU.

81 John Jay to Peter Van Shaack, 17 September 1782, JJCU.

82 Sir James Jay to Benjamin Franklin, 27 October 1782, JJCU.

83 Sir James Jay to John Adams, 21 November 1782, JJCU.

84 John Jay to Frederick Jay 7 December 1782, JJCU.

85 JJFM, 215-16.

86 Page Smith. *John Adams*. (New York, 1962) Vol. I:580.

87 John Jay to Peter Jay Munro, 26 October 1783, JJCU.

88 Wells. *The Jay Family,* Footnote 24, page 17.

89 Peter Augustus Jay to John Jay 3 March 1809, JJCU.

90 Ibid.

[91] Ibid.

[92] Ibid.

[93] John Jay to Peter Augustus Jay 16 July 1815, JJCU.

[94] Peter Augustus Jay to John Jay 16 October 1815, JJCU.

[95] John Jay to Peter Augustus Jay 16 October 1815, JJCU.

[96] JJGP, 64 - 5.

Our Mutual Esteem and Regard

We are Blessed with Many Enjoyments

CHAPTER 6

In May of 1819, at the age of seventy-three, John Jay wrote to his friend and co-Federalist, Timothy Pickering, about his children and life in general "They are Affte to me and to each other; we all have reason to be thankful to Providence for placing us in a situation where we are blessed with many enjoyments."[1] Though Jay was plagued with rheumatism, a liver ailment and a bilious stomach, his mind was sound and he had many interests which extended to his family, his farm, and intellectual and religious pursuits along with visits and correspondence with friends. These interests and pursuits sustained and enriched Jay's life during his later years. His correspondence reflects a deep love for his family, as displayed in his poignant words to his daughter Maria "...that of again seeing you and the rest of my children around me excites the most fervent wishes."[2]

Jay took a keen interest in his grandchildren, particularly in their education. He held very strong views regarding education and while in Paris for the peace negotiations with Great Britain in 1782, he paused in his diplomatic mission to express his opinion on the education of children to Robert Morris:

> ...I think the Youth of every free civilized Country should, if possible, be educated in it; & not permitted to travel out of it, 'till age has made them so cool & firm, as to retain their national & moral Impressions - Connections founded at School & College have much influence, and are to be watched even at that Period - If judiciously formed, they will often endure and be advantageous thro' Life - American Youth may possibly form proper & perhaps useful Friendships in European Semenaries, but I think not so probably as among their Fellow Citizens, with whom they are to grow

up, whom it will be useful for them to know, and be early known, to, & with whom they are to be engaged in the business of active Life; and under the Eye and Direction of Parents, whose Advice Authority & Example are frequently of more worth, than the Lesson of hireling Professors, particularly on the Subjects of Religion Morality Virtue & Prudence -I fear that the Ideas which my Countrymen in general conceive of Europe are in many Respects rather too high - [3]

Jay's high regard for an American education was borne out with his own children. Peter Augustus Jay graduated from Kings College, like his father, and William Jay graduated from Yale College. Two of his daughters, Nancy and Maria, attended the Moravian School while another daughter, Sarah Louisa, attended an academy for women in Albany, New York. Jay's interest in the education of his family continued with his grandchildren as he took more than a passing interest in all aspects of their education He delighted in a letter from Peter's daughter, Sarah, to her 'Grandpa' outlining her course of studies in geography, grammar, Arithmetic, dictionary, French and music.[4] Sarah also thanked her 'grandpa' for the stockings he gave to her and expressed her hope of visiting Jay at Christmas.[5] With regard to Peter's son, John, and the boy's education, Jay had very specific ideas when he wrote to Peter "I do not know , or at least do not recollect, that John was learning French - if he attempts to learn many things at a Time, there will be some Risque of his making only a proportional Proficiency in any of them."[6] John Jay took a particular interest in Peter's son, especially when he exhibited a weakness that his Uncle William and Aunt Nancy suffered from "John's place in his Class is as high as I expected - I hear that his Eyes continue weak - I regret it more, as his Books may retard their Recovery."[7] On another occasion, Jay sent French books to Peter's children "I herewith send (by Calhoun) some little books

We are Blessed with Many Enjoyments

which may amuse and be useful to those of your children who are learning French - I have frequently heard them commended."[8] Although Peter Augustus had a thriving and lucrative law practice, John Jay saw fit to sending his son some money for his grandson, John "Apply one hundred Dollr towards John's education."[9] His interest in the education of Peter's children and Jay's doting on them is understandable from Jay's strong views regarding the superiority of an American education as opposed to a European education but also from a personal viewpoint. Maria had lost both of her children, Nancy never married and his other daughter, Sarah Louisa, had died very young. William and Augusta lived on the farm at Bedford where a school house had been built for their children's early education and a tutor was hired for them. It seemed only natural that Jay should be so attentive to his other grandchildren who were not by his side at Bedford.

Jay's health was a matter of much concern to his family as he struggled with his ailments which often confined him to the house. Maria offered some advice to her father on his health. She "...was disappointed on hearing from Augusta that you have only walked on the Piazza; so dear Papa ride out in the chair or Coachee, exercise is so very beneficial to one that I am very solicitous you should try it."[10] Maria also offered advice that her 'Sister Ann' should have a change of scene and consult her doctor about her weak eyes.[11] Maria's request for her father to take a ride was well within reason for Jay owned several horse drawn vehicles which would have befitted a gentleman of his wealth and position. In January of 1817, John Jay wrote to Philip Smith, the Receiver of Taxes for the Town of Bedford, in payment of the carriage tax due. Jay listed four carriages that he owned at the time and other pertinent details:

> 1 Coachee on Steel Springs, which in 1807 cost 336 Dolr & with the Harness belonging to it may be worth 200.7
> 2 A Travelling waggon without springs - in 1794 it cost 125 Dolr and may with the Harness be worth 100.2
> 3 A Sulkey with wooden Springs made

We are Blessed with Many Enjoyments

> about 30 Years ago with the Harness belonging to it may be worth 50.
> 1 4 A Gig on Steel Springs, which with the Harness may Yet be worth what they cost viz 200.4[12]

The Coachee was a large horse drawn carriage; the Sulkey was a light, open two-wheeled vehicle for one person drawn by one horse; the Gig was a one-horse light carriage that was a popular form of private transportation in America and Europe during the nineteenth century. The cost of the Coachee or Gig in today's value would be about $3,500. Carriage accidents, like today's automobile accidents, were not uncommon and proved to be dangerous as John Jay related such an incident to his son Peter Augustus that occurred on the road directly in front of the Jay farm:

> Yesterday as Maria and Nancy were returning from church in the Gig, & coming down the Hill between Reynolds property and our gate, the horse which William rode at a little distance behind them pressed forward rapidly - William unable to hold him in, was thrown & his head bruised - the Horse run against the gig and overset it- Maria escaped unhurt but Nancy was bruised.[13]

Accidents of this type were a common occurrence and dangerous. The doctor was sent for and bled Nancy and William who were recuperating rapidly by the next day.

The payment of the Carriage Tax was just one of the many tasks that John Jay attended to in the management of his farm. In 1822 Jay purchased two horses from a Mr. Redon, one of which turned out to be lame. In a series of letters over a period of twelve months, Jay recounted how he made every effort to improve the condition of the lame horse by pasturing the horse during the winter but after a drive with the traveling wagon in the spring, the horse was thought to be "tender footed."

We are Blessed with Many Enjoyments

    Jay continued to make improvements to the farm with the construction of stone walls around the property extending to the main road. An ice house was constructed along with the purchase of wood lots. Nancy Jay wrote to her sister-in-law, Mrs. Peter Augustus Jay "Yesterday they completed the stone wall around the whole farm on both sides of the road excepting across the lot in front of the house - that & straightening the road ...improves the appearance of the farm more than any thing which has been done in many years --."[14] "Straightening the road" and other maintenance projects were the property owner's responsibility. 'Pathmasters' were appointed by the Town for various stretches of road to see that the property owners worked so many days a year to maintain the road and assessments were made in lieu of money.[15] When the roads were impassible with deep snow in winter, stone boats or carts were hitched to a team of oxen, or whatever farm equipment was available, to clear the road . Jay often commented on the condition of roads during the winter being impassible due to heavy snow and "teams were turned out to break the Road in this neighborhood."

    John Jay was joined in taking an interest in the improvement of the farm when Nancy informed her sister-in-law of other work done to the property "Taking an interest in our improvements here you will be pleased to hear that the Ice house is verily begun, & if a substantial stone wall will confine ice, it will be secure. - Wm [William Jay] intends having a brick cistern made,...."[16] John Jay as well took great interest in the ice house for which he ordered two "Tin Boxes - one for Flesh, the other for Fish" for use in the ice house believing that Tin would serve as a better conductor of the cold rather than wooden boxes. Once the ice was gone, the tin boxes could be painted.[17]

    An extension to the main house was built in 1818 to provide additional living space for the family with William and Augusta's ever growing family. Jay always concerned himself with new crops and his correspondence is replete with references to new fruit and vegetables grown on the farm such as acorn squash and Valpariso squash. He often relayed Nancy's request for household items to Peter Augustus for purchases such as

We are Blessed with Many Enjoyments

dessert knives and forks and a spinning wheel. For himself, Jay was precise in his instructions for mild smoking tobacco, Dutch quills, and "...<u>good</u> cloth for a winter coat and two pair of breeches and also the like quantity of casimer (<u>single</u> fulled) for <u>Summer</u>. I wish there may be nothing of <u>Purple</u> in the color of either."[18] All of these goods were delivered, as usual, by a Hudson River sloop. Most of the goods ordered by the Jay family were delivered by Squire Wood who now owned two sloops, the *Delavan* and the *Volunteer*, out of Sing Sing. The goods were then delivered over land by ox cart to the Jay farm.[19]

    Jay also indulged in a popular diversion in America at the time - he purchased a lottery ticket. Lotteries dated back to the colonial period and were an easy way to raise funds throughout the colonies rather than raise taxes. The Pennsylvania Quakers objected to lotteries but Rev. William Ames gave them a religious blessing in a textbook used at Harvard and Yale universities when he stated that lotteries were permissible if used for 'pious use'.[20] Lottery proceeds were often used to build poorhouses and expand churches. Yale, Princeton and Columbia universities used them to fund the building of new colleges. It was also not unheard of for a slave who held a winning lottery ticket to purchase his freedom. The Second Continental Congress sanctioned a lottery to pay for defense and military spending. In the 1790's, various states authorized over 2,000 lotteries which sold over four million dollars in tickets annually. By 1793 there was a federal lottery to raise funds for the construction of Washington D.C. and George Washington purchased the first ticket.[21] Lotteries for a public cause were operated by private managers who charged a commission for each ticket sold. In one instance, Congress sanctioned a Grand National Lottery in 1823 for the benefit of Washington D.C. with a top prize of $100,000. The winner of the lottery had difficulty collecting the prize. The case was taken to the Supreme Court in 1827 which ordered the city of Washington D.C. to pay the amount due.[22]

    On occasion, lotteries were set up for the benefit of an individual. In 1826 the Virginia legislature authorized a special lottery for debt-ridden Thomas Jefferson with the top prize being

We are Blessed with Many Enjoyments

Monticello which was valued at $74,000. Jefferson died before the lottery was held but 11,480 tickets were sold at ten dollars each.

Lottery offices in New York City increased from 60 to 190 between 1819 and 1827. It was 1820 when Jay asked his son to purchase a ticket in a lottery for the promotion of literature as Peter Augustus wrote to his father "I have purchased for you at the place you desired a Lottery Ticket in the Lottery for the promotion of Literature. It is No. 4759."[23]

Yet Jay also found time in his old age to see to the needs and comforts of his servants and others carrying on a family tradition of beneficence towards those less fortunate. Under the Last Will and Testament of Peter Jay, John Jay's father, Peter Jay gave one of his slaves, named Mary, her choice of which family of Peter's children she chose to live with. It is uncertain which family Mary chose but in 1823, the daughter of Peter Augustus, Sarah, wrote to John Jay about her studies at school and she also wrote that "…old Mary is sick."[24] A few months later, John Jay wrote to his son Peter Augustus "… - I omitted to desire you when here to have Old Mary comfortably provided for in every Respect at MY Expense - …as she is a poor woman she will doubtless require frequent payments - monthly ones may therefore be proper - …."[25] On another occasion, Jay made a gift to the son of an unnamed family when he wrote to Peter Augustus "…I desired you to buy for me a case of mathematical Instruments convenient for a Surveyor - I wish to present it to the Son of a Family from whom I have for a long course of years recd more than ordinary marks of good will and friendly attention - buy such as would be proper for me to give."[26]

Even in retirement, Jay's stature as a public figure hardly diminished. He was often contacted by relatives of one of Jay's contemporaries requesting that Jay write a 'memoir' or biography of his colleague or friend. Historians also contacted Jay for clarification of some event he was privy to during his years of public service. Jay always courteously declined all such offers. However, he did respond to a request for a clarification of events to furnish the grandson of Col. Charles De Witt with any

We are Blessed with Many Enjoyments

'Documents and anecdotes' of the Colonel's service during the Revolution. To this request Jay responded with great respect and appreciation for the colonel's assistance during the Revolution 'This mark of attention to the memory of your worthy ancestor is commendable;' Jay recounted when at Kingston, New York for the state convention to draft the New York constitution, he frequently visited the Colonel at his home, Greenkill "That I always met with a cordial Reception, and that under his hospitable Roof we passed many agreeable hours together."[27] The British were advancing in New Jersey where Mrs. Jay was staying with her father. Jay asked the Colonel to help him find a horse in the area but since none was available, the Colonel gave Jay his plough horse and refused any compensation from Jay.

    Jay also gave letters of introduction where he thought appropriate as in the case of Mrs. S. Sydney Hewitt, the widow of Thomas Hewitt, whom Jay had met in London. Mrs. Hewitt came to America to claim her late husband's property and to seek custody of her daughter. She was in need of legal advice and wanted to consult with Peter Augustus Jay, referring to him as "a man of extensive law knowledge". While she had letters of introduction to such distinguished men in New York as John Livingston and Archibald Gracie, this was of no importance to Jay even though he did not recollect meeting Mrs. Hewitt in London some twenty years ago. He nevertheless gave her the requested letter to present to Peter Augustus Jay. Jay reasoned that since Mrs. Hewitt "…being abroad and a Stranger, are circumstances which afford claims to Kindness and attention."[28]

    Jay never lost sight of the importance of the cause of American independence and the establishment of the federal republic nor of his contributions to the Revolution and the new republic. He also realized the impact of the revolution and how it made possible all the blessings Americans enjoyed. On two separate occasions, John Jay and his daughter, Maria, paused to reflect on the meaning of July 4th celebrations. There were Independence Day celebrations in the town of Bedford, but there is no record of any of the Jays having attended. There is one account of the 1804 Independence Day celebrations in Bedford by

We are Blessed with Many Enjoyments

a resident, Mary Guion Brown, who spoke of 250 women marching for the occasion who then went to Col. Holly's house for tea and later that evening the gentlemen dined on the Village Green under a summer house specially erected for the event and that night there was a ball at Col. Holly's house.[29] In 1823 Maria was in New York on July 4th and spoke about "the firing ringing" and "so much noise" and "my patriotism will I hope enable me to support it." She also wrote eloquently and insightfully about her father's contributions to American independence:

> Few persons amid the clamour of noisy celebration can reflect with much pleasure on the event we this day commemorate as you my dear Papa must do in your quiet retirement & while your children rejoice in the civil & religious freedom of their country, they must always feel grateful that Providence was pleased to employ you as one of its most distinguished instruments in procuring these inestimable blessings - blessings contrasted with the despotism, superstition & degradation of most other nations, seems almost a foretaste of that far more glorious freedom from sin & pain in which we hope to enjoy a better Country.[30]

A few years later, John Jay received an invitation from the Corporation of the City of New York to join them in Manhattan for the fiftieth anniversary of the signing of the Declaration of Independence "with public demonstrations of respect and joy". While Jay declined to attend due to ill health, he did express his thoughts on the occasion:

> I cannot forbear to embrace the opportunity afforded by the present occasion, to express my earnest hope

We are Blessed with Many Enjoyments

> that the peace happiness and prosperity enjoyed by our beloved Country, may induce those who direct the national councils to <u>recommend</u> a general and public return of praise and thanksgiving to Him, for whose goodness these blessings descend. The most effectual means of securing the continuance of our civil and religious liberties is always to remember with reverence and gratitude the source from which they flow.[31]

In his own dignified, quiet and reflective manner, John Jay enjoyed and celebrated the blessings of American independence being commemorated on July 4th surrounded by his family in the rural quiet he so loved and had earned after years of selfless and tireless work for his country.

Jay was also able, despite his ill health and advancing age, to maintain an interest in a number of causes such as the promotion of agriculture, religion, manumission of slaves, American history, culture and education. His interest with some organizations was in the form of a donation or subscription to books, pamphlets and journals. His library shelves contained literature on many of these subjects including *The Biographical Dictionary*, *The American Observer*, *The New York State Papers*, *Discourse on the Religion of the Indian Tribes of North America*, Botta's *History of the War of American Independence* which was translated by George Alexander Otis, and *The American Farmer*. After receiving an unsolicited pamphlet, Jay might send a donation to the organization as in the case of a pamphlet entitled *School for the Education of Healthier Youth*. During his life, Jay amassed such an extensive pamphlet collection that his son William donated the collection to the New York Historical Society after the death of his father.

In some instances, Jay responded to the author or translator as in the case of Botta's *History* in which Jay took issue with some sections of the book concerning the loyalty of the

We are Blessed with Many Enjoyments

colonies to the crown. Jay wrote to George Alexander Otis, the translator, disputing this assumption "Explicit Professions and assurances of allegiance and loyalty to the sovereign (especially since the accession of King William), and of the affection for the mother country, abound in the journals of the colonial Legislatures, and of the Congresses and Conventions, from early periods to the second petition of Congress in 1775."[32] Jay then went on to state unequivocally about the movement in the colonies for independence "During the course of my life, and until the second petition of Congress in 1775, I never did hear any American of any class, or of any description, express a wish for the independence of the colonies."[33]

Jay subscribed to Noah Webster's dictionary and in a letter of encouragement to Webster, Jay advised him to be sure the manuscript should be "very legible" since Jay heard of a gentleman's manuscript being returned by the publisher who "had neither the time nor patience to decipher much of it". Jay also wrote that Webster's forthcoming work would "excite attention in both Britain and America, and produce useful consequences."[34]

Jay received honorary memberships in many organizations. The American Antiquarian Society which Jay considered a "patriotic Institution" for its maintenance of a research library in Worcester, Massachusetts focusing on American history, literature and culture bestowed such an honorarium on Jay. Another honorary membership bestowed on him was from the American Academy of Languages and Belles Lettres which strove to promote a democratic approach to the English language. Jay was also elected to the Board of the Commission for Foreign Missions and made periodic donations to the Commission for the establishment of missions in India. Jay believed that the Commission and others like it "become the Religion we profess and the Blessing we enjoy." His health always prevented Jay from active participation in the organizations but he willingly endorsed their goals. In 1819 Jay resigned as president of the Agricultural Society of Westchester and expressed his hope that the Society would continue to work in the interest and reputation of "our respectable Country."

We are Blessed with Many Enjoyments

In 1821, despite advancing age and illness, Jay accepted the position of President of the American Bible Society. Prior to the formation of the society, there were many regional organizations striving to distribute Bibles to the poor. Denominational concerns restricted the efforts of the various groups in achieving their goal. It was Elias Boudinot who promoted the formation of the American Bible Society and helped to unite people in the cause of Bibles for the poor. During the Revolution, Boudinot was president of the Second Continental Congress, worked towards the ratification of the Constitution in his native state of New Jersey and represented the state in Congress. He was known for his support of the rights of African Americans and Native Americans.

Boudinot's work to organize the American Bible Society was hampered by his age and health. Boudinot received a 16-page 'memoir' from William Jay of the Westchester Bible Society in which he proposed a constitution for the new society based on the one used by their British counterpart, the British and Foreign Society. While the Westchester Bible Society did not meet to select delegates to the national convention, William attended the Society's convention and was seated as a representative of the Westchester branch. Elias Boudinot was elected first president of the American Bible Society and William Jay was elected one of the thirty-six lay managers. There were three vice presidents and John Jay wrote to the Society's Secretary, Rev. Dr. Romeyn, which informed Jay of his election to a vice presidency which Jay accepted:

> I rejoice in the institution of that national society, and assure the Board of Managers that I am very sensible of the honour they have done me in thus connecting me with it. The events and circumstances under which such societies have been established and multiplied, in my opinion, indicate an origin which makes it the duty of all Christians to unite in giving them

> decided patronage and zealous support.[35]

These were certainly strong words of support and encouragement from Jay who was a model of circumspection all his life. It is a definitive statement from Jay on Christian duty and charity. In a postscript to the letter Jay wrote "I shall desire my son to subscribe for me the Sum assigned for a Director of Life."[36] The sum in question was $150 which, along with Jay's reputation, stature and religious zeal, may have contributed to his appointment.[37]

In 1821, Elias Boudinot died and John Jay was offered the position of president of the American Bible Society. At first he declined the position reasoning :

> It has long and uniformly been my opinion, that no person should accept of an office or place unless he be both able and willing to do the duties of it. This principle opposes my acceptance of the one in question. My health has been dwindling for twelve years past; my excursions from home have long been limited to short distances, such are my maladies that they often confine me to the house, and at times to my chamber; combined with the necessary infirmities of age, they allow me no prospect of convalescence. As President of the society, I should think I ought to be conversant with the proceedings, and not only attend their annual meetings, but also, at least occasionally, partake in the consultations and assist in the transactions of the board of managers. Were I in capacity to do the duties of the office, I should accept it without hesitation. I say without hesitation, because I should then as much doubt my

> having a right to decline, as I now doubt my having a right to accept it.[38]

The matter did not end there. Jay's family and the Board of the Society continued in trying to persuade Jay to accept the presidency but Jay was obdurate when he wrote to his son Peter Augustus Jay:

> As sinecure Places always had my Disapprobation, it appeared to me improper to accept of one - besides would not such a Precedent lead to some appointments - whether it would be prudent to Satisfactory, to dispense with the attendance of the Presidt as a matter <u>of Course</u> and to have it so understood, is a question which in my opinion should be previously well considered.[39]

Despite Jay's sense of duty, poor health and apprehension of setting an unacceptable precedent, he reconsidered and accepted when the Society agreed to dispense with Jay's attendance of the meetings. Instead, Jay submitted an address, similar to a sermon, to the Annual Meeting each spring, in which he praised the necessity of dispensing Bibles and his desire to promote "the attainment of its great and important objects". Jay regarded the Bible and its distribution as an important element of the passage from a "short term of existence here, into a state of life of endless duration." He praised the British and their Bible Society for setting such a fine example for other nations, including America. In his first Address of May 2, 1822, he spoke about slavery and the lack of action taken by Great Britain and America in spreading the Gospel until recently:

> Throughout many generations there have been professing Christians, who, under the countenance and authority of their respective governments, treated the heathen inhabitants of certain countries in Africa as articles of commerce;

We are Blessed with Many Enjoyments

> taking and transporting multitudes of them, like beasts of burden, to distant regions; to be sold, and to toil and die in slavery. During the continuance of such a traffic, with what consistence, grace, or prospect of success, could such Christians send missionaries to present the Bible, or preach the Christian doctrines of brotherly kindness and charity to the people of those countries?[40]

Jay also spoke of the failure of Great Britain with regard to its policy in India towards the native Indians "...yet it was deemed better policy to leave them in blindness than to risk incurring the inconveniences which might result from authorizing or encouraging attempts to relieve them from it."[41] Yet he praised the efforts of missionaries to learn foreign languages, the translation of the Bible into those languages and the establishment of schools "to receive and to diffuse the light of the Gospel."

In another Address, dated May 8, 1823, Jay spoke about the treatment of "the many savage nations who still remain within our limits" and an "indifference" to alleviate their condition noting that now many religious societies and pious individuals are working to bring civilization and Christianity to these people.[42] Continuing in that vein, the next year, his Address of May 13, 1824 focused on the distribution of Bibles to those people throughout the world who are "ignorant of the revealed will of God, and that they have strong claims to the sympathy and compassion which we, who are favored with it, feel and are manifesting for them."[43] He noted that despite the many sects that have arisen as a result of the Reformation, nothing should deter Christians from distributing Bibles "without note or comment." In his last Address to the Society dated May 12, 1825, Jay focused on the attempts of pious individuals to explain the mysteries of faith. Jay believed that these people "...did not recollect that no man can explain what no man can understand."[44] Jay reiterated his credo that the Bible reveals faith to us and is not to be subjected to

We are Blessed with Many Enjoyments

reasoning or any "mental abilities for explication." To Jay, the Redeemer commanded his apostles to preach the Gospel everywhere. To prepare them for this mission, they were blessed with the Holy Spirit. Some of these apostles committed their accounts to writing which are recorded in the Bible. Jay believed that the Bible:

> ...contains these writings, and exhibits such a connected series of the Divine revelations and dispensations respecting the present and future state of mankind, and so amply attested by internal and external evidence, that we have not reason to desire or expect that further miracles will be wrought to confirm the belief and confidence which they invite and require.[45]

Viewed in this light, Jay urged the Society to continue its work and through the zealous distributions of Bibles, the Gospel will be spread throughout the world. Of this, Jay stated unequivocally "That it will proceed, and in due time be accomplished, there can be no doubt...."[46] Jay's association with the American Bible Society was an extension of his deep religious convictions and enabled him to continue to expound on the treatment of slaves and subjugated people in America and India.

Jay's family was also instilled with a sense of commitment to help those less fortunate in Bedford which his family derived in some degree from Jay himself. In the years approaching the second decade of the nineteenth century, Bedford records show that there were several spiritual and civic organizations which enjoyed the support of the Jay family. Among the organizations were the Society for the Suppression of Horse Stealing; Westchester Auxiliary Bible Society; Society for the Suppression of Vice; Westchester Agricultural Society and the Bedford Female Charitable Society. William Jay was a founding member and Secretary of the Society for the Suppression of Vice which was a temperance organization and sought, with some success, to restrict the sale of alcoholic beverages on credit.[47]

We are Blessed with Many Enjoyments

Maria Jay Banyer was a devoted member of the Bedford Female Charitable Society which strove to assist the poor in Bedford through nursing and seeing to their other needs. Nancy and Maria were active in the Sunday school at St. Matthew's Church, driving the children to church in a wagon on Sunday. Jay's deep and abiding faith and sense of Christian charity had been passed on to his children and through them to the people of Bedford who benefited from the charitable endeavors of the Jays. In later years, all of his children would distinguish themselves in their efforts for equality and justice by their involvement in many charitable and worthy social causes.

While John Jay had many friends, it was his family's relationship with the Cooper family that spanned many decades and had far-reaching effects. William Cooper and John Jay attended school together and were "always very intimate."[48] Cooper speculated in land in Otsego County in upstate New York and became a wealthy frontier developer. In his acquisitions of land he was assisted by Goldsborough Banyer, Sr., who, during the colonial period, was the provincial secretary for the allocation of wilderness lands. Banyer was renowned for his influence in business transactions in the province, particularly in land patents. For his efforts, Banyer was given payments in the form of 'kickbacks' from the speculators he assisted and he became a wealthy man.

Judge Cooper founded the town of Otsego, later renamed Cooperstown, near Otsego Lake. It was here that he built his home, Otsego Hall, on a hill overlooking the lake. He was appointed a County judge. He was a Federalist and served in Congress for three terms. A staunch supporter of John Jay's gubernatorial candidacy, Judge Cooper no doubt joined in the celebration of the election of John Jay as Governor of New York State when the citizens of Cooperstown gathered instantaneously to celebrate Jay's election.[49] After the death of Maria's husband, Goldsborough Banyer, Jr., Judge Cooper offered to assist her in the administration of the estate. Jay reflected with a measure of relief and assurance when he commented on Maria's situation "…it wd be a consolation to reflect that in case Difficulties shd arise, she might depend on his and his son's assistance - They appear to be perfectly disposed."[50] When Judge Cooper died in December of 1809, John Jay commented "...in him we have lost a Friend,....."[51]

Judge Cooper's son, James Fenimore Cooper, had attended school with William Jay and the two became good friends. James Cooper was expelled from Yale and entered the merchant trade as a 'sailor before the mast' in preparation for a career in the United States Navy. He was commissioned a Midshipman but resigned his commission when he married Susan Augusta De Lancey. They lived in Cooperstown for a while but settled in Scarsdale, in Westchester County, on property given to his wife by her father. James had issues with his family and his wife's family. The Cooper family lived at the house, Angevine, which he built on Heathcote Hill, in Scarsdale, after the collapse of his family's fortune. He was able to maintain his family with the produce from the farm and was also a member of the Westchester Agricultural Society.

His grandson, James Fenimore Cooper, related how his grandfather often read to the family in the evenings at Angevine. One evening, when Cooper was reading a new British novel to his family, he became so disgusted by the book and tossed it aside exclaiming "I could write you a better book than that myself!"[52] His wife scoffed at the idea, but Cooper, who was known to dislike writing even a letter, began to work on a novel and was later encouraged by his wife to have it published. She had read every page of the novel and thereafter, continued the practice of reading every subsequent novel her husband wrote, from cover to cover.

Prior to 1820, most Americans preferred to read novels imported from England. Copyright laws being what they were, it was more profitable for American publishers to reprint English novels than to pay American novelists royalties for their own work. Undeterred, Cooper decided to visit the Jay family at their farm in Bedford, which was twenty-five miles north of the Cooper farm in Scarsdale, for the purpose of reading his novel to them to gauge their reaction. Cooper thought that Maria Jay Banyer's

We are Blessed with Many Enjoyments

taste and judgment were critical in matters literary. Maria Banyer was a friend of the Coopers and her late husband, Goldsborough Banyer, Jr., was also well acquainted with the Cooper family. Maria and her husband spent part of their wedding trip at Otsego Hall and she spoke of her visit to the manor house and the view of Lake Otsego with warm memories. Cooper also had a great respect for John Jay and commented on his reception of local farmers at his farm in Bedford, noting how courteously Jay comported himself.[53]

On one occasion, Cooper, accompanied by his wife and daughter, Susan, and his son, James, Cooper read his novel, *Precaution* to the Jays in the parlor under a pseudonym. Only one or two people knew the true identity of the author. The Jays and their company, a Miss McDonald, approved of the book with Miss McDonald stating that the book seemed familiar and that she may have read it before. The reason for this reaction from the Jay's friend is understandable in that Cooper deliberately modeled his book after those of successful contemporary English novels written by Jane Austen and Amelia Opie. The book dealt with the "precaution" taken by three families to find suitable husbands for their daughters. The book was published but it was not a success and probably lost Cooper some money. He was undeterred and resolved to write a truly American novel.

He had been to Jay's farm at Bedford on a number of occasions and on August 31, 1820, Cooper again visited John Jay. As the two men, along with William Jay, sat on the piazza of the house, Jay spoke of a man he employed during the American Revolution to operate as a spy in Westchester County, then referred to as the Neutral Ground. Jay related the self-less patriotism of this man and according to the Cooper family, Jay never disclosed the name of the spy, even though a controversy erupted years later over the identity of this spy who some believed to be a man named Enoch Crosby. Cooper never believed the man in question was Enoch Crosby.[54] Several years after the publication of Cooper's book, *The Spy: A Tale of the Neutral Ground*, which Cooper based on his conversation with John Jay on the piazza of Jay's farm, another book appeared, *The Spy*

We are Blessed with Many Enjoyments

Unmasked; or, Memoirs of Enoch Crosby; alias Harvey Birch, the Hero of Mr. Cooper's Tale of the Neutral Ground. The book was written by H.L. Barnum who asserted that Enoch Crosby was the model for Harvey Birch, Cooper's spy in his novel. In 1832 Enoch Crosby swore in a deposition submitted for his application for a federal pension about his activities as a spy and affidavits in support of his assertions were part of the proceeding. Crosby's claim was even backed up by the minutes of the Committee for Detecting Conspiracies taken by John Jay in his own hand. As late as 1850, Cooper was still denying that Enoch Crosby was the spy, Harvey Birch, in his novel.[55] Cooper's daughter, Susan, wrote that her father's conversation with John Jay was his sole and only inspiration for the character of Harvey Birch and that Cooper had "invented every incident in the book" except for one brief anecdote related by Jay and that Cooper "never for a moment believed that Enoch Crosby was the man."[56]

Jay had employed many agents in his network of spies during the American Revolution. In 1776, the New York State Convention, fearing a Tory uprising, appointed a committee of five headed by Jay for counter-intelligence operations.[57] About ten or more agents worked for the committee gathering intelligence, including Enoch Crosby, Martin Cornwill, Nicholas Brower, John Haines, Benjamin Pitcher, William Delaney, Henry Wooden, Joseph Bennett, Elijah Frost, Samuel Hopkins and Elijah Hunter.

Only two people knew with certainty whether Enoch Crosby was the role model for Harvey Birch - Jay and Cooper. Jay never divulged the name of the agent to Cooper during their conversation nor at any other time and Cooper never believed that Enoch Crosby was Harvey Birch.

Jay's anecdote was certainly the inspiration for Cooper's novel. Cooper did incorporate much of what Jay told him about the Neutral Ground into his novel, *The Spy: A Tale of the Neutral Ground*, which became a best selling novel. The book was published in late 1820. Despite its expensive price of $2 per copy, the first 1,000 copies sold out in one month. By the end of 1821, 6,000 more copies had been ordered and Cooper's royalties of

We are Blessed with Many Enjoyments

$4,000 were a tribute to the extraordinary success of the novel. Cooper did take inspiration from Jay when he set the novel in Westchester county at a country house named the Locusts with a black servant named Caesar. The Locusts was the name of the Rye farm owned by Jay's father where Jay grew up and Caesar was a servant there. Cooper also had the countryside plagued with "Cowboys" riding and plundering for the King and the "Skinners" who did likewise for Congress as well as a spy named Harvey Birch.

After Jay's death in 1829, Cooper revised the introduction to his novel and related the facts concerning the publication of his book. Cooper also spoke of Jay's 'anecdote' in which Jay spoke of his personal encounter with one of his agents. Cooper never mentioned Jay by name in his revised introduction but referred to him as "an illustrious man." Part of the tale told to him by Jay is interesting:

> In the year ----, Mr.___ was named to a high and honorable employment at a European court. Before vacating his seat in Congress, he reported to that body an outline of the circumstances related, suppressing the name of his agent, and demanding an appropriation in behalf of a man who had been of so much use, at so great risk. A suitable sum was voted, and its delivery was confided to the chairman of the secret committee.[58]

Cooper then continued his account of Jay's meeting at midnight in a wood with the secret agent to give him the bag of gold voted by Congress. The agent refused the gold saying that "The country has need of all its means."[59] and he could always earn a livelihood. Jay left with the bag of gold in his hand and a "deep respect" for the patriotic and brave man who had risked his life on so many occasions for his country. Several years later, the agent did consent to receive "remuneration" for his efforts at a time when his country was in a position to act accordingly. This revised introduction written by Cooper appears in many editions of *The Spy* to this day.

Cooper owed Jay a great debt while never acknowledging him publicly as the person who related the 'anecdote' to him and for giving him inspiration for another novel. A letter Jay wrote to Col. John Laurens from Madrid dated May 2, 1781, details a plot to capture prisoners on the coasts of Great Britain during the Revolutionary War. The prisoners were to be exchanged for Henry Laurens, the colonel's father, who was captured by the British while on a diplomatic mission in 1780 and held captive in the Tower of London. Such a plot is detailed by Cooper in a later and successful novel entitled, *The Pilot,* which was published in 1824.[60]

In 1820 William Jay was appointed First Judge of Westchester County, a position he held until 1842 when he was removed from the bench due to his strong abolitionist views. On June 20th of that year William Jay wrote to Cooper "I see by the papers rcd by the last mail, that I am appointed First Judge. I am very sensible of the friendly part you have taken in procuring this appointment for me;"[61] It appears that Cooper was a loyal friend to William Jay throughout their lives and did what he could to assist his friend.

To this day, James Fenimore Cooper remains one of America's greatest novelists. His writings were the first to have a decidedly American plot and New World characters. Yet on another level, Cooper, from his visits to Bedford, has given us an in depth account of John Jay's farm and of Jay himself in his book *Notions of the Americans: Picked up by a Travelling Bachelor.* Cooper wrote the book at the urging of the Marquis de Lafayette as an account of his triumphal visit to America in 1824-1825. Cooper used Lafayette's visit as a backdrop for the book which closely examined American society and government in the mid to late 1820's. In the book, an unnamed Belgian bachelor, based on Lafayette, is escorted on his travels through America by an American named Cadwallader. The book is comprehensive in describing every aspect of life in America at the time. Although the book was not a commercial success, being considered too

We are Blessed with Many Enjoyments

American, Cooper's work is accurate and comprehensive. The chapters, *The Dwelling of Mr. Jay, Armorial Bearings and Liveries, Etc., Simple and Dignified Habits of Mr. Jay* and *Notions of the Employment of Mr. J*ay were based on Cooper's own observations and experiences of Jay's unassuming house and household as Cooper wrote:

> In point of size and convenience the dwelling of this distinguished American is about on a level with a third-rate English country house, or a second-rate French chateau. It has most of the comforts of the former, with some luxuries that are not easy to obtain in your island, and it is consequently both inferior and superior to the latter, in very many particulars. There is a mixture of use and appearance in the disposition of the grounds, that I am inclined to think very common about the residences of gentlemen of this country. The farm buildings, &c., though a little removed, were in plain view, as if their proprietor, while he was willing to escape from the inconveniences of a closer proximity, found a pleasure in keeping them at all times under his immediate eye. The house itself was partly of stone, and partly of wood, it having been built at different periods; but, as is usual here, with most of the better sort of dwellings, it was painted, and having a comfortable and spacious piazza along its façade, another common practice in this climate, it is not without some pretension externally; still its exterior, as well as its internal character, is that of respectable comfort,

We are Blessed with Many Enjoyments

rather than of elegance, or show. The interior arrangement of this, no less than of most of the houses I have entered here, are decidedly of an English character. The furniture is commonly of mahogany, and carpets almost universally prevail, summer and winter. There is a great air of abundance in the houses of the Americans generally, and in those of the wealthy, it is mingled with something that we are apt to consider luxurious. I might have counted ten or twelve domestics about the establishment of Mr. Jay, all quiet, orderly, and respectful. They were both white and black. You probably know that the latter are all free here, slavery having been virtually abolished in New York. The servants wore no liveries, nor did I see many that did out of the city of New York. Though sometimes given, even there, they are far from frequent. They are always exceedingly plain, rarely amounting to more than a round hat with a gold or a silver band, and a coat, with cuffs and collars faced with a different cloth. Armorial bearings on carriages are much more frequent, though Cadwallader tells me it is getting to be more genteel to do without them. He says the most ancient and honorable families, those whose descent is universally known, are the first to neglect their use. I saw the carriages of Mr. Jay, but their pannels were without blazonry. I remarked, however, ancient plate in the house that

We are Blessed with Many Enjoyments

> bore those European marks of an honorable name, and which I did not hesitate to refer to the period of the colonial government. Mr. Jay himself is of French descent, his ancestor having been a refugee from the religious persecution that succeeded the revocation of the edict of Nantes.[62]

Cooper then turned his attention to Jay and his family:

> I scarcely remember to have mingled with any family, where there was a more happy union of quiet decorum, and high courtesy, than I met beneath the roof of Mr. Jay. The venerable statesman himself is distinguished, as much now, for his dignified simplicity, as he was, formerly, for his political sagacity, integrity, and firmness. By one class of his countrymen, he is never spoken of without the profoundest respect. It is evident that there are some who have been accustomed to oppose him, though it is not difficult to see that they begin to wonder why. During my short stay beneath this hospitable roof, several of the yeomanry came to make visits of respect, or of business, to their distinguished neighbour. Their reception was frank and cordial, each man receiving the hand of the "Governor," as he is called, thought it was quite evident that all approached him with the reverence a great man can only inspire. For my own part, I confess, I thought is a beautiful sight to see one who had mingled in the councils of nations, who had instructed

> a foreign minister in his own policy, and who had borne himself with high honour and lasting credit in the courts of mighty sovereigns, soothing the evening of his days by these little acts of bland courtesy, which, while they elevated others, in no respect subtracted from his own glory. His age and infirmities prevented as much intercourse as I could have wished with such a man, but the little he did communicate on the scenes in which he had been an actor, was uttered with so much clearness, simplicity, modesty, and discretion, that one was left to regret he could hear no more."[63]

Cooper also commented on a mistaken impression that had arisen regarding Jay's interests during retirement which were generally believed to be "writing on the prophesies" concerning recent English books on the Apocalypse. Cooper adamantly argued that Jay had a "sense of the fruitlessness of any inquiry, at the present hour, into their hidden meaning." Cooper then expounded on Jay, his retirement avocations and his character:

> I am rather inclined to think, that as this eminent man has endeavoured so to model his life, that he may be prepared for any and every development of the mighty mystery, some curious, but incompetent observers of his habits have mistaken his motive, attributing that to a love of theory, which might, with more justice, be ascribed to the humbler and safer cause of practice. And here I must bid adieu to this estimable statesman; but before I take leave of you, I will mention a queer enough instance of the vagaries of the

We are Blessed with Many Enjoyments

> human mind, which has recently come under my observation, and which is oddly enough recalled by the connexion between Mr. Jay and his fancied avocations in retirement. It furnishes another proof of the precarious quality of all conjecture.[64]

Cooper certainly gave an insightful rendering of John Jay in retirement, evincing an estimable respect and admiration for Jay. Such first hand accounts of Jay and his farm in Bedford are rare and support the evidence that John Jay lead a life in the country of many varied interests and occupations, despite his physical handicaps. Cooper wrote of Jay's "dignified simplicity" and his "clearness, simplicity, modesty, and discretion," with which Jay spoke to visitors and of the "respectable comfort" of his house. It is in these passages that Cooper reinforces the assessment of John Jay by some of his contemporaries and future biographers as that of a Founding Father living in quiet simplicity and enjoying the liberties he worked so long and hard to achieve for his country while retaining a deep interest and commitment to varied social causes.

Jay had achieved his goal of retirement in the country. He was surrounded by his family, whom he doted on, and attended by loyal servants. Jay maintained an active interest in the management of his farm. He received visits from former colleagues and admirers from near and far. Jay also gave of his time to various organizations and causes and in several cases, his active participation. He lived simply but well and passed on his compassion for those in lesser circumstances to his family as well as setting an example for them to work for equality and justice. Jay continued to be a deeply pious individual in a quiet and respectful way. He was relieved of his long-term commitment to his country and devoted himself to living a simple life with his family in the country. He was a person who was truly blessed with 'many enjoyments' during his retirement years on his beloved farm in Bedford.

We are Blessed with Many Enjoyments

1 John Jay to Timothy Pickering, 17 May 1819, JJCU.

2 John Jay to Maria Jay Banyer, 22 February 1814, JJCU.

3 John Jay to Robert Morris, 13 October 1782, JJCU.

4 Sarah Jay to John Jay, 11 November 1823, JJCU.

5 Ibid.

6 John Jay to Peter Augustus Jay, 17 February 1818, JJCU.

7 John Jay to Peter Augustus Jay, 30 October, 1820, JJCU.

8 John Jay to Peter Augustus Jay, 6 January 1824, JJCU.

9 John Jay to Peter Augustus Jay, 16 November 1824, JJCU.

10 Maria Jay Banyer to John Jay, 3 May 1821, JJCU.

11 Ibid.

12 John Jay to Philip Smith, Town of Bedford Receiver of Taxes, 7 January 1817, JJCU.

13 John Jay to Peter Augustus Jay, 7 September 1818, JJCU.

14 Ann Jay to Mary Rutherford Clarkson Jay, 21 September 1819, JJH.

15 Duncombe et al. *Katonah The History of a New York Village and its People,* 59-60.

16 Ann Jay to Mary Rutherford Clarkson, Jay 31 September 1819, JJH.

We are Blessed with Many Enjoyments

[17] John Jay to Maria Jay Banyer, 1 May 1821, JJCU.

[18] John Jay to Peter Augustus Jay, 10 May 1824, JJCU.

[19] Duncombe et al. *Katonah The History of a New York Village and its People,* 90-1.

[20] David G. Schwartz. *The History of Gambling Roll the Bones.* (New York 2006), 144.

[21] Ibid 145-8.

[22] Ibid. 148.

[23] Peter Augustus Jay to John Jay, 12 May 1820, JJCU.

[24] Sarah Jay to John Jay, 11 November 1823, JJCU.

[25] John Jay to Peter Augustus Jay, 4 November 1824, JJCU.

[26] John Jay to Peter Augustus Jay, 27 November 1821, JJCU.

[27] John Jay to Charles Gerrit De Witt, 18 August 1823, JJCU.

[28] John Jay to Mrs. S. Sydney Hewitt, 20 May 1816, JJCU.

[29] Massi. *The Story of Mary Guion Brown From Her Diary of 1800-1852,* 70.

[30] Maria Jay Banyer to John Jay 4 July 1823, JJCU.

[31] John Jay to Jacob Morton, Clerk The Corporation of the City of New York, 29 June 1826, JJCU.

[32] John Jay to George Alexander Otis, 13 January 1821, JJCU.

[33] Ibid.

[34] Johnston. *The Correspondence and Public Papers of John Jay.* IV: 458.

[35] John Jay to Rev. Dr. John Brodehead Romeyn 12 June 1816, JJCU.

[36] Ibid.

[37] Budney. *William Jay Abolitionist and Anticolonial,* 17.

[38] Johnston. *The Correspondence and Public Papers of John Jay.* IV: 460.

[39] John Jay to Peter Augustus Jay, 14 January 1822, JJCU.

[40] Johnston. *The Correspondence and Public Papers of John Jay.* IV: 483.

[41] Ibid, 484.

[42] Ibid, 491.

[43] Johnston. *The Correspondence and Public Papers of John Jay.* IV: 493.

[44] Johnston. *The Correspondence and Public Papers of John Jay.* IV: 502.

[45] Ibid, 504.

[46] Ibid.

47 Bayard Tuckerman. *William Jay and the Constitutional Movement for the Abolition of Slavery.* (New York, 1893), 10; Budney. *William Jay Abolitionist & Anticolonialist,* 16.

48 Cooper ed.. *Correspondence of James Fenimore Cooper.* I: 40.

49 Alan Taylor. *William Cooper's Town Power and Persuasion on the Frontier of the Early American Republic.* (New York 1995), 196.

50 John Jay to Ann Jay, 19 July 1806, JJCU.

51 John Jay to Peter Augustus Jay, 10 January 1810, JJCU.

52 Cooper ed.. *Correspondence of James Fenimore Cooper.* I: 38.

53 Taylor. *William Cooper's Town Power and Persuasion on the Frontier of the Early American Republic,* 144.

54 Cooper ed.. *Correspondence of James Fenimore Cooper.* I: 42.

55 Morris. *John Jay The Making of a Revolutionary,* 334.

56 Ibid.

57 Monaghan. *John Jay,* 91.

58 James Fenimore Cooper. Introduction to *The Spy; A Tale of the Neutral Ground.* (New York 1831).

59 Ibid.

60 Jack Kligerman. *Notes on Cooper's Debt to John Jay.* American Literature 41:3, 415-19 (1969).

[61] Cooper ed.. *Correspondence of James Fenimore Cooper.* I: 88.

[62] James Fenimore Cooper. *Notions of the Americans Picked Up By a Traveling Bachelor, Vols. I &II.* (New York 1828) I:85-6.

[63] Ibid, I: 88.

[64] Ibid, I: 89.

The Last Inn

CHAPTER 7

In the first years of his retirement to Bedford, John Jay wrote to his friend Lindley Murray "I flatter myself that this is the last inn at which I am to stop in my journey through life."[1] He once again commented on "...the necessity and value of patience and resignation."[2] During Jay's years at Bedford, death had claimed his six siblings, his wife, his youngest daughter and Maria's husband and children. Many of his friends and compatriots had passed to a 'better place' including Washington, Hamilton, Judge Cushing of the Supreme Court, Judge William Cooper, Robert Morris and Pres. John Adams. In 1821 Jay wrote to Adams reflecting on their station in life and expounded on the virtues of 'patience and resignation':

> At the age in which you have arrived, I believe very few enjoy an equal Exemption from its usual Infirmities - Your Hand indeed is not now as formerly the Hand of a ready Writer, but you still retain a more than common degree of general Health - In these Respects I have been less favored - For twelve years past I have not had one well Day - an incurable obstruction of the Liver has gradually reduced me to an emaciated and feeble state; and severe attacks of Rheumatism frequently produce much pain. It rarely happens that the maladies and infirmities which generally accompany old age, will yield to medical Skill - but happily for us Patience & Resignation are excellent Palliatives.[3]

While Jay's maladies were treated with 'patience and resignation', he retained his intellectual acumen and exhibited an interest in diverse projects.

One interest of his was the construction of the much

The Last Inn

anticipated Erie Canal begun in 1817 and completed in 1825. Peter Augustus Jay, a representative to the New York State Assembly, was an ardent supporter of the canal realizing that trade with the west consisting of Ohio, Indiana, Illinois and much of Kentucky would be centered in Albany. Peter's brother, William Jay, was also a supporter of the Erie Canal. He visited the construction site and thought the canal was awesome and one of the most praiseworthy undertakings in North America.[4] William also realized the vast opportunities for investment in roads, canals, turnpikes and railroads that the canal afforded though he preferred a 'coach and four' to the rattling wheels, smoke and the 20 mile and hour speed of a train engine.[5]

The 363 miles of the canal ran from Albany to Buffalo and created a navigable water route from New York City and the Atlantic Ocean to the Great Lakes. The canal made it possible for New York City to surpass Philadelphia as the largest city and port on the eastern seacoast. During his tenure as governor, Jay supported the construction of canals in New York State but on a modest scale. As parts of the Erie Canal were completed, they were opened to the public and for trade. In 1821, Maria wrote to her father about her trip to upstate New York and Niagara Falls and her ride on the Erie Canal:

> ... we embarked on the Canal in a neat boat about 70 feet long; it was towed by two horses which are exchanged every two miles; - we glided along very pleasantly at the rate of 4 miles an hour. We passed thro' six locks, the first in the night which I saw thro' the window of my berth; it looked as if we were sinking into a large dungeon. Having traveled 56 miles in this way we left the canal, but as all who love their Country feel an interest in its success, I know you will be pleased to hear that so far it has answered the most sanguine expectations of its friends.[6]

The Last Inn

Maria also commented on the difficulties of the construction of the canal "It seems almost incredible that the Canal can be carried thro'; near Genesee river it must be dug 25 feet deep thro' solid rock for 3 miles."[7] Her extensive description of the canal no doubt delighted Jay. As governor, some of his friends had invested in the construction of canals but with little profit. Jay must have been gratified with the letter from Maria and her account of its immediate success. When the Erie Canal was officially opened in 1825, the Corporation of the City of New York sent John Jay a medal "...as a tribute of respect for your distinguished public services , and private virtues." along with a copy of a memoir on the New York Canals.[8]

He continued his interest in agriculture with a subscription to the *American Farmer* and when a storm in September of 1821 destroyed fifty fruit trees, willows and a locust grove at Bedford and Rye, Jay undoubtedly took an interest in the restoration.

Yet Jay was discreet with regard to his subscriptions to journals as when the editor of the *Columbian* sent Jay a paper entitled *The New York Journal a Patron of Industry.* Jay declined the latter stating "Having still more weekly news papers than are useful or interesting" and instructed his son Peter Augustus to discontinue another journal *The American* after the expiration of his subscription.[9]

Jay continued to be consulted on matters of importance and in 1821 Gov. Ethan Allen Brown of Ohio sent Jay a Report on the Joint Committee of both houses of the Ohio Legislature concerning the Second Bank of the United States. Brown was born in Connecticut on July 4, 1776 to loyal supporters of the Revolution and was named after Ethan Allen, who lead the Green Mountain Boys who distinguished themselves in capturing Fort Ticonderoga for the Americans. He studied law under Alexander Hamilton and left New York for Ohio to claim some land his father wanted for investment purposes. He established a law practice in Cincinnati and in 1810 was soon elected to the state's Supreme Court. Although Hamilton, his mentor, was a Federalist, Brown became a member of the Democratic-Republican party . He was lauded for his integrity and the fairness of his rulings, but

The Last Inn

he chose to run for governor of Ohio and was easily elected in 1818.

At the time Gov. Brown wrote to Jay, the country was in the midst of a post-war depression precipitated by the Panic of 1819. The Second Bank of the United States had engaged in inflationary practices with the issuance of paper money. Specie was scarce since American imports of foreign goods exceeded its exports. Unemployment was exacerbated by low-cost imports which caused many American factories to close. The Bank was also a part of the sale of public land in the west which was encouraged by the federal government. Land was auctioned at a price of about $2 per acre with a down payment of one-fourth of the total cost. The balance was to be paid in four annual payments with forfeiture if the loan was not paid in full after five years.[10] The public debt rose from $3 million to $17 million by 1818.[11]

The Bank had eighteen branch offices which were operated with very little oversight from the main branch in Philadelphia rather than by the U.S .Treasury.[12] These banks accepted bank notes as loan payments and issued paper money lacking sufficient specie reserves.[13] By 1818 the Bank had liabilities of $22.4 million with specie funds of $2.4.[14] It was then that the Bank tightened its credit policies and ordered its branch offices to reject all state chartered bank notes.[15] State chartered banks called in the loans on the mortgaged land financed by them. Cash poor farmers, unable to pay their loans found the banks foreclosing on their loans. President Monroe tried to alleviate some of the problems for the farmers by proposing legislation that was passed by Congress in 1821 - the Relief for Public Land Debtors Act. The act allowed debtors to keep the land they had paid for and to surrender the remaining land. Debtors were also given more time to pay off their loans with a discount for early payment. All of these factors contributed to the Panic of 1819 which was sparked by the precipitous drop in the price of American cotton by 25% in one day due to England flooding the U.S. market with inexpensive cotton.

Gov. Brown and many people in the country blamed the Panic on the Bank. The Bank's local branch in Chillicothe, Ohio

The Last Inn

refused to take state issued paper money unless it was backed by specie. Many farmers in the state could not pay their debts due to the shortage of specie in circulation. The Ohio State Legislature sought to reduce the power of the Bank's Ohio branch by passing a law taxing the local branches in Ohio. The legislature authorized the seizure of $50,000 from the two branches of the Bank in payment of taxes due. The federal government sued the state of Ohio in the U.S. Supreme Court, *Osborn v. Bank of the United States (1824)*. The Court ruled that taxing the National Bank was unconstitutional.[16]

    Gov. Brown had sent Jay a report of the joint committee of both houses of the Ohio legislature regarding certain proceedings of the Bank of the United States. Jay responded to Brown's letter and the report in April of 1821 with an insightful discussion of taxation of property, income and the need for those powers given to the State governments and the national government to be "well ascertained and observed":

> However extensive the constitutional Power of a Govermt to impose Taxes may be, I think it should not be so exercised as to impede or discharge the lawful & <u>useful</u> Industry and Exertions of Individuals. Hence the Prudence of taxing Products should extend only to Property - or only to Income - or to both - are Points on which opinions have not been uniform. I am inclined to think that both should not be taxed - If the first is preferred, then tax the Land and the Stock of a Farmer, but not his Crops - tax his milk cows, but not their milk, nor the butter and cheese made of it whether the same to be sent to market or consumed by his Family - Tax the real and personal Estate of a Physician and a Lawyer, but not the conjectural and varying Profits they derive from the

The Last Inn

>skillful and industrious Exercise of their
>Professions - &c &c [17]

From his tenure as President of the Continental Congress and later as Governor of New York State, Jay deplored the unbridled printing of paper money and believed that the states and the people should provide funds through loans and taxes. While Jay was governor of New York, the legislature levied taxes for improvements and expansion of the state's infrastructure, a move favored by Jay who was upset that some individuals believed that they were exempt from paying taxes. Jay also believed that the fortification of New York Harbor and the construction of an arsenal for the purchase of weapons were to provide for security and the means to achieving this was through increased taxation. As a Federalist, he believed in a strong central government and the subordination of the states, including broad powers of taxation. Years later in retirement, Jay still seemed to advocate that taxation must have a purpose and in his letter to Gov. Brown, he distinguished between direct and indirect taxation - one or the other, but not both was Jay's position.

By 1821, some of the state's were holding conventions to amend their state constitutions. Pres. John Adams sent Jay a copy of the Proceedings of the Convention to amend the Massachusetts Constitution. Peter Augustus Jay was elected a delegate from Westchester County to the New York State Constitutional Convention of 1821. The move towards democratic principles in the country resulted in a number of amendments to various state constitutions. The main reasons for the desire to amend the New York State Constitution, adopted in 1777 which John Jay helped to draft, were the growing dissatisfaction with the property qualifications for electors, which had been abolished in other states, and the political power of the judiciary. Recent settlement of western New York State and the western lands in Ohio, pitted the old landed gentry against the new interests of the rural settlers. When Thomas Jefferson was elected president in 1800, most states had property requirements for voting. The push for white male suffrage began in earnest in 1807, when New Jersey abolished the property restrictions for voting followed by Maryland in 1810.[18]

The Last Inn

Between 1816 and 1821 six new states were admitted to the Union - Indiana, Illinois, Mississippi, Alabama, Missouri and Maine. All the states' constitutions provided for universal white male suffrage.[19]

New York State's population had quadrupled between 1790 and 1820 and two-thirds of the state's population lived on land that was considered the frontier. Many of the settlers in New York's rural areas had come from other states where white male suffrage requirements were more moderate than those of New York State. New York City had the largest African American population north of the Chesapeake.[20] In 1799, then Gov. John Jay, signed into law a statute that provided for the gradual emancipation of slaves and by 1821, free African Americans were exercising their right to vote in New York State. This called into question John Jay's belief that "those who own the country ought to govern it".[21] The propertied and educated elite ran the government but the surge in the call for greater democracy could not be unheeded. Gov. De Witt Clinton was opposed to the Convention along with his Federalist allies in the state. Yet a small faction of his party, the Democratic-Republicans called the Bucktails, wanted to transfer powers from the executive to the legislative branch of the state government. Clinton realized the broad support for a state constitutional convention and the voters of New York City and the state's western areas provided strong support when the population voted on the issue.

Male suffrage to include blacks and whites was one of the questions debated during the convention. While opposed to universal male suffrage, Peter Augustus Jay, a delegate to the Convention, favored suffrage for the "colored population " and he distinguished himself in eloquent speeches in support of his position. Peter Jay rose to address the insertion of the word "white" in a proposed amendment to the state's constitution as a condition to extending suffrage to a greater number of males in the state when he said that he had faith in the committee to honor certain principles including equality.[22] Jay's comments were direct and eloquent. Jay wondered why free blacks were denied the same rights as other men, since they were born free like everyone else.[23] Jay then cited the examples of Virginia, North Carolina and Pennsylvania as extending suffrage to "free people of colour". Defying politics, Jay confronted the belief of the inferiority of "people of colour" stating that when a person is enslaved they lose most of their worth being denied the ability to support themselves, viewing labor as an evil and passing this on to their children who are punished for the crimes society inflicted on their parents.[24]

Jay's piercing remarks resulted in a vote of 63 to 59 not to disenfranchise free African Americans. Yet a few weeks later, the delegates who were opposed to black suffrage, voted for the imposition of a $250 freehold payment while removing this requirement for whites.[25] The irony of a convention called to address the issue of extending the franchise to a greater number of people in the state while denying it to others is puzzling. This disenfranchisement was most likely the result of the rise of the Jeffersonian Democratic-Republican party and the loss of power by the Federalists and the predominant belief in white superiority.[26]

Changes were made to the Constitution which included a limited veto power for the governor and the elimination of the Council of Appointment which held wide patronage of more than six thousand appointed jobs.[27] Peter Augustus Jay was one of eight delegates to vote against the Constitution which was adopted by the Convention and he wrote to his father about the changes to the Constitution citing as defects universal suffrage without property qualifications, empowering the legislature to make appointments, the independence of the judges of the State Supreme Court and his prediction of the adverse effects on society when people without property are more numerous than those who have property.[28]

John Jay followed the proceedings of the New York and Massachusetts conventions with great interest and at the outset of the New York proceeding he expressed his regret over the positions of some of the delegates to the New York convention to Pres. Adams:

It is honorable to Massachusetts that

> their political Parties have been so attentive to Moderation and Decorum - I wish the like remark was equally applicable to those in this State. Certain of our Demagogues seem to resent checks and balances as inconvenient Obstacles; and there is Reason to fear that the kind of Constitution which it is said they prefer, will if adopted and established retard the Prosperity of the State.[29]

Jay was kept informed of the Convention's progress by his son Peter and in responding to one of Peter's letters Jay was troubled by the political influences " It is to be regretted that the Temper and Proceedings of the convention are not more promising - a constitution formed under the Influence of improper motives and Feelings may not be approved by the People, unless a majority of them should be actuated by similar Excitements."[30] However, Jay was pleased with his son's participation in the Convention when he wrote about a newspaper article that contained a short speech given by Peter " - which in my opinion does you credit."[31]

Jay and Adams continued their interest in their state Constitutional Conventions by exchanging copies of the proceedings. Jay instructed his son, Peter Augustus, to purchase a copy of the New Convention for Adams, complete with explicit instructions for the binding of the document "Let it be decently but not splendidly bound;...I intend to transmit it with a few lines to Mr. Adams - "[32] When Jay did transmit the document to Adams, it was with his remark "To you any Remarks I might make relative to it, would be superfluous."[33]

The New York State Constitutional Convention was held at a time when the new principles of democracy, such as universal male suffrage, were taking root throughout the country. The newly adopted constitution for New York was ratified in a special election by a vote of 75,422 to 41,497.[34] The convention was considered revolutionary for its time with the expansion of the franchise for white voters with property requirements being

The Last Inn

removed and free African Americans were given limited suffrage with property qualifications. The Council of Revision was abolished and its power to veto legislation was transferred to the governor, whose veto could be overcome by a two-thirds vote of the legislature. Eight Circuit Courts were created in the state relieving the justices of the New York Supreme Court of having to ride circuit. Jay must have approved of this latter provision. During his tenure as Chief Justice, he and the other justices of the U.S. Supreme Court petitioned Congress to abolish the practice of circuit riding.[35] The practice of riding circuit would not be abolished by Congress for U.S. Supreme Court justices until it was done officially in 1911.[36]

    John Jay was part of the committee to draft New York's first state constitution, which provided for a bicameral legislature, veto power by the executive over legislation and executive appointments to State positions approved by the Senate. He must have approved of the revisions made by the 1821 State Constitutional Convention to the powers of the executive and the legislature. Given his views on suffrage for freeholders, it is probable that he did not approve of the new suffrage requirements for white males which removed property qualifications and it is questionable what he thought about the requirements for free African Americans who were now freeholders. This may account for his comment to Pres. Adams when sending him the account of the convention's proceedings.

    Jay was always welcoming old friends and compatriots to his farm and the Marquis de Lafayette was no exception receiving an invitation to visit Jay. In 1824-25 the Marquis, after an absence of almost fifty years, visited all twenty-four states after receiving an invitation from Pres. James Monroe to visit America. Lafayette's visit was to contribute to the nation's impending fiftieth anniversary and to instill the "spirit of 1776" in the younger generation of Americans. During his triumphal visit, Lafayette traveled more than 6,000 miles via stagecoach, horseback, canal barge and steamboat. It was the hope and intention of Jay and Lafayette that the two men would meet, but Peter Augustus Jay wrote to John Jay in September, 1824, several

The Last Inn

months after the Marquis' arrival in America that "General Lafayette will have so many places to visit, & so much ceremony to undergo, that I think it doubtful whether he will pay you his promised visit this Fall."[37] However, a few days later after Lafayette's itinerary was changed and he traveled directly from New York City to Boston, Jay commented that he heard the Marquis had traveled the entire distance in "a thick cloud of dust" and Jay applied the Latin maxim of *"nulla sine Pulvere Palmo"* to the situation.[38] Jay expressed his deep regret that Lafayette could not visit him "Had not the state of my health detained me here, I should immediately after your arrival at New York have had the gratification of seeing you here."[39] Jay stated his appreciation to the Marquis "Your attachment and services to the United States and the friendly attentions with which you have honored me, are fresh in my memory; and it will always give me pleasure to manifest the sense which I entertain of both."[40]

The Marquis was accompanied by his son, Georges Washington de Lafayette, who later visited Jay. When Lafayette received Jay's letter, he expressed heartfelt sentiments to Jay:

> As soon as I found myself once more on the happy shore of America, one of my first inquiries was after you, and the Means to greet my old friend. The pleasure to see your Son was great indeed, but I regretted the distance, engagements, and duties which obliged me to postpone the high gratification to meet you after so long an absence.[41]

As much as Lafayette wished to meet with Jay once more, he could not anticipate when this might happen and begged Jay to "receive the grateful respects of my Son" and signed the letter "Your old revolutionary Companion And constant friend, LAFAYETTE."[42] While the two men never met during Lafayette's trip, their high regard and friendship for each other was palpable. It must have been some degree of consolation and pleasure to both men that they met with each other's son.

However, Maria Jay Banyer had her own encounter with the Marquis and gave her father an account of Lafayette's sermon at her church in New York City. Maria wrote that she feared "he had forgotten his sacred office & was going to give us an Oration instead of a Sermon, but far other was his intention - he took for his Text the verse in Proverbs "better is he that ruleth his Spirit than he that taketh a City" and drew an animated contrast between an Earthly Conqueror and a Christian soldier."[43] Afterwards the Marquis "shook hands with the Preacher & told him he had chosen the wiser path." Maria then went on to relate that while she had not correctly quoted the text in her letter to her father, she expressed every confidence that the verse was familiar to John Jay. She then spoke of a ball for the Marquis in New York City attended by 5,000 people. John Jay was probably comforted by his daughter's account of Lafayette's sermon and its message alluding to Lafayette's approach to his visit to America.

In 1826, the Jay family received a visit from Henry Van der Lyn who was an attorney and noted diarist. Henry's brother, the neo-classical painter John Van der Lyn, had been commissioned by the Common Council of New York City in 1802 to paint a full-length portrait of John Jay. Jay had received notification from a member of the Common Council, Robert Lenox, that Van der Lyn was ready to begin Jay's portrait, whereupon Jay set out for New York in February, but was delayed at Rye due to a snow storm where he contracted a fever. Jay returned to Bedford where he continued in poor health but nevertheless expressed the honor done to him by the Common Council:

> This delay is unavoidable as well as embarrassing, and I regret it the more, as it may countenance conjectures not consistent with the sense I entertain of the honour intended me by the corporation of my native city - a corporation which, for many years, has been entitled, not only to my respect, but to my sincere and grateful attachment.[44]

Later that month, Peter Augustus wrote to his father that Van der Lyn was leaving for Washington. He described Van der Lyn as such "He is said to be one of the best portrait painters in

The Last Inn

the world - far superior to [Gilbert] Stuart."[45] As a result, Van der Lyn never painted any portrait of John Jay.

When Henry Van der Lyn visited the Jays, John Jay was eighty years old and Van der Lyn described Jay as follows:

> He is 80 years old looks thin & infirm, but has his memory hearing & understanding He spoke considerably & sensibly & inter alia said, that he thought the act of the late State Convention, re-moving the Sup. Ct. Judges, before their constitutional time had expired, a very dangerous precedent & violation of the most solemn compact. He must have been a pattern of polite hospitality, as he yet evinced as his great age the most particular attention to us. His manners are mild & gentle. After the cloth was removed at dinner, He did us the honour to drink our health & soon after withdrew a short distance from the table, & his servant brot (sic), his long pipe, which he smoked once. He offered us Segars & the ladies kindly pressed us to smoke, saying they were used to the flavor of the smoke, which we thus urged could not decline. There were no Gentlemen at table but us & the Governor, & the ladies politely remained in the room after dinner out of Respect to us.[46]

Van der Lyn's description of Jay's mental and physical health does not reflect the mild paralytic stroke that he suffered in May of 1825. William Jay noted his father's seizure at dinner on May 31, 1825, "...he complained of dizziness, his ideas seemed confused and some of his expressions were incoherent. We soon discovered that he was under the influence of a paralytick attack."⁴⁷ William continued with a description of his father's symptoms "Neither his face or limbs were in the least affected. His articulation was perfect but he found it difficult to express himself from a forgetfulness of the words he wished to use. He frequently called things by wrong names, was conscious of his mistakes but unable to correct it."⁴⁸ William noted that his father was willing to submit to whatever treatment the doctor prescribed. A few days later, William wrote that his father was better and spoke a few words coherently.

    Jay must have recovered to the degree noted by Van der Lyn during his visit to Bedford for in 1826, Jay finally resolved to end a debate that had been growing for almost two decades over the authorship of one of the most revered documents in American history - George Washington's *Farewell Address*. Was the author of the document Washington or Alexander Hamilton? It would fall to John Jay, with the assistance of his friend, Judge Richard Peters, to unequivocally settle the debate.

    Near the end of his second presidential term, Washington decided to write his *Valedictory* for the nation. A draft of an address had been drafted near the end of Washington's first term of office, but was tabled when Washington decided to run for a second term. With his second term coming to an end, Washington drafted a document and asked Hamilton to review it as Washington had relied on Hamilton's judgment dating back to the Revolution when Hamilton was on Washington's staff. On those occasions and with the *Valedictory Address*, Hamilton served as an editor preserving the content of the document as Washington instructed him "…all of the ideas and observations are confined, as you will readily perceive, to my *draft* of the valedictory Address. If you form one anew, it will, of course, assume such a shape as you may be disposed to give it, predicated upon the Sentiments contained in the enclosed Paper."⁴⁹ However, Washington had such a high regard for Jay, he asked Hamilton to consult with Jay on the matter saying "…as I have great confidence in the abilities, the purity of Mr. Jay's views, as well as his experience, I should wish his sentiments on the purport of this letter."⁵⁰ Jay and Hamilton met at Jay's house on Broadway in

The Last Inn

New York City to review Washington's draft. The two men worked from a copy of Washington's draft made by Hamilton and the changes made to the Address were "none of much importance" as Jay later noted. Jay and Hamilton made no changes to Washington's draft which was published on September 15, 1796 in the *American Daily Advertiser* and many other American and international journals under different titles. It was George Hough of the *Courier of New Hampshire* in Concord who reprinted the *Valedictory* under the title of "*Washington's Farewell Address*." Yet, it was the meeting of Hamilton and Jay that was to have national ramifications in one of the most curious episodes in American history.

With Hamilton's death in 1804, one of the Executors of his estate, Nathaniel Pendleton, was examining some of the estate's papers in 1810 and discovered a draft of Washington's Address in Hamilton's hand. Mrs. Hamilton and members of her family took the position that it was Hamilton and not Washington who was the author of the *Address*. Pendleton did not want to compromise his position as Executor and he delivered the papers to Rufus King for safe keeping. Both men were Federalists and of the opinion that Washington wrote the *Address*. They were fearful of Mrs. Hamilton gaining access to the papers and tarnishing George Washington's reputation by asserting that it was her husband, and not Washington, who wrote the *Address*.

As the controversy grew over the next few years, Judge Richard Peters wrote to Jay in 1811 about the rumors being circulated by the claim of Hamilton's supporters in New York and Philadelphia, many of whom were Democratic-Republicans. Both men remained great admirers of Washington as Peters stated to Jay "I am always hurt when I hear anything which tends to break with what remains of the *Charm* his [Washington's] name once possessed."[51] Jay was greatly disturbed by what Peters had to say about the growing controversy and his response to Peters of March 29, 1811 thrust Jay into the forefront of the authorship debate and his letter to Peters became the focal point of the authorship controversy. Jay still retained a high degree of credibility with the public and he was the sole surviving participant in the *Address* episode. He found the news about the rumors being spread "unpleasant and unexpected". Jay then embarked on a long discourse of Washington's character and his skill in writing the *Address*. He asserted in a very legal manner that the premise of Hamilton's authorship:

> ...will be found too slight and shallow, to resist that strong stream of counter-evidence which flows from the conduct and character of that great man; a character not blown up into transient splendor by the breath of adulation, but which, being composed of his great and memorable deeds, stands, and will forever stand a glorious monument of human excellence.[52]

Jay then succinctly discussed his meeting with Hamilton stating in his circumspect and lawyerly manner "Thus much for presumptive evidence, I will now turn to some that is direct."[53] Jay was convinced that if Washington was alive, he would want Jay to commit the facts of the episode to writing for disclosure when it became necessary. While Jay did not want the contents of the letter to Peters made public at this time, and he sent the letter to Peters for his 'care and discretion'. Peters, a federal judge and leading citizen of Philadelphia, disclosed Jay's crucial role in the editing of the *Farewell Address* to influential Philadelphians but followed Jay's instructions not to make the letter public until such time as Jay deemed it necessary. Peters wrote to Jay "Nothing can be a stronger bulwark against their Attacks than your letter. I shall not use it indiscreetly or busily. But when I shall believe that *you* would think it right, I will use it."[54] Jay's response to Peters was characteristic. "I endeavoured to write those Facts with great Precision - In affairs of this kind there cannot be too much Circumspection."[55] Circumspection was a major aspect of Jay's personality and in his approach to matters both personal and public.

Mrs. Hamilton, in the meantime met with several people in the hopes of finding someone to write a biography of her

The Last Inn

husband and publish the letters found in his estate. However, Peters' judicious use of Jay's letter helped to forestall such an event and even helped to dissuade Joseph Hopkinson from undertaking such a project for Mrs. Hamilton. Hopkinson was a federal judge and distinguished trial constitutional law attorney who argued several landmark cases before the Supreme Court including *Dartmouth College v. Woodward* and *McCullough v. Maryland*.

Mrs. Hamilton even visited Jay at Bedford in 1818 and stated that Hamilton was the author of the *Farewell Address* since Washington had sent Hamilton a draft of the *Address* and asked Hamilton to make "alterations" to the document. In true legal style, Jay replied in a letter to Peters about his meeting with Mrs. Hamilton and made the distinction between editing and writing a document "This is certainly very different from desiring him to compose one."[56]

That same year, Mrs. Hamilton visited Justice Bushrod Washington, a member of the Supreme Court and George Washington's nephew and executor, for the purpose of borrowing some of Washington's letters for copying. Justice Washington stated that Mrs. Hamilton never brought up the subject of the *Farewell Address* but was later informed by a friend of the ever growing controversy. Judge Peters allowed Justice Washington to make a copy of the section of Jay's 1811 letter concerning the meeting with Hamilton. This was not the first occasion that Justice Washington had loaned the president's correspondence to another person for research. In 1800 the papers were loaned to future Chief Justice John Marshall for the purpose of writing a biography of the president which was ultimately published in five volumes from 1806-1807.

Jay and Peters continued their correspondence and in 1820 Peters wrote to Jay for clarification about Jay's meeting with Hamilton to review the *Address*. Jay responded by reiterating his position that it was Washington who wrote the *Farewell Address* which contained his 'Sentiments' and that Jay and Hamilton respected the confidential nature of their work for Washington by never speaking publicly about their meeting.

The Last Inn

Remaining constant in his views on the *Farewell Address*, Jay was later approached by Prof. John McVikcar of Columbia University about the authorship controversy. Prof. McVickar's sister, Augusta, had married Jay's son, William. His account of the meeting with Jay was "When the slow-puffing pipe and the deaf ear turned were no longer an apology for not hearing, the answer came out with a quiet smile: 'My opinion my dear sir, you shall freely have. I have always thought General Washington competent to write his own addresses.'"[57]

In 1823 the debate had begun to take on national implications when Presidents Jefferson and Madison, both Democratic-Republicans, commented on the issue though neither were privy to the all important Jay/Hamilton meeting. Both had participated in the drafting of a valedictory address for Washington at the end of his first term in 1792. Jefferson stated that Madison recognized several passages in the 1796 draft as being his own composition and other passages to be that of Washington with some revisions by Hamilton.[58] Madison agreed with Jefferson's assessment and replied "If there be any circumstantial inaccuracy, it is imputing to him [Washington] more agency in composing the document than he probably had."[59]

By 1825, the debate entered the national arena when James Hamilton, on behalf of his mother, brought a suit in Chancery to compel Rufus King to relinquish the Hamilton papers in his custody for almost twenty years. This alarmed Bushrod Washington so that he wrote to Chief Justice John Marshall for advice. Marshall replied with confidence and wisdom in Jay's enduring credibility "It is extremely fortunate that Mr. Jay was privy to the whole transaction and that he has lived long enough to explain it."[60] Marshall further stated that he did not believe that Hamilton retained the documents in question for the purpose to which Hamilton's family is using them "Mrs. Hamilton and her son appear to be more to blame than I had supposed, since they must know that the *Address* was written by General Washington and revised by his friends."[61] Marshall also stated that Washington's supporters should not oppose the publication of Hamilton's papers relative to the *Farewell Address* stating with reference to Jay's letter about his meeting with Hamilton that he believed Jay's statement to be correct.[62] Marshall went on to state that when writing Washington's biography, he never saw anything in the president's papers to suggest anything other than Washington was the author of the *Address*.

The suit brought in Chancery gave the issue of the authorship of the *Farewell Address* national prominence and was taken up by the prestigious Historical Society of Pennsylvania. The Society's president, William Rawle, wrote to David Claypoole, the original publisher of the Farewell Address. Claypoole was asked to produce the draft of the *Address* written in Washington's own hand which Washington had given to Claypoole after he had finalized the draft of the *Address*. Rawle was familiar with the handwriting of both Washington and Hamilton and was convinced that the draft of the *Address* which Claypoole had produced for their meeting was the document written by Washington. Claypoole's Certification and a report written by Rawle were later published in the Society's journal, *Memoirs*.

However, the Society wanted more proof of the authorship of the *Farewell Address* and formed an *ad hoc* committee to clarify the matter. Letters were sent to Richard Peters, Bushrod Washington, John Marshall and John Jay to shed light on the issue of the authorship of the *Address*. Washington and Marshall replied that they had not seen any documentation to prove that the *Farewell Address* was written by anyone other than Washington. Peters, who still had possession of Jay's 1811 letter, wrote to the Society that he could not do anything with Jay's letter without Jay's permission.[63] Peters also criticized the Hamilton family for asserting that Hamilton had betrayed Washington's confidence when they knew that such was not the case and that Hamilton did not write the *Address*. Peters then bemoaned the injury the nation would suffer by having the name of Washington discredited.[64] Peters had also corresponded with Washington during the Revolutionary War being a member of the Board of War. He too was familiar with Washington's handwriting and his style of writing and he wrote to Rawle that Washington always wrote

The Last Inn

himself what he deemed to be of consequence.[65] Jay's trust in Peters had not been misplaced but had been repaid with loyalty, patriotism and the utmost discretion as Jay was about to make an important decision that would alter the course of the authorship controversy. Jay's reply to the Society was succinct and he stated that he first learned of the controversy from Peters in 1811 and Peters had his letter of March 29, 1811 "I therefore take the liberty to refer you to Judge Peters who will readily communicate to you the entire contents of that letter. Permit me to add, that should any copies be taken, it is my desire that they may be copies of the *whole*, and not merely of *parts* of the letter."[66] At last, Jay had given his consent to having his letter to Peters of March, 1811 published. Perhaps the confluence of events, the escalation of the debate to a national level, Mrs. Hamilton's suit in Chancery and John Jay's mild stroke the year before, prompted Jay to agree to the publication of his letter. On October 5, 1826, the *New York American* published Jay's 1811 letter to Judge Richard Peters in its entirety. A statement from the newspaper followed the letter:

New York American
Thursday Evening, October 5, 1826
The letter of Mr. Jay, which we will publish this day, on the subject of Washington's Farewell Address, will be read with great interest. It is marked with the characteristic force and elegance of that gentleman's style, and in its facts and reasoning, is conclusive.[67]

Considering that the *New York American* was a Republican/Whig newspaper, this was high praise and well earned for it was members of the Republican/Whig party, in an attempt to discredit Washington, who initially took the position that it was Hamilton and not Washington who wrote the *Farewell Address*. The publication of Jay's letter convinced Rufus King and James Hamilton that King had been exonerated and King gave Hamilton's papers to Mrs. Hamilton. Mrs. Hamilton withdrew her suit from Chancery realizing that Jay's letter made the law suit unnecessary. However, to her death, Mrs. Hamilton never wavered in her belief

The Last Inn

that it was her husband who wrote the *Farewell Address* and she attested to that belief in her Last Will and Testament. The Pennsylvania Historical Society published its findings on the matter of the *Farewell Address* in 1826 and stated:

> The facts in Mr. Jay's letter to Judge Peters well account for the *mistake* which has accompanied this question. The whole *Address* appears to have been copied by General Hamilton, whose affectionate attachment to the President prevented him from thinking any trouble on his account too great, and this copy having, we know not how, returned to his possession, was probably the cause of the opinion that he was the original author.[68]

The publication of Jay's 1811 letter to Peters put an end to the debate over the authorship of Washington's *Farewell Address*. Jay most likely did not want to wait too long to make his letter public, fearing another stroke or death, and no doubt wanted to have some control over the publication process. Throughout the years that Peters followed Jay's instructions about the all important letter, Jay remained steadfast in waiting for the appropriate time to have the truth come to light. His actions throughout the controversy revealed his great admiration and respect for Washington. Indeed, Jay's character, integrity and credibility, were highly respected even by his political opponents, and aided in the settlement of the debate. Jay was also a major participant in the editing of the *Farewell Address* and he, among the three participants, was the sole survivor and had full knowledge of the facts of the episode. He remained circumspect, lawyerly and patient throughout and even a stroke could not diminish his faculties and resolve to have the facts emerge that it was George Washington who wrote the *Farewell Address*.

As the nation approached the fiftieth anniversary of the signing of the Declaration of Independence, Jay, though aging and

The Last Inn

infirm, was still regarded by many as a Founding Father and his contribution to the cause of American Independence was still revered. The Corporation of the City of New York invited Jay to attend the celebration "to you, sir, this anniversary must return with feelings grateful to a patriot heart. ... By your firmness and the wisdom of your counsels, you eminently contributed to the glorious and happy issue which has placed our country in a rank with the most favored nation of the earth."[69] Jay declined the invitation due to ill health but had the following reverential observation to make about the nation he helped to create:

> I cannot forbear to embrace the opportunity afforded by the present occasion, to express my earnest hope that the peace, happiness, and prosperity enjoyed by our beloved country, may induce those who direct her national councils to *recommend* a general and public return of praise and thanksgiving to HIM from whose goodness these blessings descend. The most effectual means of securing the continuance of our civil and religious liberties, is always to remember with reverence and gratitude the source from which they flow.[70]

It was on this particular Independence Day that John Adams and Thomas Jefferson died, making John Jay one of the last surviving individuals who rose to the occasion in the early days of the Revolution. Two years later, Jay would be the only survivor of all the members of the First Continental Congress.[71]

Despite his age and failing health, Jay was determined to complete a project that began in 1813 when he loaned Joseph Cusno, his waiter from Sicily, $750 to buy a house in the Cantitoe Corners section of Bedford. Although Joseph purchased the land in 1815 from Annanias Westcott, Jay executed a deed in his name. At the time, Joseph was an immigrant and, under the law, could not own real property until he became a naturalized citizen. He

The Last Inn

became a citizen of the United States on September 22, 1834 in the presence and under the supervision of Judge William Jay. However, in 1825, the New York Legislature passed a law that made it legal for a resident alien to buy, own and sell real property. What Joseph had to do was execute a deposition that included his name, residence and the date and place of the deposition which would be filed in Albany with the office of the Secretary of State. Joseph also had to become a naturalized citizen within six years. The deed, dated December 15, 1828, included the numerous transfers of title to the property owned by Joseph. Jay wanted his waiter to have clear title to the property. The deed was executed in the presence of Jay's son, William, and his daughter, Maria, who signed their names to the document as witnesses. However, Jay did not sign the deed but made his 'mark' **X** on the deed. Jay no doubt was mindful of the importance of the due execution of the deed and the following words appear on the deed below Jay's 'mark' "John Jay in consequence of an injury to his right hand executed the above instrument by affixing his mark thereto in the presence of Maria Jay Banyer and William Jay."[72]

In 1827, probably March 26th, John Jay injured his hand while drawing a piece of firewood and his condition quickly deteriorated as attested to by his daughter Nancy:

> ...[Jay] recd a scratch & bruise from an upper piece falling on the back of his hand, which took off some skin, & soon caused much discoloration -- he put on court plaister, & came in the parlor to tea as usual & said but little about his hand -- The next morning his hand was very painful & excessively swelled -- The plaister was removed with difficulty & a poultice applied -- but the pain & swelling increased --the Dr. was sent for, & he added lead water to the poultice -- but without good effect -- Chills & loss of appetite & fever

The Last Inn

> followed --On Wednesday he was much
> worse, Dr.N.K. [Keeler] was sent for,
> yeast, poultice, & wine & quinine &
> porter were ordered -- mortification was
> apprehended --[73]

Realizing the gravity of the situation, William wrote to his brother Peter Augustus on March 28th "On the whole Papa's situation is so critical that I shall dispatch Blake [the Jay's coachman] with this letter although I well know the shock you will feel on receiving it."[74] William also noted Jay's extreme lethargy which made it "difficult to get him to answer questions or to take instructions." William then asked Peter to contact other family and friends to summon them to Jay's bedside where Nancy and Maria were "as well as can be expected." A few days later Peter and his wife, Mary, arrived along with Dr. Watts and Mr. Munro by which time "the hand was dreadfully swelled, of a dark purple color and extremely painful." Gangrene had set in and even though it should be checked, the doctors feared that he would succumb to the discharge from the ulcers. It fell to William to inform his father of the prognosis which "was received without the slightest perceptible emotion". Nancy observed that her father "...looked like a saint & spoke like one" as Jay assured Nancy and Maria who were by his side to "...look to Jesus for faith & hope & trust." After six weeks in bed and looking "dreadfully emaciated" Jay stated that this life would be of no value and spoke of the life to come. By June 29th, Jay had recovered to a degree where he was able to walk and sit on the piazza for two hours. William later stated unequivocally "The strength of his constitution, aided perhaps by the serenity of his mind, triumphed over his disease; and he was spared to his family and friends for about two years longer."[75].

During the last two years of Jay's life, he was a virtual invalid. By December of 1828 William noted in a letter to his brother that his father's "debility continues to increase but very gradually" and he was now taking laudanum every night for his pain and he walked with great difficulty. Yet despite his condition, he managed to make his mark on the deed for Joseph

The Last Inn

Cusno.

Jay also kept up a correspondence primarily with his old friends and Federalists. Since the injury to his hand left his fingers stiff and unable to use a pen, William wrote the letters for him. In 1828, Judge Richard Peters wrote to Jay about many political subjects and stated that he believed the authorship controversy of Washington's *Farewell Address* had been 'put to rest'. He went on to state *"Washington's Address* is our political Bible. Its principles should guide this and future generations of our Country."[76] He also believed that he was free of "envy, hatred and malice." Peters departed this life with no enmities a few months later on August 22nd. His friendship with Jay had lasted more than fifty years.

Given his age and failing health, Jay seemed determined to reach closure on certain matters, to put his affairs in order, and to prepare himself for the end which he must have sensed was finally imminent. It was in keeping with Jay's character to address every issue and task with thoroughness and commitment and to see it through to completion. Two important matters had been settled - the authorship of Washington's *Farewell Address* was clarified and Joseph Cusno now had clear title to his property at Cantitoe Corners.

During the remainder of his life, Jay needed assistance when walking and spent much of each day in his room. During the evening hours he had the companionship of his family and friends and took pleasure in listening to books which were read aloud. Although he could not attend services at St. Matthew's church, he received communion in his room along with his family. In March of 1829 William wrote to his brother Peter about their father's condition "Papa is unusually comfortable complaining of little or no pain; but for this, the peperine has no credit since he discontinued the use of it after a few doses, imagining it disagreed with him."[77] Maria also made a favorable report of her father's condition "Papa appeared more cheerful than usual yesterday, conversed with us till nearly 4 o'clock & sat up till ½ past 8 - had a good appetite & in every respect appeared better - this morning he had difficulty in expressing himself tho' perfectly composed &

self possessed - "[78] In attending her father during his last days, Maria said that he could barely speak and at one point he spoke about the Lord being good and better than people merit.[79] He remained in bed, silent and nursed by his daughters with an expression on his face that Maria described as saintly.[80] Then, as related by William:

> On the evening of May 14th, 1829, he retired to bed as well as usual, but in the course of the night was seized with palsy. The disease affected his articulation, and almost entirely deprived him of the power of conversing. It was evident, however, from the few sentences he succeeded in uttering, that his mind was unimpaired by the shock. Medical skill proved unavailing, and he lingered till noon on Sunday, the 17th when he expired in the eighty-fourth year of his age.[81]

A few weeks after John Jay's death, Peter Augustus Jay wrote to James Fenimore Cooper "My good old father has paid the debt of nature."[82] Peter also wrote that Jay was "much loved and venerated by his children."

In accordance with John Jay's wishes and as attested to in his Last Will and Testament, Jay wanted a simple funeral "I would have my funeral decent, but not ostentatious. No scarfs - no rings. Instead thereof, I give two hundred dollars to any one poor deserving widow or orphan of this town, to whom my children shall select."[83] Eschewing the traditional practice of having commemorative items such as scarves and rings made for the funeral participants, Jay instead chose to make a bequest to a deserving person in Bedford in his last act of charity to those in true need. During his lifetime, Jay was charitable to those less fortunate by forgiving some debts or seeing to the needs of those 'deserving' charity.

Jay's Will also reflects his undying belief in God from whom all blessings are derived even the "unmerited blessings" and

The Last Inn

for salvation through God's "beloved Son." Jay gave thanks for all that he had received from God during his life:

> He has been pleased to bless me with excellent parents, with a virtuous wife, and with worthy children. His protection has accompanied me through many eventful years, faithfully employed in the service of my country; and his providence has not only conducted me to this tranquil situation, but also given me abundant reason to be contented and thankful.[84]

His papers were left to his sons, William and Peter Augustus, with the instructions that all non-essential documents be destroyed. The two brothers left no record to account for their actions in carrying out their father's wishes. John Jay was always very sensitive about the publication of any of his papers and his Will directed his sons to thoroughly sort all the documents left to them before any were made public. Harvard president and historian, Jared Sparks, had requested access to the papers upon learning that the two brothers had possession of the documents, but his requests were always denied by William and Peter Augustus.[85] Perhaps Jared Sparks' critical opinion of John Jay allowed the two brothers to exercise their denial of access without any hesitation.

Jay appointed as Executors of his estate, his children, and further expressed his contentment with the pleasure he derived from their admirable behavior and their attachment to Jay and each other.

Jay wanted certain properties to remain in the family and his beloved 'farm in Bedford' was left to William. William resided with his family for the remainder of his life in Bedford.

Peter Augustus was left the Stone House on Broadway where John Jay and his wife Sarah had entertained the political and social elite of the new republic.

Nancy and Maria were left personalty from the estate, among other testamentary provisions for them. The two sisters

The Last Inn

remained with William for a short while in Bedford until they moved to Maria's house in Manhattan next to Peter's house. A few years later, Nancy and Maria would move across town to 20 Bond Street where Peter's son, Dr. John Clarkson Jay, resided at 21 Bond Street and acted as advisor to his aunts.

John Jay also made provision in his Will for some of his loyal servants. James Roe and Peter Blake received bequests of two hundred dollars each and Joseph Cusno was given a devise of real property. Jay's Will also directed that Clarinda, a very old servant, be given to the care of his son, William, thereby carrying on a family tradition of providing for the needs of deserving servants.

Jay's Will was a reflection of the life he had lived with a consistent and unwavering devotion to God, love for his family, patriotism for his country and helping those in need. His funeral was held in St. Matthew's Church with his family, friends and gentlemen from various parts of the country in attendance. The pastor preached a sermon and John Jay was then laid to rest in the Jay Family Cemetery in Rye, a short distance from the house where he spent his childhood. A simple monument was later erected over his grave with an epitaph written by his son, Peter Augustus:

IN MEMORY OF JOHN JAY,
EMINENT AMONG THOSE WHO ASSERTED
THE LIBERTY
AND ESTABLISHED THE INDEPENDENCE
OF HIS COUNTRY,
WHICH HE LONG SERVED IN THE MOST
IMPORTANT OFFICES,
LEGISLATIVE, EXECUTIVE, JUDICIAL AND
DIPLOMATIC
AND DISTINGUISHED IN THEM ALL BY HIS
ABILITY, FIRMNESS, PATRIOTISM AND
INTEGRITY.
HE WAS IN HIS LIFE AND IN HIS DEATH
AN EXAMPLE OF THE VIRTUES,
THE FAITH AND THE HOPES

The Last Inn

OF A CHRISTIAN [86]

There were obituaries for Jay with one newspaper stating that Jay, deserved the great reputation he enjoyed during his lifetime.[87] Another journal honored Jay by saying that his exceptional talents he exhibited during his public career stemmed from his sense of duty to his country.[88]

Members of the judiciary also paid tribute to Jay with Chief Justice Jones of the New York Supreme Court honoring his memory "...few men in any country, and perhaps scarce one in this, have filled a larger space, and few ever passed through life with such perfect purity, integrity and honor."[89] Upon receiving news of Jay's death, the New York Supreme Court, as a mark of respect, adjourned for the day. One week after his death, the Court of Common Pleas adopted a tribute to John Jay and resolved to wear 'crape' on the left arm for a period of thirty days as a sign of respect for Jay's memory.[90]

On May 19, 1829, just two days after Jay's death, the Bar of the State of New York adopted a Resolution, *Action of the New York Bar on the Death of John Jay.* The Resolution outlined Jay's political, executive, judicial and diplomatic contributions to the founding of his country noting that Jay was an "...early agent in laying the foundations of this nation, of which he soon became one of the brightest, and continued one of its fairest pillars."[91] Jay was also recognized for "...his great talents, discretion, firmness and skills"[92] The Bar also paid tribute to Jay's years of retirement which among other pursuits involved "..the signal observance of that religion which had been the bright beam of the morning and the evening of his life, the rights and toleration of which he had secured to this people in one of the most important articles of our Constitution."[93] The Bar then adopted the following Resolutions:

> *Resolved,* That the members of this Bar are impressed with deep grief upon the decease of their illustrious brother, John Jay. They find, however, a consolation in the reflection that his conduct through a long and useful life, has given a luster

The Last Inn

to our profession and this Bar, and that while his character for private virtues and public worth has justly endeared him to the nation, his patriotism, his great talents as a statesman, and his great acquirements as a jurist, his eminent piety as a Christian, and probity as a man, all unite to present him to the public as an example whose radiance points to the attainment of excellence.

Resolved, That in respect for the character of the deceased, the members of this Bar will wear crape during the period of thirty days.

Resolved, That the Chairman and Secretary are desired to transmit a copy of the proceedings of this meeting to the family of the deceased.

Resolved, That the proceedings be signed by the Chairman and Secretary, and Published in the different newspapers of this city.[94]

Congressman Gulian C. Verplank, whose ancestral home in Fishkill dated to the days of the Dutch settlement of the Hudson River Valley, delivered an address shortly after Jay's death in which he echoed Maria's description of her dying father as having the aura of a saint. He said of Jay:

A halo of veneration seemed to encircle him as one belonging to another world, though lingering among us. When the tidings of his death came to us, they were received through the nation, not with sorrow or mourning, but with solemn awe,...."[95]

Even Sen. Daniel Webster was also among those who honored Jay for his purity of character [96]

In 1831 Congress honored Jay by appropriating sums for a

bust of John Jay to be executed by the noted sculptor, John Frazee, for the Supreme Court Chamber in the Capitol in Washington, D.C. where it remains on exhibit to this day. Frazee was honored stating that this was the first time that the Government voluntarily honored an 'American genius'.[97]

Perhaps George Pellew in his biography of John Jay expressed the very essence of Jay:

> He might for a time be uncertain as to what his duty was, but the moment it was clear to him, he acted accordingly, promptly, fearlessly, without regard to personal considerations, undeterred by the consequences to his friends or his family.[98]

The Last Inn

---

[1] John Jay to Lindley Murray, 12 June 1805, JJCU.

[2] Ibid.

[3] John Jay to John Adams, 7 May 1821, JJCU.

[4] Robert A. Trendel, Jr. *William Jay. Churchman, Public Servant and Reformer.* (New York 1982), 112.

[5] Ibid, 112-13.

[6] Maria Jay Banyer to John Jay, 27 June 1821, JJCU.

[7] JJCU.

[8] John Agnew, Thomas Bolton, William A. Davis and R. Riker to John Jay, 25 September 1825, JJCU.

[9] John Jay to Peter Augustus Jay, 9 July 1821, JJH.

[10] Harry Ammon. *James Monroe: The Quest for National Identity.* (New York 1971), 465.

[11] George Dangerfield. *The Awakening of American Nationalism: 1815-1828.* (New York 1965), 86.

[12] Dangerfield. *The Awakening of American Nationalism: 1815-1828,* 80-81; Ammon. *James Monroe: The Quest for National Identity,* 466-67.

[13] Dumas Malone and Basil Rauch. *Empire for Liberty: The Genesis and Growth of the United States of America.* (New York 1960), 416.

The Last Inn

[14] Murray Rothbard. *The Panic of 1819: Reactions and Policies.* (New York 1962), 8.

[15] Susan Wilentz. *The Rise of American Democracy: Jefferson to Lincoln.* (New York 2008), 206-7; Ammon. *James Monroe: The Quest for National Identity.* 466.

[16] *Ethan A. Brown.* http://www.ohiohistorycentral.org.

[17] John Jay to Ethan Allen Brown, 30 April 1821, JJCU.

[18] *The Clash of Political Philosophies: The Debate Over Universal Suffrage in New York, 1821,* www.montgomerycollege.edu/Departments/hpolscrv/nysuffra.html, 4.

[19] Ibid.

[20] Ibid, 5.

[21] Ibid, 5-6.

[22] Paul J. Polgar. *Whenever They Judge it to be Expedient: Politics of Partisanship and Free Black Voting Rights in Early National New York,* American Nineteenth Century History, 12: 1, 1-23, 3.

[23] *The Clash of Political Philosophies: The Debate Over Universal Suffrage in New York, 1821,* www.montgomerycollege.edu/Departments/hpolscrv/nysuffra.html, 13.

[24] *The Clash of Political Philosophies: The Debate Over Universal Suffrage in New York, 1821,* www.montgomerycollege.edu/Departments/hpolscrv/nysuffra.html, 14.

The Last Inn

[25] Polgar. *Whenever They Judge it to be Expedient: Politics of Partisanship and Free Black Voting Rights in Early National New York,* 2.

[26] Ibid.

[27] Jay, ed.. *Memorials of Peter A. Jay Compiled for his Descendants,* 108.

[28] Ibid, 109.

[29] John Jay to John Adams, 7 May 1821, JJCU.

[30] John Jay to Peter Augustus Jay , 16 October 1821, JJCU.

[31] Ibid.

[32] John Jay to Peter Augustus Jay, 4 February 1822, JJCU.

[33] John Jay to John Adams, 11 March 1822, JJCU.

[34] Jay, ed.. *Memorials of Peter A. Jay Compiled for his Descendants,* 109.

[35] John Jay and the Justices of the U.S. Court to Pres. George Washington, 9 August 1792, Library of Congress, The George Washington Papers 1741-1799, Washington D.C.

[36] Joshua Glick. *Comment: On the Road: The Supreme Court and the History of Circuit Riding,* Cardozo Law Review 19: 1-68.

[37] Peter Augustus Jay to John Jay, 3 September 1824, JJCU.

[38] John Jay to Peter Augustus Jay, 6 September 1824, JJCU; *Nulla sine Pulvere Palmo* translation, "not without dust on the palms".

[39] John Jay to General Lafayette, 20 September 1824, JJCU.

[40] Ibid.

[41] General Lafayette to John Jay, 10 November 1824, JJCU.

[42] Ibid.

[43] Maria Jay Banyer to John Jay, 12 September 1824, JJCU.

[44] John Jay to Robert Lenox, 3 April 1802, HPJ IV: 294.

[45] Peter Augustus Jay to John Jay, 8 March 1802, JJCU.

[46] Diary of Henry Van der Lyn, I:91, JJCU.

[47] William Jay to Peter Augustus Jay, 31 May 1825, JJCU.

[48] Ibid.

[49] Carol Brier. *John Jay and George Washington's Valedictory.* The Supreme Court Historical Society Quarterly XXXII:1, 7 (2010).

[50] Brier. *John Jay and George Washington's Valedictory.* The Supreme Court Historical Society Quarterly XXXII:1, 7 (2010).

[51] Carol Brier. *Tending Our Vines: From the Correspondence and Writings of Richard Peters and John Jay.* Pennsylvania History: A Journal of Mid-Atlantic Studies 80:1, 102 (2013).

[52] John Jay to Richard Peters, 29 March 1811, JJCU.

[53] Ibid.

[54] Brier. *John Jay and George Washington's Valedictory.* The Supreme Court Historical Society Quarterly XXXII :1,9 (2010).

[55] John Jay to Richard Peters, 23 April 1811, JJCU.

[56] John Jay to Richard Peters, 25 January 1819, JJCU.

[57] Professor John Mc Vickar, in *N.Y. Review,* October, 1841; JJGP 319-20.

[58] Victor Hugo Paltsits. *Washington's Farewell Address,* (New York 1935) 82

[59] Paltsits. *Washington's Farewell Address,* 82.

[60] John Marshall to Bushrod Washington, 7 July 1825, Paltsits. *Washington's Farewell Address,* 285; Brier. *John Jay and George Washington's Valedictory.* The Supreme Court Historical Society Quarterly Vol. XXXII : 2, 9 (2010).

[61] Ibid.

[62] John Marshall to Bushrod Washington, 7 July 1825, Paltsits. *Washington's Farewell Address,* 282.

[63] Richard Peters to Historical Society of Pennsylvania, 21 February 1826, *Memoirs of the Historical Society of Pennsylvania,* I: 247.

[64] Ibid.

[65] Ibid.

[66] John Jay to Historical Society of Pennsylvania, 21 February 1826, JJCU; Brier. *John Jay and George Washington's Valedictory.* The Supreme Court Historical Society Quarterly XXXII:2:10 (2010).

[67] *New York American*, 5 October 1826.

[68] Report of the Committee, *Memoirs of the Historical Society of Pennsylvania,* I: 242-43.

[69] Committee of the Corporation of the City of New York to Jay, 22 June, 1826, HPJ, IV: 475.

[70] Jay to the Committee of the Corporation of the City of New York 29 June 1826, HPJ, IV: 477.

[71] JJFM, 435; JJGP, 315.

[72] Deed, John Jay to Joseph Cusno, 15 December 1828, recorded in the Office of the Westchester County Clerk on 20 December, 1828, Liber 33, p.313-314.

[73] Ann Jay to Peter Augustus Jay, March 1826, JJCU.

[74] William Jay to Peter Augustus Jay, 28 March 1827, JJCU.

[75] JJWJ, I:256.

[76] Richard Peters to John Jay, 10 June 1828, JJCU.

[77] William Jay to Peter Augustus Jay, 2 March 1829, JJCU; Peperine is a porous volcanic rock.

[78] Maria Jay Banyer to Ann Jay 11 May 1829, JJCU.

[79] JJWS, 384.

80 Ibid.

81 JJWJ, I: 256.

82 Peter Augustus Jay to James Fenimore Cooper, 29 May 1829, Cooper, ed.. *Correspondence of James Fenimore Cooper.* I:171.

83 Extracts from the Will of John Jay. HPJ IV: 515.

84 Ibid.

85 Budney. *Wiliam Jay Abolitionist and Anticolonialist,* 28.

86 Jay, ed.. *Memorials of Peter A. Jay Compiled for his Descendants.* 128.

87 JJWS, 384.

88 Ibid.

89 *New York Mirror: A Weekly Gazette,* 30 May 1829; Pellew. *John Jay.* 315.

90 Donald W. Marshall, Town Historian, Town of Bedford, NY. *Bedford Tricentennial 1680-1980* (Town of Bedford 1980), 48.

91 Action of the New York Bar on the Death of John Jay, 19 May, 1829.HPJ IV: 517.

92 Ibid.

93 Ibid, 518.

[94] Ibid, 517-18.

[95] JJWJ, I: 259.

[96] French. *History of Westchester County, New York Vols. 1-5.* II: 909.

[97] https://ww.senate.gov/vtour/jay.htm.

[98] JJGP, 316.

The Last Inn

Legacy

CHAPTER 8

John Jay's legacy to his country relates primarily to his achievements in his diplomatic, judicial and executive roles. The qualities that were the basis for his success during his career as a public official also sustained him during his retirement. One of his biographers, George Pellew, wrote "Jay's principles of conduct were so unvarying, and his actions so consistent with them and with one another, that the most careless reader of his life, if it has been fairly presented, must be already familiar with the dignified and simple character of the man."[1] Jay's actions were governed by a sense of moral duty with a firm belief in God and Jay's conviction to do his duty with a disregard for popular praise or condemnation. Many of his contemporaries praised him. George Washington admired Jay for his 'purity' of views and John Adams called Jay "a Roman". Jay always strove to be wise and prudent and believed "to act accordingly, is to be wise". He also acted from a belief "To avoid mistakes it is necessary to see things as they really are."[2] With Jay prudence and circumspection were hallmarks of his character as he noted in a his letters to his children "The longer we live, and observe what passes in the world, the more we become sensible of the value and of the necessity of prudence."[3] Some people, primarily his political adversaries, deemed these qualities of Jay's character to render him aloof, distant and austere.

Throughout his life, there was a constancy in Jay's commitment to his endeavors and a preference for a simple life with "neatness and utility" his guiding principles. He and his wife longed for a quiet life in the country and when his wife departed this life in the early days of their retirement, he refrained from publicly expressing any regret for her loss for he believed she was in a better place. He desired an Episcopalian church in Bedford and took an active role and interest in the construction and operation of St. Matthew's Church. During his life in Bedford, he and his two sons were active in the administration of St. Matthew's, a tradition that was carried on by succeeding generations. Jay passed on this moral commitment to his two

Legacy

daughters, Nancy and Maria, who were active in the Sunday School at the church and in other charitable endeavors in Bedford.

Jay himself was not indifferent to the plight of those in need, seeing to the comfort of his servants and neighbors and supporting numerous charities with financial contributions. It was not until after his death that Jay's family learned of one of his philanthropic endeavors of supporting six impoverished New Rochelle boys from the same area where Jay himself was raised by seeing to their education.[4] His dedication to the abolition of slavery never wavered in his old age and he prepared manumission papers for residents of Bedford who wished to manumit their slaves. William Jay wrote of his father "Age and infirmities, instead of blunting, seemed to quicken his sensibility to the sufferings of others, and various were his modes of administering to their relief."[5] This sense of moral duty that Jay had and his piety gave him inspiration and comfort.

Jay once said "All depended on churches and schoolhouses."[6] and his dedication to the American Bible Society during his final years is ample proof of his moral character and beliefs in religious and lay education. Yet as a Christian and a republican, he disdained ostentation and strove to be "temperate in all things" which extended to his personal life and his children. He saw to his own comfort and that of his children without extravagance.

Jay was also steadfast in his friendships. Though the Revolutionary War may have interrupted his relationships with some of his friends, such as Peter Van Schaack, Lindley Murray and Benjamin Vaughan, Jay respected these men and others for their views on American independence, although their views may have been different from his own. His friendship with Judge Richard Peters lasted almost fifty years and was solidified by their common views on many subjects including the American republic, slavery, horticulture and agriculture. Jay readily shared Peters' writings on his agricultural experiments with his neighbors and fellow farmers by placing copies of Peters' treatises in the Bedford Town Library. Jay often addressed Peters as "my good and constant friend." Their mutual trust for each other was evident when the two men labored to protect the name of George Washington and his accomplishments during the *Farewell Address* debate. Captain John Paul Jones, who never met Jay, had the highest personal regard for Jay when he wrote to him from Paris in 1787 "As there is no man who inspires me with more esteem than yourself, I beg you to accept my bust as a mark of my affection;"[7] To this day, the bust of John Paul Jones is often on display in Jay's house in Bedford. Although Jay once said "Separate yourself from your enemies,..."[8] he adhered to this doctrine when dealing with adversaries. He remained loyal to his friends and counted many during his lifetime some of whom he received with great pleasure at his farm in Bedford. William Jay said of his father "'...in the whole course of his life he never deserted a friend...'"[9]

After Jay's death, William wrote a two volume biography of his father which some have said to be hagiographical. However, some of his simple yet insightful observations about his father and the advice that John Jay gave to his children are nevertheless constructive and interesting, and reveal much about Jay's character and the legacy he left to his children. Some of Jay's advice is taken from his letters to his youngest daughter, Sarah Louisa, when she was a teenager attending boarding school in Albany while staying with her sister, Maria Jay Banyer.

Jay's first piece of advice was on the subject of writing letters as he had good reason to be extremely concerned with letter writing when he wrote to Sarah Louisa in 1805 "It is better not to write, than to write what ought not to be written."[10] Jay was concerned that "letters sometimes miscarry" and that they are often read "by persons we have no reason to trust."[11] He continued in this vein by advising that he and his family should "reserve confidential matters for confidential conversation" and that "Even in this, circumspection is necessary; for there are many persons who, although friendly and honorable, are in the habit of imprudently talking about any thing and every thing, to everybody and before anybody."[12] Once again, Jay's hallmark characteristic of 'circumspection' came to the fore as he gave his daughter some basic and fatherly advice. During his career as a public official, Jay no doubt learned the virtues of being discreet and circumspect in all matters even when he wrote to his wife in 1775 and advised her to "...avoid writing any thing which if published, may give you a moment's uneasiness or concern."[13] This is a trait that it is said Jay inherited from his father and perhaps his schooling with Rev. Mr. Stoupe when attending his school for boys in New Rochelle. This attribute Jay willingly displayed and shared in his letters to his young daughter while passing on his invaluable experience and wisdom to his children.

Continuing in a slightly different vein on the subject of 'prudence' Jay's next piece of advice to his daughter, Sarah Louisa, in 1806 "There is a wide difference between confiding sentiments to me, and confiding sentiments to a letter to me."[14] Concerned with letters 'miscarrying' Jay advised his daughter "Prudence is one of the cardinal virtues, and well deserves our constant attention. The longer we live, and observe what passes in the world, the more we become sensible of the value, and of the necessity of prudence."[15] In a fatherly manner, Jay observed that this all-important quality is usually acquired through 'experience' and he also noted the advantage that Sarah Louisa had when he explained to her "I mean that of obtaining, upon every occasion, the advice and opinion of an affectionate, sincere, and judicious sister."[16] As a single and retired parent, Jay obviously was glad to have his eldest daughter, Maria, taking an important role in the development of Sarah Louisa. Maria, who lived in Albany where Sarah Louisa attended school, no doubt guided Sarah Louisa in many ways drawing upon her own life experience and the advice she no doubt received from her parents.

Jay wrote another letter to Sarah Louisa in 1808 when his daughter was sixteen and touched upon a number of subjects ranging from life on earth and the next world, common sense and self-command:

> I am particularly solicitous that they [his children] should be well versed in the science of living agreeably and comfortably here, and happily hereafter. The first includes whatever is taught by prudence, or common sense,

> and by the maxim 'never to buy anything at too great a price, whether it be pleasure, or riches, or ornaments. Hence it becomes necessary that we should endeavour to see persons and things as being what they really are, to estimate them at their true value, and to act accordingly.
>
> To do this effectually, self-command is absolutely indispensable. To look at objects through our passions, is like seeing through coloured glass, which always paints what we view in its own, and not in the true colour.[17]

By the time Sarah Louisa had reached adulthood, Jay was still counseling his daughter on moral issues particularly of the subject of ingratitude and maintaining her faith. Jay advised her:

> We should nevertheless proceed in doing good, because it is our duty; and not from the hope or expectation of grateful returns. Except in certain cases, it is better to cast our bread on the waters, 'that is, on many; here a little and there a little, according to our abilities and opportunities, and leave the rest to Providence.'"[18]

Jay's advice to his daughter was according to Christian principles and also stemmed from his experience during his long career as a public official. He cared deeply for the welfare of his family and strove to impart what he called 'perfect wisdom and perfect goodness' combined with 'practical prudence and real common sense' to his children. Sadly though, Jay would see Sarah Louisa die at the age of twenty-six.

In his biography of his father, William Jay chose to publish excerpts from two letters that Jay wrote to his daughter, Maria. After the loss of her husband and children, Maria's health was plagued by headaches and somber moods. Jay wrote to Maria on many occasions and the two letters selected by William Jay are yet additional proof of Jay's devotion to his family and his pragmatic approach to life. Jay and Maria had been exchanging letters about a course of action Maria should take, but the letters are vague, as Jay advised his family to be cautious when writing letters. Concerned about Maria's overall health 'corporeal or mental' and the need for a proper outlook, Jay advised Maria "Cheerfulness promotes health, and health promotes cheerfulness."[19] He advised her to treat her problems and 'indispositions' equally "They who neglect to cultivate the one and resist the other, are not wise."[20] Jay then addressed the issue of 'habitual melancholy' and that their religion does not 'countenance' such behavior "Our religion not only permits, but directs us to rejoice; and although it does not forbid occasional sorrow or grief, yet it marks the limits beyond which they are not to be indulged."[21] He then encouraged his daughter to employ "prudential truths and principles" for if they are neglected, "they are as unproductive as gold locked up in a miser's chest."[22] He then exhorted her to persevere "Virtuous exertions are never neglected by Providence; and I am persuaded that yours will be blessed if you persevere."[23] Jay continued to moralize to his daughter "To me, nothing appears more strange and unaccountable, than that a Christian should consider afflictions as evidence of Divine displeasure and dereliction."[24] According to Jay, "God loves those whom he chastises, and that he chastises them because he loves them."[25] He believed the Scriptures and the sufferings of holy men throughout the ages bore ample testimony to the truth of the doctrine of suffering. A life of unbridled prosperity, without chastisement "whereof all are partakers, then are ye bastards and not sons." God's love is in his forgiveness of sinners and their redemption in coming to Him. Jay then reasoned that 'religious melancholy' is produced by poor health and bad nerves and not in our minds and he advises Maria to take the cure by tending to her physical and mental health to cure her 'melancholy'.

    John Jay wrote many letters to all his children giving them advice. The letters are illustrative of Jay's devotion to his children

Legacy

and their well being, which continued throughout his retirement. Throughout their adulthood, Jay's children consulted their father for advice on a wide range of matters - personal, social, economic, political and religious. His advice is punctuated with common sense, his life experience and his pious adherence to the Episcopal church and its teachings. In a sense, Jay set an example for his children through his own life and his beliefs and instilled in them his strong sense of moral duty. This was part of Jay's legacy to his children.

Nancy and Maria spent their lives in numerous charitable endeavors that aided the poor and indigent. It was said that no one in need of help was turned away from Maria's home at 20 Bond Street in Manhattan. One of Nancy and Maria's most notable achievements occurred when ten ladies, including Nancy and Maria, all members of a prominent philanthropic group known as the Society for the Relief of Worthy Aged Indigent Colored Persons, met in the living room of Maria's house in the autumn of 1839 and formed the Colored Home for the "relief of the sick and respectable Colored aged." Maria donated one thousand dollars for the founding of the institution. The Colored Home was so successful that the New York State Legislature later expanded the scope of the organization to include "disabled colored sailors and other infirm and destitute colored people." Other members of the Jay family who participated in the work of the Colored Home included John Jay II [William Jay's son] and Elizabeth Clarkson Jay [the daughter of Peter Augustus Jay]. Members of other notable New York families who aided the Home included the Livingstons, Hamiltons and Roosevelts. In time, the Colored Home expanded its operations and is now Lincoln Hospital.[26]

Over the years Nancy and Maria were associated with other worthy philanthropic organizations. Nancy died on November 13, 1856. Her sister Maria died eight days later. Maria's account book summed up her charitable donations during the last nine years of her life which totaled $71,397 or roughly eight thousand dollars a year.[27] Nancy Jay's notebook also revealed donations to worthy charities of roughly six to eight thousand dollars a year.[28] In their Wills, the sisters made

Legacy

numerous bequests to the charities they had worked for over the years; the Ladies Depository, the Colored Orphan Asylum, the New York Medical Dispensary and the Association for the Relief of Respectable Aged Indigent Females, to name a few.

William Jay distinguished himself as one of the nation's leading exponents for the abolition of slavery. He was a skilled writer and wrote extensively on the subject. One of William's most influential writings *"Inquiry Into the Character and Tendency of the American Colonization and American Anti-Slavery Societies"* was widely read and reprinted in London.[29] William was so outspoken regarding the abolition of slavery, that he was forced to resign his position as Westchester County Judge. He was one of the founding members of the New York City Anti-Slavery Society and was active in assisting slaves traveling north via the Underground Railway.[30]

William followed his father's belief in settling disputes through arbitration to avoid hostilities. He was fervent in his conviction that war should be eliminated through arbitration and he worked tirelessly through the American Peace Society, of which he was a president, to that end. His essay *"War and Peace: the Evils of the First with a Plan for Securing the Last"* outlined his plan for securing his goals.

When William died in 1858, members of the Jay family were joined by neighbors, friends, old servants, the poor and former slaves in paying homage to him. Many people in farm wagons lined the road to St. Matthew's Church and fell into line with the hearse, along with the numerous other mourners along the road to St. Matthew's Church. William Jay was buried on the Sabbath and the services were conducted by the Rector, the Rev. Edward B. Boggs, assisted by Dr. McVickar of New York, who was Augusta McVickar Jay's brother, and a former pastor of the church, Mr. Partridge. There was no eulogy, and in keeping with William's wishes, the usual Sunday services were conducted but stressed William's Christian virtues. Afterwards, William was buried in the cemetery adjoining the church, along side his wife, Augusta. The words carved on the tombstone in accordance with William's wishes are from the New Testament "Verily, verily, I

Legacy

say unto you, he that believeth on me hath everlasting life."[31] In future years several loyal servants were buried in the Jay family plot at St. Matthew's. Although William desired no eulogies, Frederick Douglass delivered a eulogy at the Shiloh Presbyterian Church in New York City the following year. Douglass praised William Jay and said "…impartial history will accord to William Jay the credit of having affirmed all the leading principles of modern abolitionism."[32]

John Jay's legacy to his family continued with William's son, John Jay II. John was active in the anti-slavery movement while a student at Columbia University and was president of the New York Young Men's Antislavery Society. He became a lawyer and served as United States Minister to Austria-Hungary. John Jay II strove to abolish slavery. He was a member of the Anti-Slavery Convention in New York and wrote a report on the constitutional right and duty of Congress to ban slavery in all the territories being admitted to the Union as states. Jay was also president of a New York anti-slavery organization, the Free Democratic Club. In 1855 he helped organize the Republican Party in New York with its opposition to the extension of slavery in America. Like his father, John Jay II wrote and made speeches on the subject of abolition. Two essays written by Jay *"America Free or America Slave"* and *"The American Church and the American Slave Trade"* proved to be influential in the movement to abolish slavery.[33]

John Jay II worked tirelessly for social justice for African Americans in attempting to persuade the Bishop of the New York Diocese of the Episcopal Church to admit black congregations to its then all-white congregations in the New York Diocese. As a result of his efforts, St. Phillip's Church, a black congregation, was admitted to the Protestant Episcopal Convention. John Jay II tried, unsuccessfully, to have the Convention pursue an investigation into the slave trade from the port of New York and to have the Convention preach against slavery. These actions cost Jay his positions as a delegate to the Convention and as Vestryman of St. Matthew's Church in Bedford.[34]

He gained a reputation as an attorney working on behalf of

Legacy

African Americans who were excluded from the Episcopal Theological Seminary, and defending African Americans who had been arrested as fugitives. In this last instance, he is perhaps best remembered as co-counsel, along with Erastus Culver, who was a well-known anti-slavery attorney in Brooklyn, in a case before New York Superior Court - *Lemmon v. the People*.[35]

In 1852, Jonathan Lemmon, a slave owner from Virginia, and his wife, Juliet, brought eight slaves to New York City. The next day, Louis Napoleon, one of Lemmon's slaves, filed a writ of habeas corpus. The following day, the other slaves were brought into court and taken into police custody. Louis Napoleon's case was based on the 1846 *Revised Statutes of New York* which stated that any person who entered New York State as a slave will be considered a free person.[36] Lemmon asserted in court that the slaves were his wife's inherited property under the laws of Virginia and that he and his wife were in transit to Texas, a slave state, and were only in New York City as long as they could book passage on a ship bound for Texas. However, the Court ruled that the slaves were free and were discharged from police custody[37]. The decision was appealed and upheld by all the New York courts, including the state's highest court, the New York Court of Appeals, formerly the New York Supreme Court, over which John Jay had presided as the state's first Chief Justice. An appeal by Lemmon was filed in 1860 with the U.S. Supreme Court in Washington, D.C. This aroused anti-slavery activists who were concerned that the Supreme Court would base its decision on the *Dred Scott* decision handed down by the Court a few years earlier in 1857. Anti-slavery groups were concerned about the *Lemmon* case since the Supreme Court, led by Chief Justice Roger Taney, had declared the Missouri Compromise unconstitutional in the *Dred Scott* decision. The Court held that the Fifth Amendment prohibited any law that would deprive a slaveholder of his property, which included slaves, upon journeying to a free territory. However, the outbreak of the Civil War allowed the decision of the New York Court of Appeals to stand in the *Lemmon* case. The brief submitted to the Supreme Court asserted that freedom is a normal state for all men but slavery is in

Legacy

opposition to the intent of the Constitution.[38] The New York Court of Appeals had concurred with these basic truths when it upheld the freedom of Louis Napoleon. As co-counsel in the *Lemmon* case, John Jay II carried on the legacy passed on to him by his grandfather and father in striving for justice for African Americans.

Peter Augustus Jay was no less committed to his father's legacy of social justice and rights for African Americans. Like his father before him, Peter was president of the New York Manumission Society. Peter also was president of the New York Public School Society, an anti-slavery institution, which strove to aid the poor. It is worth mentioning again his impassioned speech for African American suffrage as a delegate to the New York State Constitutional Convention in 1821.

Peter inherited the Locusts, the farm in Rye, in 1822, where his grandfather, Peter Jay, brought up his family to escape the scourge of the yellow fever epidemics in New York City. In 1836, Peter hired a builder, Edwin Bishop, to tear down the Locusts which had been ravaged by the British during the Revolutionary War. A Greek Revival mansion was built in its place. The house survives to this day as the Jay Heritage Center and is a National Historic Landmark. It should be noted that John Jay's beloved 'farm in Bedford' was home to six generations of Jays. Today it is the John Jay Homestead New York State Historic Site. Both the John Jay Homestead and the Jay Heritage Center are open to the public as a testament to the Jay family's legacy which is being preserved for future generations. Both sites are also part of the Westchester County African American Heritage Trail.

John Jay strove to instill in his family integrity, strong character and a sense of moral duty. He wrote to Jonathan Trumbull who served as a commissioner for the Treaty of Paris and as Jay's secretary during the negotiations:

> Firmness…as well as integrity and caution, will be requisite to explore and preserve in the path of justice. They who, in following her footsteps, tred on

Legacy

> popular prejudices, or crush the
> schemes of individuals, must expect
> clamor and resentment. The best way to
> prevent being perplexed by
> considerations of that kind is to dismiss
> them all, and never to permit the mind
> to dwell upon them for a moment.[39]

John Jay instilled in his family a commitment to the moral duty for social justice and the 'firmness' to commit themselves in their efforts. In this, he passed on an invaluable legacy not only to his family and their descendants, but to his country.

Legacy

[1] JJGP, 316.

[2] Ibid, 318.

[3] Ibid; JJWJ, II: 428.

[4] Judith S. Kaye. *Kaye on Jay: New York's First Chief The Family Man.* Judicial Notice of the Historical Society of the Courts of the State of New York 8:7 (2012).

[5] JJWJ, I: 258.

[6] Ibid.

[7] JJGP, 317.

[8] JJWJ, I:257.

[9] Ibid.

[10] John Jay to Sarah Louisa Jay, 5 December 1805, JJCU.

[11] Ibid.

[12] Ibid.

[13] John Jay to Sarah Livingston Jay, 11 October 1775, JJCU.

[14] John Jay to Sarah Louisa Jay, 20 November 1806, JJH.

[15] Ibid.

[16] Ibid.

Legacy

[17] John Jay to Sarah Louisa Jay, 18 January, 1808, JJCU.

[18] John Jay to Sarah Louisa Jay, 16 February, 1813, JJCU.

[19] John Jay to Maria Jay Banyer, 3 January, 1812, JJCU.

[20] Ibid.

[21] Ibid.

[22] Ibid.

[23] Ibid.

[24] Ibid.

[25] Ibid.

[26] Rev. J.F. Richmond. *New York and Its Institutions 1609-1871.* (New York 1871), 439-40; Carol Brier. *Nancy Jay The Lady of the House.* Friends of John Jay Homestead, (Bedford 2010).

[27] John McVickar. *A Christian Memorial to Two Sisters.* (Memphis, TN 2012) 23.

[28] Ibid.

[29] Jennifer P. McLean. *The Jays of Bedford.* (Friends of John Jay Homestead, Katonah NY 1984), 17.

[30] Kaye. *Kaye on Jay: New York's First Chief The Family Man:* 15.

Legacy

[31] Last Will and Testament of William Jay, Westchester County Surrogate's Court.

[32] Douglass, Frederick. *Eulogy of the Late Hon. Wm. Jay.* (Rochester NY 1859) 23.

[33] McLean. *The Jays of Bedford,* 24-5.

[34] Jay, John II and the Vestry of St. Matthew's Church, Bedford, NY. *Correspondence between John Jay, Esq. and the Vestry of St. Matthew's Church, Bedford, NY,* (St. Matthew's Church Bedford 1862), 11-12.

[35] Kaye. *Kaye on Jay: New York's First Chief The Family Man;* 15.

[36] John D. Gordon III. *The Lemmon Slave Case.* Judicial Notice of the Historical Society of the Courts of the State of New York 4: 1(2006).

[37] Ibid, 9-10.

[38] Kaye. *Kaye on Jay: New York's First Chief The Family Man:* 16.

[39] JJGP, 322.

Legacy

NOTES AND BIBLIOGRAPHY

The following abbreviations are used for frequently cited works.

Letters cited at Columbia University are either in manuscript in the Rare Book and Manuscript Room of the Butler Library, Rare Book and Manuscript Division, or the John Jay Papers website, http://www.columbia.edu/cu/lweb/digital/jay/.

DHSC   Marcus, Maeva, ed. *The Documentary History of the Supreme Court of the United States 1789-1800.*

HPJ   Johnston, Henry P., ed. *The Correspondence and Public Papers of John Jay.*

JJCU   *The John Jay Papers,* Butler Library Rare Book and Manuscript Division, Columbia University
The John Jay Papers website
http://www.columbia.edu/cu/lweb/digital/jay/.

JJFM   Monaghan, Frank. *John Jay: Defender of Liberty Against Kings and People, Author of the Constitution and Governor of New York, President of the Continental Congress, Co-Author of the Federalist, Negotiator of the Peace of 1783 & the Jay Treaty of 1794, First Chief Justice of the United States.*

JJGP   Pellew, George. *John Jay.*

JJH   *Jay Family Papers,* John Jay Homestead State Historic Site, Katonah, New York.

1JJRM Morris, Richard B., ed. *John Jay the Making of a Revolutionary, Unpublished Papers 1745-1780.*

2JJRM Morris, Richard B., *The Peacemakers The Great Powers & American Independence.*

JJWS   Stahr, Walter. *John Jay.*

NOTES AND BIBLIOGRAPHY

JJWJ   William Jay. *The Life of John Jay: With Selections from His Correspondence and Miscellaneous Papers*, I-II.

NOTES AND BIBLIOGRAPHY

BOOKS

Ammon, Harry. *James Monroe: The Quest for National Identity.* New York: Mc Graw-Hill, 1971.

Baker, Leonard. *John Marshall A Life in Law.* New York and London: MacMillan Publishing Co., Inc., 1974.

Bakeless, John. *Turncoats, Traitors & Heroes Espionage in the American Revolution.* New York: Da Capo Press, 1998.

Banner, James M. Jr.. *To the Hartford Convention: The Federalists and the Origins of Party Politics in Massachusetts 1789-1815.* New York: Alfred A. Knopf, 1969.

Barnum, H.L. *The Spy Unmasked; or Memoirs of Enoch Crosby, alias Harvey Birch, the hero of Mr. Cooper's tale of the Neutral Ground.* New York: J&J Harper, 1828.

Bemis, Samuel Flagg, ed. *The American Secretaries of State and Their Diplomacy 1-X.* New York: Pageant Book Co., 1958.

Budney, Stephen P. *William Jay Abolitionist and Anti-Colonialist.* Westport, CT and London: Praeger Publishers, 2005.

Burroughs, Edwin G. and Wallace, Mike. *Gotham A History of New York City to 1898.* New York: Oxford University Press, 1999.

Casto, William R. *The Supreme Court in the Early Republic: The Chief Justiceships of John Jay and Oliver Ellsworth.* Columbia, SC: University of South Carolina Press, 1995.

Cooper, James Fenimore.
Precaution. New York: A.T.Goodrich, 1820.
The Spy: A Tale of the Neutral Ground. New York and London: H. Colburn and R. Bentley, 1821.
The Pilot: A Tale of the Sea. I-II. New York: Charles Wiley, 1824.
Notions of the Americans Picked Up By a Traveling Bachelor, I-II. New York: Frederick Ungar Publishing Co., 1863.

NOTES AND BIBLIOGRAPHY

Cooper, James Fenimore (Grandson), ed. *Correspondence of James Fenimore Cooper, I-II.* New York: Haskell House Publishers, Ltd., 1922.

Dangerfield, George. *The Awakening of American Nationalism: 1815-1828.* New York: Harper & Row, 1965.

Dekay, James T. *A Rage for Glory - The Life of Com. Stephen Decatur.* New York: Free Press, 2004.

Dixon, Ryan Fox. *The Decline of Aristocracy in the Politics of New York.* New York: Columbia University Press, 1918.

Duncombe, Frances and other Members of the Historical Committee Katonah Village Improvement Society. *Katonah the History of a New York Village and Its People.* Katonah, NY: The Colonial Press, 1974.

East, Robert A. and Judd, Jacob eds. *The Loyalists of America: A Focus on Greater New York.* Tarrytown, NY: Sleepy Hollow Restorations, 1975.

Ellet, Mrs. *The Queens of American Society.* Philadelphia: Henry T. Coates & Co., 1867.

Ellis, David M., Frost, James A., Syrett, Harold C. and Carman, Harry J. *A History of New York State.* Ithaca, NY and London: New York Historical Association by Cornell University Press, 1957.

Fens-de Zeeuw, Lyda. *Lindley Murray 1745-1826 Quaker and Grammarian.* Utrecht, Netherlands: Lot Dissertation Series, 2011.

Flexner, James Thomas,
Steamboats Come True American Inventors in Action. Boston, Toronto: Little Brown and Company, 1944.
George Washington, I-IV. Boston, Toronto: Little Brown and Company, 1969.

Frank, Elizabeth. *Memoirs of the Life and Writings of Lindley Murray: in a Series of Letters, Written by Himself.* New York and Philadelphia: New York, Samuel Wood and Sons; Philadelphia, B. and T. Kite, 1827.

NOTES AND BIBLIOGRAPHY

French, Alva P. ed. *History of Westchester County, New York I-V*. New York and Chicago: Lewis Historical Publishing Company, 1925.

Hamlin, Paul M. *Legal Education in Colonial New York*. New York: New York University Press, 1939.

Hinit, Dorothy Humphreys and Duncombe, Frances Riker. *The Burning of Bedford 1779*. Bedford, NY: Bedford Historical Society, 1974.

Howard, Hugh and Strauss, Roger III. *Houses of the Founding Fathers the Men Who Made America and the Way They Lived*. New York: Artisan, 2007.

Jay, John (Grandson) ed. *Memorials of Peter A. Jay Compiled for his Descendants*. G.J. Thieme for Private Circulation, 1929.

Jay, William. *The Life of John Jay: With Selections from His Correspondence and Miscellaneous Papers, I-II*. New York: J. J .Harper, 1833.

Johnston, Henry P. *The Correspondence and Public Papers of John Jay, I-IV*. New York: Lenox Hill Pub. and Dist. Co. (Burt Franklin) 1890.

Keller, Allan. *Life Along the Hudson*. Tarrytown, NY: Sleepy Hollow Restorations, 1985.

Knight, Franklin, ed.. *Letters on Agriculture from His Excellency George Washington President of the United States to Arthur Young, Esq. F.R.S. and Sir John Sinclair, Bart., M.P. with Statistical Tables and Remarks, by Thomas Jefferson, Richard Peters, and Other Gentlemen on the Economy and Management of Farms in the United States:* Washington, Franklin Knight: Philadelphia: William S. Martiem: New York: Baker & Scribner, and William S. Martiem, 1847.

Larkin, John, *The Reshaping of Everyday Life 1790-1840*. New York: Harper & Row Publishers, Inc., 1989.

Leckie, Elizabeth Betts. *A Furnishing Plan for John Jay Homestead State Historic Site*. Katonah, NY: Friends of John Jay Homestead, 1992.

Lewis, Tom. *The Hudson A History*. New Haven, CT and London: Yale University Press, 2005.

NOTES AND BIBLIOGRAPHY

Long, Robert Emmet. *James Fenimore Cooper*. New York: Continuum, 1990.

Love, Robert W. *History of the U.S. Navy 1775-1941*. Harrisburg, PA: Stackpole Books, 1992.

Luquer, Thatcher T.P. *An Historical Sketch of St. Matthew's Church, Bedford, NY 1634-1938*. Bedford, NY: Katonah Bedford Press, 1938.

Malone, Dumas and Rauch, Basil. *Empire for Liberty: The Genesis and Growth of the United States of America*. New York: Appleton-Century-Crofts, 1960.

Marcus, Maeva, ed. *The Documentary History of the Supreme Court of the United States, 1789-1800*. New York: Columbia University Press, 1992.

Marvin, Mary Vaughan. *Benjamin Vaughan*. Hallowell, ME: Hallowell Printing Co., 1979.

Massi, Barbara S. *The Story of Mary Guion Brown from her Diary of 1800-1852*. North Castle, NY: The North Castle Millennium Committee, Town of North Castle, NY, 2000.

McManus, Edgar J.. *A History of Negro Slavery in New York*. Syracuse, NY: Syracuse University Press, 1966.

Mc Vickar, John. *A Christian Memorial to Two Sisters*. Memphis, TN: General Books, 2012.

Monaghan, Charles. *The Murrays of Murray Hill*. New York: Urban History Press, 1998.

Monaghan, Frank. *John Jay: Defender of Liberty Against Kings & People, Author of the Constitution & Governor of New York, President of the Continental Congress, Co-Author of the Federalist, Negotiator of the Peace of 1783 & the Jay Treaty of 1794, First Chief Justice of the United States*. New York and Indianapolis, IN: The Bobbs-Merrill Company, 1935.

Moore, Glover. *The Missouri Controversy, 1819-1821*. Lexington, KY: University of Kentucky Press, 1953.

Morris, Richard B., ed.
The Peacemakers The Great Powers & American Independence. New York: Harper & Row, 1965.
John Jay The Nation and the Court. Boston: Boston University Press, 1967.
John Jay the Making of a Revolutionary Unpublished Papers 1745-1780. New York, Evanston, San Francisco and London: Harper & Row, 1975.
John Jay the Winning of the Peace Unpublished Papers 1780-1784. New York: Harper & Row, 1980.

Nichols, George Warner. *Fragments from the study of a pastor.* New York: H. B. Price, 1860.

Norton, Mary Beth. *Liberty's Daughters The Revolutionary Experience of American Women, 1750-1800.* Boston: Little, Brown, 1980.

Paltsits, Victor Hugo. *Washington's Farewell Address.* New York: The New York Public Library, 1935.

Parish Family Members. *A Sesquicentennial History of St. Matthew's Protestant Episcopal Church, Bedford, NY.* Bedford, NY: n.p., 1960.

Pellew, George. *John Jay.* Boston: Houghton Mifflin, 1898.

Peterson, Merrill D. ed. *Democracy, Liberty & Prosperity: The State Constitutional Conventions of the 1820,s.* Indianapolis, New York and Kansas City: The Bobbs-Merrill Company, Inc., 1966.

Richmond, Rev. J.F. *New York and Its Institutions 1609-1871.* New York: E.B. Treat, 1871.

Rothbard, Murray N.. *The Panic of 1819: Reactions and Policies.* New York and Chicago: New York, Columbia University Press; Chicago, W.T. Keener, 1962.

Scharf, Thomas J. *History of Westchester County I-II.* Camden, ME: Picton Press, 1992.

Shonnard, Frederick and Spooner, W.W. *History of Westchester County.* New York: New York History Company, 1900.

Schwartz, David G. *The History of Gambling, Roll the Bones.* New York: Gotham Books, 2006.

Smith, Page. *John Adams.* New York: Doubleday, 1962.

Stahr, Walter. *John Jay*. New York and London: Hambledon and London Press, 2005.
Swanson, Susan Cochran and Fuller, Elizabeth Green. *Westchester County*. Elmsford, NY: Arcadia Publishing, 1989.
Taylor, Alan. *William Cooper's Town Power and Persuasion on the Frontier of the Early American Republic*. New York: First Vintage Books, 1995.
Taylor, Elizabeth Dowling. *A Slave in the White House: Paul Jennings and the Madisons*. New York: Palgrave MacMillan, 2012.
Tuckerman, Bayard. *William Jay and the Constitutional Movement for the Abolition of Slavery*. New York: Dodd, Mead, 1894.
Van Schaack, Henry Cruger. *Memoirs of the Life of Henry Van Schaack*. Chicago: A.C. McClure, 1892.
Waite, John G., Huey, Paul R. and Truax, Martha. *John Jay House an Historic Structure Report*. New York: New York State Historic Trust, 1972.
Warren, Charles. *The Supreme Court in United States History I-II*. Boston: Little Brown, and Company, 1922.
Wells, Laura Jay. *The Jay Family of La Rochelle and New York Province and State: A Chronicle of Family Tradition*. New York: Order of the Colonial Lords of Manors in America, 1938.
Wilentz, Susan. *The Rise of American Democracy: Jefferson to Lincoln*. New York: Norton, 2005.
Wood, James. *The History of the Town of Bedford*. Bedford, NY: [s.n.], 1925.
Weyant, Charles H. *The Sacketts of America: Their Ancestors and Descendants 1630-1907*. Newburgh, NY: [Journal Print], 1907.
Williams, George W. *History of the Negro Race in America from 1619 to 1880 I-II,* New York: G. P. Putnam Sons, 1883.

NOTES AND BIBLIOGRAPHY

MANUSCRIPT COLLECTIONS

American Philosophical Society, Philadelphia, PA
    John Jay Correspondence
Bedford, New York Town Book. Bedford Town House, Bedford, NY
Columbia University, Butler Library, Rare Book and Manuscript Division, New York, NY
    John Jay Papers
     Watts Special Miscellaneous Collection
Historical Society of Pennsylvania, Philadelphia, PA
    Richard Peters Papers 1697-1845
    Memoirs by Richard Peters for the Philadelphia Society for Promoting Agriculture
John Jay Forum. Carol Brier, Author, Publisher and Administrator. www.jjforum@blogspot.com .
John Jay Homestead State Historic Site, Katonah, NY
    Jay Family Papers
Keeler Tavern Museum, Ridgefield CT.
    Keeler Family Papers
Library of Congress, Washington, D.C.
    The George Washington Papers 1741-1799
    The Thomas Jefferson Papers Series1. General Correspondence
Massachusetts Historical Society. Boston, MA
    Adams Family Papers
    Portraits of American Abolitionists
    Timothy Pickering Papers 1731-1827
National Archives, Washington, D.C.
    John Jay Papers
New York County Surrogate's Court, New York, NY
    Abstracts and Wills
New York Historical Society, New York, NY
    Gilder Lehrman Institute of American History
    John Jay Papers
New York Public Library, New York, NY
    John Jay Papers
St. Matthew's Episcopal Church, Bedford, NY

NOTES AND BIBLIOGRAPHY

United States Census Reports
> Populations Schedules of the Fourth Census of the United States 1820, No.33, Roll 75, Vol. 14, Washington, D.C. National Archives

U.S. Constitution.
> National Archives, Washington, D.C.

Westchester County Archives, Elmsford, NY.
Westchester County Division of Land Records, Mortgages, White Plains, NY
Westchester County Historical Society, Elmsford, NY.

NOTES AND BIBLIOGRAPHY

ARTICLES, JOURNALS, PERIODICALS and PAMPHLETS

Baird, Charles W. "History of Rye, NY Chronicle of a Border Town, Westchester County, New York Including Harrison and White Plains till 1788." New York (1871).

Brier, Carol.
"John Jay and George Washington's Valedictory." *The Supreme Court Historical Society Quarterly* Vol. XXXII, no. 1 (2010): 6-9; Vol. XXXII, no. 2 (2010):8-11.
"Nancy Jay the Lady of the House." Friends of John Jay Homestead, Bedford (2010).
"Joseph Cusno: The Sicilian Immigrant and the Jays of Bedford." *The Westchester Historian*, Vol. 87, no. 2 (Spring 2011): 40-51.
"Tending Our Vines: From the Correspondence and Writings of Richard Peters and John Jay." *Pennsylvania History: A Journal of Mid-Atlantic Studies*, Vol. 80, no. 1, (Winter 2013): 85-111.

Brown, Ethan A. http:/www.ohiohistorycentral.org.

"The Clash of Political Philosophies: The Debate Over Universal Suffrage in New York 1821." http:/www.Montgomery college.edu/Departments/hpolscrv/suffra.html,4.

Cornell, Greta A. "The Ossining Story 175 Years on the Hudson, The History of the Village of Ossining." Ossining, NY (1988).

Douglass, Frederick. "Eulogy of the Late Hon. Wm. Jay" Rochester, NY (1859).

"Encounters with America's Premier Nursery and Botanic Garden" *Thomas Jefferson's Monticello*, Twinleaf Journal, January (2004).

Glick, Joshua. "Comment: On the Road: The Supreme Court and the History of Circuit Riding." *Cardozo Law Review*, April (2003): 1753.

Gordon, John D. III. "The Lemmon Slave Case." *Judicial Notice of the Historical Society of the Courts of the State of New York*, Issue 4 (2006): 2-13.

NOTES AND BIBLIOGRAPHY

Horne, Philip Field. "A Land of Peace - The Early History of Sparta a Landing town on the Hudson." Ossining: NY 1976.

Horton, Jan. "Three Sisters." John Jay Homestead, Katonah, NY.

Janson, Jennifer. "Sarah Jay Livingston 1756-1802: Dynamics of Domesticity, Patriotism and the American Revolution." *West Virginia University* (Spring 2007):1-82.

Jay, Sir James. "Reflections and Observations on the Gout." London: G.Kearsley, H.Parker, J.Ridley, 1772.

Jay, John II.
"America Free or America Slave." New York: Office of the New York Tribune, 1856.
"The American Church and the American Slave Trade." New York: R. Lockwood & Sons 1860; Mr. Jay's speech in the New York diocesan convention of the Protestant Episcopal Church, September 27, 1860.
"Correspondence between John Jay, Esq., and the Vestry of St.Matthew's Church, Bedford, NY 1862-1863." Bedford, NY [s.n.] 1863.

Jay, William.
"Inquiry Into the Character and Tendency of the American Colonization and American Slavery Societies." New York: American Anti-Slavery Society 1840.
"War & Peace: The Evils of the First with a Plan for Saving the Last." London: T. Ward and Company 1842.

"Jay Cemetery, Rye New York." Privately published 1947.

Johnson, Herbert Alan. "John Jay 1745-1829." Albany: The University of the State of New York, The State Education Department, 1970.

Kaminski, John P. and Lawton, C. Jennifer. "Duty and Justice at 'Every Man's Door': The Grand Jury Charges of Chief Justice John Jay, 1790-94." *Journal of Supreme Court History*, Vol. 31, Issue 3 (Nov. 2006): 235-51.

Kaye, Judith S. "Kaye on Jay: New York's First Chief, The Family Man." *Judicial Notice of the Society of the Courts of the State of New York*, Issue 8 (Spring 2012): 3-13.

NOTES AND BIBLIOGRAPHY

Kligerman, Jack. "Notes on Cooper's Debt to John Jay". *American Literature*, Vol. 41, no. 3 (November 1969): 415-19.

"Laws of Yale College in New Haven, in Connecticut: Enacted by the President and Fellows". New Haven, CT 1808.

Marcus, Maeva. "George Washington's Appointments to the Supreme Court." *Journal of Supreme Court History*, Vol. 4, Issue 3 (Dec. 1999): 244-54.

McVickar, Professor John in *New York Review*. October, 1841.

Mintz, Max M. "Robert Morris and John Jay on Education: Two Letters." *Pennsylvania Magazine for History and Biography*, Vol. 4, no. 3 (July, 1950):340-47.

The New York American.

The New York Mercury.

The New York Mirror: A Weekly Gazette.

Peters, Richard and Breck, Samuel. 'A Collection of Puns and Witticisms of Judge Richard Peters." *The Pennsylvania Magazine of History and Biography*, I, no. 3. The Historical Society of Pennsylvania (1901): 366-69.

Peters, Richard. "Memoir on the Tunis broad-tailed Sheep." *Philadelphia Society for Promoting Agriculture, II Philadelphia 1811*; *The Annual Register, or a View of the Politics and Literature, For the Year 1810* (London 1812):624-50.

Polgar, J. Paul. "Whenever They Judge it to be Expedient: Politics of Partisanship and Free Black Voting Rights in Early National New York." *American Nineteenth Century History* 12:1: 1-23.

"Prince Family Nurseries ca. 1737-post-185." *Bulletin of the Hunt Institute for Botanical Documentation, Carnegie Mellon Institute*, 21(1) Spring 2009.

The United States Senate, John Jay.
https:/www.senate.gov.vtour/jay.htm .

NOTES AND BIBLIOGRAPHY

About the Author

Carol Brier is a graduate of Queens College, CUNY with an honors degree in History and is a member of Phi Alpha Theta, the National History Honor Society. She is the author of several articles about John Jay published by the Supreme Court Historical Society, the Pennsylvania Historical Association, the Westchester County Historical Society and Friends of John Jay Homestead. The author is a long-time volunteer at the John Jay Homestead State Historic Site and a former Trustee of the Friends of John Jay Homestead. She is also a member of the Supreme Court Historical Society and a subscriber to the White House Historical Association. More recently, she is the Author, Publisher and Administrator of the JOHN JAY FORUM, a blog that is a bibliography devoted to researching John Jay and his family with information about books, articles, manuscripts, pamphlets, events and links. One of the first certified paralegals in the country, Ms. Brier is now retired from the legal profession and devotes her time to writing about John Jay and continuing her volunteer work at the John Jay Homestead State Historic Site.

INDEX

Adams, John, 15, 18-20, 36, 40, 43, 45, 71, 115, 151, 198-199, 210, 245, 250, 266, 276, 278, 285, 307
Address to the People of Great Britain, 9, 41, 112, 139, 145, 149
African Free School, 126, 132, 145
Agriculture, 33, 50, 72, 74, 77, 93, 192, 222, 247, 286, 305, 309, 313
American Bible Society, 65-66, 112, 224-225, 228, 286
American Revolution, 3, 38, 42, 87, 116, 121, 124, 157, 173, 184, 186, 188-189, 193, 231-232, 303, 312
Articles of Confederation, 22, 24, 72, 125
Banyer, Sarah (Maria Jay Banyer's daughter), 80
Banyer Jr., Goldsborough, 37, 48, 58, 81-82, 229, 231
Banyer Sr., Goldsborough, 81-82, 94, 229

Banyer, Maria Jay (see Maria Jay), vii, 58, 65, 89-95, 110, 122, 135-137, 139-140, 165, 170, 171(f), 229-230, 240-241, 255, 267, 276, 279, 281, 287, 298
Bayard, Anna Maria (Jay's grandmother), 1
Beaulah Affair, 179, 183
Bedford Academy, 112
Bedford, New York, vii, xi-xii, 1, 25, 36, 38-39, 47-48, 51-59, 61, 63-66, 68, 71, 77, 84, 86-87, 98, 100-101, 103-105, 107-108, 110, 112, 116, 118, 120, 123, 131-134, 138, 143-144, 160-161, 165, 171(h), 177, 192-193, 198, 202, 215, 220, 228-231, 234, 239-240, 245, 247, 256, 258, 261, 266, 270-272, 282, 285-287, 293, 295, 299, 305-309, 312
Bedford Female Charitable Society, 100, 228-229
Boudinot, Elias, 127-128, 132, 142, 224-225

315

Boundary Disputes, 6, 13, 38
Brown, Ethan Allen,
　Governor of Ohio,
　247-250, 277
Chambers, Judge John, 4
Chisholm v. Georgia, 31
Circuit Riding, 28, 34, 39, 45,
　254, 278, 311
Claypoole, David, 263
Clarkson, Mary Rutherford
　(see Mary Rutherford
　Clarkson Jay), 65, 91,
　240
Clinton, De Witt, 158, 251
Clinton, George, 24, 34, 196
Colored Home, 291
Committee of Fifty, 9, 173
Committee of Fifty-one, 9,
　159
Committee of Sixty, 179
Committee of Twenty-five, 8
Committee for Detecting
　Conspiracies, 232
Constitution, New York
　State, 12-13, 23-25, 36,
　38, 67, 132, 220,
　250-254, 273, 295
Constitution, United States,
　12, 23, 25-26, 28, 30-32,
　44, 114-115, 128, 132,
　150, 163, 191, 310
Continental Congress, First,
　9, 173, 266
Continental Congress,
　Second, 10, 218, 224
Cooper, James Fenimore,
　viii, 58, 64, 88-89,

Cooper, James Fenimore,
　(cont.)
　171(n), 230, 234,
　243-244, 270, 282, 304,
　306
Cooper, William, 229, 243,
　245, 308
Corporation of the City of
　New York, 221, 241,
　247, 266, 281
Crosby, Enoch, 231-232, 303
Cusno, Joseph, 86, 120, 141,
　143, 266, 269, 272, 281,
　311
Debating Club, 178
Democratic-Republican
　Party, 247, 252
Duane, James, 6, 115, 140,
　173
Duyckinck, Polly, 47, 57
Dwight, Rev. Timothy, 57,
　64, 129
Embargo Act, 152, 154
Erie Canal, ix, 67, 171(r),
　246-247
Federalist Papers, 38
Federalist Party, 3, 34, 127,
　165
Felch, Nathan, 108-109,
　111
Fens-de Zeeuw, Lyda, 181,
　183, 206
First Barbary War, 121
Franklin, Benjamin, 18, 42,
　115, 177, 186, 198, 210
Free African Americans, 67,
　251-252, 254

INDEX - *MR. JAY OF BEDFORD*

French Revolution, 64, 149-152, 163, 189
Fulton, Robert, 113
Ground Shells fertilizer, 73
Ha-Ha, 106
Hamilton, Alexander, 7, 23-24, 36, 107, 115, 125, 163, 247, 258
Hamilton, Mrs. (Elizabeth Schuyler Hamilton), 117, 259-262, 264
Hartford Convention, 163-164, 171, 303
Historical Society of Pennsylvania, 92, 263, 280-281, 309, 313
Hudson River Sloop, 54, 218
Huguenots, 1, 107, 112
Hunter, Capt. Elijah, 48, 53, 232
Invisible Ink, 11, 195-196
Izard Jr., Ralph, 121-122
Jay, Ann (Nancy) (Jay's daughter), vii, 55, 66, 90-94, 135, 171(e), 217, 240, 243, 281, 291, 298, 311
Jay, Anna Maria Bayard (Jay's grandmother), 1
Jay, Anna Marika (Jay's sister), 56, 130, 142
Jay, Augusta McVickar (William Jay's wife), 65-66, 92, 108, 292
Jay, Augustus (Jay's grandfather), 1
Jay, Eve (Jay's sister), 98
Jay Family Cemetery, Rye, New York, 84, 95, 106, 272, 312
Jay, Sir James (Jay's brother), 11, 193-194, 196-197, 199-200, 209-210
Jay, John, iii, vii-viii, xi-xiii, 1-5, 9, 12, 15-16, 20, 26-27, 29, 33-34, 37-38, 40-45, 47-48, 51-59, 61, 65-71, 74-75, 77-81, 83-95, 97-99, 105-109, 111-114, 117-118, 120-123, 130-132, 134-143, 145-146, 152-153, 159-161, 165, 167-171, 171(a), 171(b), 171(c), 171(e), 171(f), 171(g), 171(h), 173, 175-179, 185, 189-190, 192-211, 213-217, 219-222, 224-225, 229-232, 234, 239-243, 245, 247, 250-252, 254, 256-258, 263-264, 266-267, 270-273, 275-282, 285, 287, 290-291, 293-299, 301-303, 305-309, 311-314
Jay, John II (Jay's grandson by William), vii, 113, 122-123, 132, 134, 171(g), 291, 293, 295
Jay, Maria (Jay's daughter), vii, 58, 65, 89-95, 110,

Jay, Maria (Jay's daughter), (cont.) 122, 135-137, 139-140, 165, 170, 171(f), 229-230, 240-241, 255, 267, 276, 279, 281, 287, 298

Jay, Mary Rutherford Clarkson (wife of Peter Augustus Jay), 65, 240

Jay, Mary Van Cortlandt (Jay's mother), 2, 47

Jay, Peter (Jay's father), 3-4, 7, 40, 47, 86, 129-130, 142, 194, 200-201, 219, 295

Jay, Peter "Blind Peter" (Jay's brother), 56-57, 78, 97

Jay, Peter Augustus (Jay's son), vii, 11, 29, 33, 50-51, 54-55, 58, 65, 68, 78-79, 81, 83, 86, 88-89, 91-94, 98, 101-102, 104-106, 108, 110-111, 116-118, 121, 123, 127, 131, 135-140, 143, 152, 155, 159, 161-162, 168-171, 171(d), 177, 193, 200-202, 209-211, 214-217, 219-220, 226, 240-243, 246-247, 250-254, 256, 268, 270-272, 276, 278-279, 281-282, 291, 295

Jay, Sarah Livingston (Jay's wife), vii, xiii, 1, 42,

Jay, Sarah Livingston (Jay's wife), (cont.) 60-61, 86-90, 106, 140, 171(b), 297

Jay, Sarah Louisa (Jay's daughter), 58, 63-64, 78-80, 82, 84, 90-91, 102-103, 105, 112, 114, 139-140, 160, 170, 214-215, 287-289, 297-298

Jay, Susan (Jay's daughter), 17

Jay, William (Jay's son), vii, xii, 1, 40, 55, 58, 64-65, 69, 71, 77, 84, 92-93, 104-108, 114, 119, 122-123, 127, 132, 134, 137, 140, 142-143, 157, 170, 171(c), 177, 214-217, 222, 224, 228, 230-231, 234, 242-243, 246, 257-258, 262, 267-272, 276, 279, 281, 286-287, 289-290-293, 299, 302-303, 305, 308, 312

Jay Treaty: Treaty of Amity Commerce and Navigation, 21, 33, 39, 126, 145, 149, 301, 306

Jefferson, Thomas, 18, 23, 25, 36, 43, 70, 72, 92, 130, 192, 200, 209, 218, 250, 266, 305, 309, 311

Johnson, Samuel, 3

July 4th Celebrations, 220-221
Keeler, Dr. Walter, 101, 104-105
Kinderhook, New York, 173-174, 176-177
King, Rufus, 103, 136-137, 150, 158, 165, 168, 259, 262, 264
Kings College, 3-6, 11, 14, 64, 173, 178, 193-194, 203, 214
Kissam, Benjamin, 4-6, 40, 146, 178
Lafayette, Georges Washington de, 255
Lafayette, Marquis de, viii, 18, 171(o), 234, 254-255
Laurens, Henry, 14, 18, 234
Lemmon v. People, 294-295, 299, 311
Livingston Jr., Robert R., 3, 6, 24-26, 44, 173, 197-198, 209-210
Livingston, William, 6-7, 9, 40, 42
Livingston, Susannah French, 16, 42, 197, 209
Locusts, Peter Jay's farm in Rye, NY, 2, 233, 295
Lotteries, 218
Loyalists, 9-10, 19, 179-180, 193, 195, 203, 205, 304
Lyons, Major Samuel, 48, 50, 63, 90
Maddison, James, 156

Madison, James, 23, 70, 72, 130, 154, 192
Marshall, John, 31, 37, 46, 164, 261-263, 280, 303
McVickar, Augusta (see Augusta McVickar Jay), 65-66, 92, 108, 292
Medicine, 100-102, 193, 196, 199, 202
Missouri Compromise, 127, 294
Monaghan, Charles, 167, 180, 183, 306
Moot, 6-7, 14, 38
Moravian School Bethlehem, Penn., 67, 91
Morris, Gouveneur, 13, 42, 158, 170, 173, 197, 209-210
Munro, Peter Jay, 16, 98, 104, 106-107, 135, 137, 199, 210
Murray Jr., John, 145-146, 156, 167
Murray, Lindley, viii, 5, 38, 85, 95, 171(j), 177, 181, 206-207, 245, 276, 286, 304
Napoleon Bonaparte, viii, 76, 103, 150-152, 160, 163, 171(l)
New York State Constitutional Convention of 1821, 67, 250, 254, 295

New York Manumission Society, 66-67, 125, 132, 145, 295
New York Provincial Congress, 10-13, 38, 145, 174
New York State Supreme Court of Judicature, 13
New York Sunday School Society, 111
Olive Branch Petition, 10, 41, 145, 149
Panic of 1819, 248, 277, 307
Perry, Commodore Oliver Hazard, 160
Peters, Richard, viii, 49, 72, 74-75, 90, 92-93, 97, 135, 162-163, 168, 170-171, 171(k), 258-259, 263-264, 269, 279-281, 286, 305, 309, 311, 313
Philadelphia Society for the Promotion of Agriculture, 74, 93, 309, 313
Pickering, Timothy, 48, 75, 86, 139, 153, 161, 169-170, 213, 240, 309
Plaister of Paris, 73-74
Price, Dr. Richard, 43, 124, 141
Putrid Fever, 103
Rawle, William, 263
Republican Party, 247, 252, 293
Sackett, Dr. William H., 101

St. Matthew's Church, Bedford, NY, 107-109, 122, 132, 138, 229, 269,
St. Matthew's Church, Bedford, NY, (cont.) 272, 285, 292-293, 299, 306, 312
Servants, 58, 68, 107, 117-119, 122, 132, 202, 219, 233, 236, 239, 257, 272, 286, 292-293
Sheep, 50, 74-77, 93, 106, 313
Sinclair, Sir John, 33, 50, 73, 92, 305
Sing Sing, viii, 53-55, 165, 171(i), 218
Slaves and Slavery, 10, 13, 16, 22, 36, 65, 122-134, 143, 146, 163, 188, 218-219, 222, 226-228, 236, 243, 251-252, 286, 292-295, 299, 306, 308, 311-312
Smith, Philip, Receiver of Taxes, Town of Bedford, 215, 240
Social Club, 7
Society for the Relief of Worthy Aged Indigent Colored Persons, 291
Stoupe, Rev. Mr., 3, 288
Toll Roads, 52-53
Treaty of Ghent, 161, 163-164
Treaty of Paris, 20-21, 25, 31-33, 38, 115, 121, 145,

Treaty of Paris, (cont.)
149, 176, 181, 186-187,
199, 295
Trinity Church, New York
City, 3, 66, 111, 201
United States Supreme
Court, xi, 37, 44, 114,
249, 254, 294, 301, 306,
308
Van der Lyn, Henry,
256-257, 279
Van Schaack, Peter, 3, 5-6,
40, 157, 169, 173, 175,
178, 198, 205-206, 286
Vaughan, Benjamin, ix, 19,
42, 172, 185, 190, 193,
208-209, 286, 306
War of 1812, viii, 152, 156,
163-164, 171(m), 185,
192
Ware v. Hilton, 31
Washington, Bushrod,
261-263, 280

Washington, George, 9, 12,
24, 43-45, 52, 70-71, 75,
87, 92, 146, 160, 180,
196-197, 209-210, 218,
258-259, 261, 265,
278-281, 285, 287,
304-305, 309, 311, 313
Washington, George,
Farewell Address,
258-265, 269, 280, 287,
307
Watts, Dr. John, 101, 136
Way Mail, 52
Westchester Agricultural
Society, 74, 77, 228, 230
Westchester Bible Society,
224
Wilberforce, William, 60,
126-127, 141, 151, 168
William Prince Nursery,
Flushing, NY, 71
Yale College, 64, 90, 214,
313

www.ingramcontent.com/pod-product-compliance
Lightning Source LLC
Chambersburg PA
CBHW070718160426
43192CB00009B/1234